PENGUIN BOOKS

ELEVEN RINGS

Phil Jackson is arguably the greatest coach in the history of the NBA. His reputation was established as head coach of the Chicago Bulls from 1989 to 1998; during his tenure, Chicago won six NBA titles. His next team, the Los Angeles Lakers, won five NBA titles from 2000 to 2010. He holds the record for the most championships in NBA history as a player and a head coach. He also has the highest winning percentage of any NBA coach (704). Jackson was a player on the 1970 and 1973 NBA champion New York Knicks. In 2007 Jackson was inducted into the Basketball Hall of Fame.

A former editor for *Sports Illustrated* and *People*, Hugh Delehanty is the coauthor with Phil Jackson of the bestselling memoir *Sacred Hoops*.

ELEVEN RINGS

THE SOUL OF SUCCESS

PHIL JACKSON

AND HUGH DELEHANTY

PENGUIN BOOKS

PENGUIN BOOKS
Published by the Penguin Group
Penguin Group (USA) LLC
375 Hudson Street
New York, New York 10014

USA | Canada | UK | Ireland | Australia | New Zealand | India | South Africa | China
penguin.com
A Penguin Random House Company

First published in the United States of America by The Penguin Press,
a member of Penguin Group (USA) Inc., 2013
Published with a new afterword in Penguin Books 2014

ISBN 978-1-59420-511-8 (hc.)
ISBN 978-0-14-312534-1 (pbk.)

Printed in the United States of America
3   5   7   9   10   8   6   4

Book design by Stephanie Huntwork

Photo insert designed by Emily Herrick

*Penguin is committed to publishing works of quality and integrity.
In that spirit, we are proud to offer this book to our readers;
however, the story, the experiences, and the words
are the author's alone.*

FOR RED HOLZMAN, TEX WINTER,
AND ALL THE PLAYERS I'VE COACHED
WHO HAVE TAUGHT ME SO MANY LESSONS.

When you do things from your soul,
you feel a river moving in you, a joy.

RUMI

CONTENTS

ELEVEN RINGS

1

THE CIRCLE OF LOVE

Life is a journey. Time is a river. The door is ajar.
JIM BUTCHER

Cecil B. DeMille would have loved this moment.

Here I was sitting in a limo at the ramp leading into the Los Angeles Memorial Coliseum, waiting for my team to arrive, while an ecstatic crowd of ninety-five thousand plus fans, dressed in every possible combination of Lakers purple and gold, marched into the stadium. Women in tutus, men in *Star Wars* storm-trooper costumes, toddlers waving "Kobe Diem" signs. Yet despite all the zaniness, there was something inspiring about this ancient ritual with a decidedly L.A. twist. As Jeff Weiss, a writer for *LA Weekly*, put it: "It was the closest any of us will ever know what it was like to watch the Roman Legions returning home after a tour of Gaul."

Truth be told, I've never really felt that comfortable at victory celebrations, which is strange given my chosen profession. First of all, I'm phobic about large crowds. It doesn't bother me during games, but it can make me queasy in less controlled situations. I've also never really loved being the center of attention. Perhaps it's my inherent shyness or the conflicting messages I got as a kid from my parents, who were both ministers. In their view, winning was fine—in fact, my mother was one of the most fiercely competitive people I've ever met—but reveling in your own success was considered an insult to God. Or as they would say, "The glory belongs to Him."

This celebration wasn't about me, though. It was about the remarkable transformation the players had undergone en route to the 2009 NBA championship. You could see it in their faces as they descended the long purple and gold staircase into the coliseum dressed in rally caps and championship T-shirts, laughing, jostling, beaming with joy, while the crowd roared with delight. Four years earlier the Lakers hadn't even made the playoffs. Now they were masters of the basketball universe. Some coaches are obsessed with winning trophies; others like to see their faces on TV. What moves me is watching young men bond together and tap into the magic that arises when they focus—with their whole heart and soul—on something greater than themselves. Once you've experienced that, it's something you never forget.

The symbol is the ring.

In the NBA, rings symbolize status and power. No matter how gaudy or cumbersome a championship ring may be, the dream of winning one is what motivates players to put themselves through the trials of a long NBA season. Jerry Krause, the former general manager of the Chicago Bulls, understood this. When I joined the team as an assistant coach in 1987, he asked me to wear one of the two championship rings I'd earned playing for the New York Knicks as a way to inspire the young Bulls players. This is something I used to do during the playoffs when I was a coach in the Continental Basketball Association, but the idea of sporting such a big chunk of bling on my finger every day seemed a bit much. One month into Jerry's grand experiment the ring's centerpiece rock fell out while I was dining at Bennigan's in Chicago, and it was never recovered. After that I went back to wearing the rings only during the playoffs and on special occasions like this triumphant gathering at the coliseum.

On a psychological level, the ring symbolizes something profound: the quest of the self to find harmony, connection, and wholeness. In Native American culture, for instance, the unifying power of the circle was so meaningful that whole nations were conceived as a series of interconnected rings (or hoops). The tepee was a ring, as were the campfire, the village, and the layout of the nation itself—circles within circles, having no beginning or end.

Most of the players weren't that familiar with Native American psychology, but they understood intuitively the deeper meaning of the ring. Early in the season, the players had created a chant they would shout before each game, their hands joined together in a circle.

One, two, three—RING!

After the players had taken their places on the stage—the Lakers' portable basketball court from the Staples Center—I stood and addressed the crowd. "What was our motto on this team? The ring," I said, flashing my ring from the last championship we won, in 2002. "The ring. That was the motto. It's not just the band of gold. It's the circle that's made a bond between all these players. A great love for one another."

Circle of love.

That's not the way most basketball fans think of their sport. But after more than forty years involved in the game at the highest level, both as a player and as a coach, I can't think of a truer phrase to describe the mysterious alchemy that joins players together and unites them in pursuit of the impossible.

Obviously, we're not talking romantic love here or even brotherly love in the traditional Christian sense. The best analogy I can think of is the intense emotional connection that great warriors experience in the heat of battle.

Several years ago journalist Sebastian Junger embedded himself with a platoon of American soldiers stationed in one of the most dangerous parts of Afghanistan to learn what enabled these incredibly brave young men to fight in such horrifying conditions. What he discovered, as chronicled in his book *War*, was that the courage needed to engage in battle was indistinguishable from love. Because of the strong brotherhood the soldiers had formed, they were more concerned about what happened to their buddies than about what happened to themselves. Junger recalls one soldier telling him that he would throw himself on a grenade for any one of his platoonmates, even those he didn't like all that much. When Junger asked why, the soldier replied, "Because I actually love my brothers. I mean, it's a brotherhood. Being able to save their life so they can live, I think is rewarding. Any of them would do it for me."

That kind of bond, which is virtually impossible to replicate in civilian life, is critical to success, says Junger, because without it nothing else is possible.

I don't want to take the analogy too far. Basketball players don't risk their lives every day like soldiers in Afghanistan, but in many ways the same principle applies. It takes a number of critical factors to win an NBA championship, including the right mix of talent, creativity, intelligence, toughness, and, of course, luck. But if a team doesn't have the most essential ingredient—love—none of those other factors matter.

Building that kind of consciousness doesn't happen overnight. It takes years of nurturing to get young athletes to step outside their egos and fully engage in a group experience. The NBA is not exactly the friend-liest environment for teaching selflessness. Even though the game it-self is a five-person sport, the culture surrounding it celebrates egoistic behavior and stresses individual achievement over team bonding.

This wasn't the case when I started playing for the Knicks in 1967. In those days most players were paid modestly and had to take part-time jobs in the summer to make ends meet. The games were rarely televised and none of us had ever heard of a highlight reel, let alone Twitter. That shifted in the 1980s, fueled in large part by the popu-larity of the Magic Johnson–Larry Bird rivalry and the emergence of Michael Jordan as a global phenomenon. Today the game has grown into a multibillion-dollar industry, with fans all over the world and a sophisticated media machine that broadcasts everything that happens on and off the court, 24-7. The unfortunate by-product of all this is a marketing-driven obsession with superstardom that strokes the egos of a handful of ballplayers and plays havoc with the very thing that attracts most people to basketball in the first place: the inherent beauty of the game.

Like most championship NBA teams, the 2008–09 Lakers had struggled for years to make the transition from a disconnected, ego-driven team to a unified, selfless one. They weren't the most tran-scendent team I'd ever coached; that honor belongs to the 1995–96 Chicago Bulls, led by Michael Jordan and Scottie Pippen. Nor were they as talented as the 1999–2000 Lakers team, which was loaded with clutch shooters including Shaquille O'Neal, Kobe Bryant, Glen Rice, Robert Horry, Rick Fox, and Derek Fisher. But the 2008–09 Lakers had the seeds of greatness in their collective DNA.

The players looked hungrier than ever when they showed up for training camp in August 2008. At the end of the previous season, they'd made a miraculous run to the finals against the Celtics, only to be humiliated in Boston and lose the decisive game 6 by 39 points.

Clearly the beating we'd received at the hands of Kevin Garnett and company—not to mention the torturous ride to our hotel afterward through mobs of Celtics fans—had been a brutal experience, especially for the younger players who hadn't tasted Boston venom before.

Some teams get demoralized after losses like that, but this young, spirited team was energized by getting so close to the prize only to have it batted away by a tougher, more physically intimidating opponent. Kobe, who had been named the NBA's most valuable player that year, was particularly laser focused. I've always been impressed by Kobe's resilience and ironclad self-confidence. Unlike Shaq, who was often plagued by self-doubt, Kobe never let such thoughts cross his mind. If someone set the bar at ten feet, he'd jump eleven, even if no one had ever done it before. That's the attitude he brought with him when he arrived at training camp that fall, and it had a powerful impact on his teammates.

Still, what surprised me the most was not Kobe's ruthless determination but his changing relationship with his teammates. Gone was the brash young man who was so consumed with being the best player ever that he sucked the joy out of the game for everyone else. The new Kobe who had emerged during the season took his role as team leader to heart. Years ago, when I'd first arrived in L.A., I'd encouraged Kobe to spend time with his teammates instead of hiding out in his hotel room studying videotape. But he'd scoffed at the idea, claiming that all those guys were interested in were cars and women. Now he was making an effort to connect more closely with his teammates and figure out how to forge them into a more cohesive team.

Of course, it helped that the team's other cocaptain—Derek Fisher—was a natural leader with exceptional emotional intelligence and finely tuned management skills. I was pleased when Fish, who had played a key role as a point guard during our earlier run of three consecutive championships, decided to return to L.A. after free-agent gigs with the Golden State Warriors and the Utah Jazz. Though Fish wasn't as quick or as inventive as some of the younger point guards in the league, he was strong, determined, and fearless, with a rock-solid character. And despite his lack of speed, he had a gift for pushing the ball up court and making our offense run properly. He was also an excellent three-point shooter when the clock was running down. Most of all, he and Kobe had a solid bond. Kobe respected Derek's mental discipline and dependability under pressure, and Derek knew how to get through to Kobe in a way that nobody else could.

Kobe and Fish kicked off the first day of training camp with a speech about how the upcoming season would be a marathon, not a sprint, and how we needed to focus on meeting force with force and not allowing ourselves to be intimidated by physical pressure. Ironically, Kobe was beginning to sound more and more like me every day.

In their groundbreaking book, *Tribal Leadership*, management consultants Dave Logan, John King, and Halee Fischer-Wright lay out the five stages of tribal development, which they formulated after conducting extensive research on small to midsize organizations. Although basketball teams are not officially tribes, they share many of the same characteristics and develop along much the same lines:

STAGE 1—shared by most street gangs and characterized by despair, hostility, and the collective belief that "life sucks."

STAGE 2—filled primarily with apathetic people who perceive themselves as victims and who are passively antagonistic, with the mind-set that "my life sucks." Think *The Office* on TV or the *Dilbert* comic strip.

STAGE 3—focused primarily on individual achievement and driven by the motto "I'm great (and you're not)." According to the authors, people in organizations at this stage "have to win, and for them winning is personal. They'll outwork and outthink their competitors on an individual basis. The mood that results is a collection of 'lone warriors.'"

STAGE 4—dedicated to tribal pride and the overriding conviction that "we're great (and they're not)." This kind of team requires a strong adversary, and the bigger the foe, the more powerful the tribe.

STAGE 5—a rare stage characterized by a sense of innocent wonder and the strong belief that "life is great." (See Bulls, Chicago, 1995–98.)

All things being equal, contend Logan and his colleagues, a stage 5 culture will outperform a stage 4 culture, which will outperform a 3, and so on. In addition, the rules change when you move from one culture to another. That's why the so-called universal principles that appear in most leadership textbooks rarely hold up. In order to shift a culture from one stage to the next, you need to find the levers that are appropriate for that particular stage in the group's development.

During the 2008–09 season the Lakers needed to shift from a stage 3 team to a stage 4 in order to win. The key was getting a critical mass of players to buy into a more selfless approach to the game. I didn't worry so much about Kobe, even though he could go on a shooting spree at any second if he felt frustrated. Still, by this point in his career I knew he understood the folly of trying to score every time he got his hands on the ball. Nor was I concerned about Fish or Pau Gasol, who were naturally inclined to be team players. What concerned me most were some of the younger players eager to make a name for themselves with the ESPN *SportsCenter* crowd.

But to my surprise, early in the season I noticed that even some of the most immature players on the team were focused and single-minded. "We were on a serious mission, and there wasn't going to be any letup," says forward Luke Walton. "By the time we got to the finals, losing just wasn't going to be an option."

We got off to a roaring start, winning twenty-one of our first twenty-five games, and by the time we faced the Celtics at home on Christmas, we were a far more spirited team than we'd been during the previous year's playoffs. We were playing the game the way the "basketball gods" had ordained: reading defenses on the move and reacting in unison like a finely tuned jazz combo. These new Lakers beat the Celtics handily, 92–83, and then danced through the season to the best record in the Western Conference (65-17).

The most troubling threat came in the second round of the playoffs from the Houston Rockets, who pushed the series to seven games, despite losing star Yao Ming to a broken foot in game 3. If anything, our biggest weakness was the illusion that we could cruise on talent alone. But going to the brink against a team that was missing its top three stars showed our players just how treacherous the playoffs could be. The close contest woke them up and helped them move closer to becoming a selfless stage 4 team.

No question, the team that walked off the floor in Orlando after winning the championship finals in five games was different from the team that had fallen apart on the parquet floor of the TD Garden in Boston the year before. Not only were the players tougher and more confident, but they were graced by a fierce bond.

"It was just a brotherhood," said Kobe. "That's all it is—a brotherhood."

Most coaches I know spend a lot of time focusing on *X*'s and *O*'s. I must admit that at times I've fallen in that trap myself. But what fascinates most people about sports is not the endless chatter about strategy that fills the airwaves. It's what I like to call the spiritual nature of the game.

I can't pretend to be an expert in leadership theory. But what I do know is that the art of transforming a group of young, ambitious individuals into an integrated championship team is not a mechanistic process. It's a mysterious juggling act that requires not only a thorough knowledge of the time-honored laws of the game but also an open heart, a clear mind, and a deep curiosity about the ways of the human spirit.

This book is about my journey to try to unravel that mystery.

2

THE JACKSON ELEVEN

*You can't break the rules until you know
how to play the game.*

RICKI LEE JONES

Before we go any further, I'd like to give you an overview of the basic principles of mindful leadership that I've evolved over the years to help transform disorganized teams into champions. You won't find any lofty management theories here. With leadership, as with most things in life, the best approach is always the simplest.

1. LEAD FROM THE INSIDE OUT

Some coaches love to run with the lemmings. They spend an inordinate amount of time studying what other coaches are doing and trying out every flashy new technique to get an edge over their opponents. That kind of outside-in strategy might work in the short term if you have a forceful, charismatic personality, but it inevitably backfires when the players grow weary of being browbeaten and tune out or, even more likely, your opponents wise up and figure out a clever way to counter your latest move.

I am antilemming by nature. It goes back to my childhood, when I was force-fed religious dogma by my parents, both Pentecostal ministers. I was expected to think and behave in a rigidly prescribed manner. As an adult, I've tried to break free from that early conditioning and develop a more open-minded, personally meaningful way of being in the world.

For a long time, I believed I had to keep my personal beliefs separate from my professional life. In my quest to come to terms with my own spiritual yearning, I experimented with a wide range of ideas and practices, from Christian mysticism to Zen meditation and Native American rituals. Eventually, I arrived at a synthesis that felt authentic to me. And though at first I worried that my players might find my unorthodox views a little wacky, as time went by I discovered that the more I spoke from the heart, the more the players could hear me and benefit from what I'd gleaned.

2. BENCH THE EGO

Once a reporter asked Bill Fitch, my coach at the University of North Dakota, whether dealing with difficult personalities gave him heartburn, and he replied, "I'm the one who gives people heartburn, not them." Fitch, who later became a successful NBA coach, represents one of the most common styles of coaching: the domineering "my way or the highway" type of leader (which, in Bill's case, was tempered by his devilish sense of humor). The other classic type is the suck-up coach, who tries to mollify the stars on the team and be their best friend—a fool's exercise at best.

I've taken a different tack. After years of experimenting, I discovered that the more I tried to exert power directly, the less powerful I became. I learned to dial back my ego and distribute power as widely as possible without surrendering final authority. Paradoxically, this approach strengthened my effectiveness because it freed me to focus on my job as keeper of the team's vision.

Some coaches insist on having the last word, but I always tried to foster an environment in which everyone played a leadership role, from the most unschooled rookie to the veteran superstar. If your primary objective is to bring the team into a state of harmony and oneness, it doesn't make sense for you to rigidly impose your authority.

Dialing back the ego doesn't mean being a pushover. That's a lesson I learned from my mentor, former Knicks coach Red Holzman, one of the most selfless leaders I've ever known. Once when the team was flying out for a road trip, a player's boom box started blaring some heavy rock. Red went over to the guy and said, "Hey, do you have any Glenn Miller in your mix?" The guy looked at Red as if he were out of his mind. "Well, when you get some, you can play a little of my music and a little of yours. Otherwise, shut that damn thing off." Then Red sat down next to me and said, "You know, players have egos, but sometimes they forget that coaches have egos too."

3. LET EACH PLAYER DISCOVER HIS OWN DESTINY

One thing I've learned as a coach is that you can't force your will on people. If you want them to act differently, you need to inspire them to change themselves.

Most players are used to letting their coach think for them. When they run into a problem on the court, they look nervously over at the sidelines expecting coach to come up with an answer. Many coaches will gladly accommodate them. But not me. I've always been interested in getting players to think for themselves so that they can make difficult decisions in the heat of battle.

The standard rule of thumb in the NBA is that you should call a time-out as soon as an opposing team goes on a 6–0 run. Much to my coaching staff's dismay, I often let the clock keep running at that point, so that the players would be forced to come up with a solution on their own. This not only built solidarity but also increased what Michael Jordan used to call the team's collective "think power."

On another level, I always tried to give each player the freedom to carve out a role for himself within the team structure. I've seen dozens of players flame out and disappear not because they lacked talent but because they couldn't figure out how to fit into the cookie-cutter model of basketball that pervades the NBA.

My approach was always to relate to each player as a whole person, not just as a cog in the basketball machine. That meant pushing him to discover what distinct qualities he could bring to the game beyond taking shots and making passes. How much courage did he have? Or resilience? What about character under fire? Many players I've coached didn't look special on paper, but in the process of creating a role for themselves they grew into formidable champions. Derek Fisher is a prime example. He began as a backup point guard for the Lakers with average foot speed and shooting skills. But he worked tirelessly and transformed himself into an invaluable clutch performer and one of the best leaders I've ever coached.

4. THE ROAD TO FREEDOM IS A BEAUTIFUL SYSTEM

When I joined the Bulls in 1987 as an assistant coach, my colleague Tex Winter taught me a system, known as the triangle offense, that aligned perfectly with the values of selflessness and mindful awareness I'd been studying in Zen Buddhism. Tex learned the basics of the system as a student at the University of Southern California under legendary coach Sam Barry. As head coach at Kansas State, Tex refined the system and used it to lead the Wildcats to eight league titles and two Final Four appearances. He also relied on it when he was head coach of the Houston Rockets. (Tex's USC teammates Bill Sharman and Alex Hannum used their own versions of the triangle en route to winning championships with the Lakers and 76ers, respectively.)

Despite Tex's and my extraordinary success using the triangle with the Bulls and the Lakers, there are still a lot of misconceptions about how the system works. Critics call it rigid, outdated, and complicated to learn, none of which is true. In fact, the triangle is a simpler offense than most NBA teams run today. Best of all, it automatically stimulates creativity and teamwork, freeing players from having to memorize dozens of set plays.

What attracted me to the triangle was the way it empowers the players, offering each one a vital role to play as well as a high level of creativity within a clear, well-defined structure. The key is to train each player to read the defense and react appropriately. This allows the team to move together in a coordinated manner—depending on the action at any given moment. With the triangle you can't stand around and wait for the Michael Jordans and Kobe Bryants of the world to work their magic. All five players must be fully engaged every second—or the whole system will fail. That stimulates an ongoing process of group problem solving in real time, not just on a coach's clipboard during time-outs. When the triangle is working right, it's virtually impossible to stop it because nobody knows what's going to happen next, not even the players themselves.

5. TURN THE MUNDANE INTO THE SACRED

As a boy I used to marvel at the way my parents created community, transforming the hardscrabble life on the plains of Montana and North Dakota into a sacred experience.

You know the hymn:

Blest be the tie that binds
Our hearts in Christian love;
The fellowship of kindred minds
Is like to that above.

That's the essence of what it means to bring individuals together and connect them to something greater than themselves. I heard that hymn thousands of times when I was growing up, and I witnessed what happens when the spirit touches people and unites them. The rituals had a profound effect on me—and on my approach to leadership—even though later I drifted away from the Pentecostal faith and found a new direction spiritually.

Once when the Bulls were getting on the team bus after a close come-from-behind win, my trainer Chip Schaefer said he wished we could bottle that late-game energy like a magic potion so we could bring it out whenever we needed it. That's a nice idea, but what I've learned is that the forces that join people harmoniously aren't that clear-cut. They can't be manufactured at will, though you can do your best to create the conditions that will promote that sort of transformation—very similar to what my parents tried to do every Sunday in church.

As I see it, my job as a coach was to make something meaningful out of one of the most mundane activities on the planet: playing pro basketball. Despite all the glamour surrounding the sport, the process of playing day after day in one city after another can be a soul-numbing exercise. That's why I started incorporating meditation into practices. I wanted to give players something besides X's and O's to focus on. What's more, we often invented rituals of our own to infuse practices with a sense of the sacred.

At the start of training camp, for instance, we used to perform a ritual that I borrowed from football great Vince Lombardi. As the players formed a row on the baseline, I'd ask them to commit to being coached that season, saying, "God has ordained me to coach you young men, and I embrace the role I've been given. If you wish to accept the game I embrace and follow my coaching, as a sign of your commitment, step across that line." Wonder of wonders, they always did it.

We did this in a fun way, but with a serious intent. The essence of coaching is to get the players to wholeheartedly agree to being coached, then offer them a sense of their destiny as a team.

6. ONE BREATH = ONE MIND

When I took over the Lakers in 1999, they were a talented but highly unfocused team. They often fell apart in the playoffs because their attack was so confused and undisciplined and the better teams, such as the San Antonio Spurs and the Utah Jazz, had figured out how to neutralize the Lakers' most potent weapon: Shaquille O'Neal.

Yes, we could make a number of tactical moves to counter these weaknesses, but what the players really needed was a way to quiet the chatter in their minds and focus on the business of winning basketball games. When I was head coach of the Bulls, the players had to deal with the Michael Jordan media caravan. But that was nothing compared to the distractions the Lakers faced in the belly of celebrity culture. To get the players to settle down, I introduced them to one of the tools I'd used successfully with the Bulls: mindfulness meditation.

I've taken a lot of ribbing from other coaches for my experiments with meditation. Once college basketball coaches Dean Smith and Bobby Knight came to a Lakers game and asked me, "Is it true, Phil, that you and your players sit around in a dark room before games and hold hands?"

All I could do was laugh. Though mindfulness meditation has its roots in Buddhism, it's an easily accessible technique for quieting the restless mind and focusing attention on whatever is happening in the present moment. This is extremely useful for basketball players, who often have to make split-second decisions under enormous pressure. I also discovered that when I had the players sit in silence, breathing together in sync, it helped align them on a nonverbal level far more effectively than words. One breath equals one mind.

Another aspect of Buddhist teachings that has influenced me is the emphasis on openness and freedom. The Zen teacher Shunryu Suzuki likened the mind to a cow in a pasture. If you enclose the cow in a small yard, it will become nervous and frustrated and start eating the neighbor's grass. But if you give it a large pasture to roam around in, it will be more content and less likely to break loose. For me, this approach to mental discipline has been enormously refreshing, compared to the restricted way of thinking ingrained in me as a child.

I've also found that Suzuki's metaphor can be applied to managing a team. If you place too many restrictions on players, they'll spend an inordinate amount of time trying to buck the system. Like all of us, they need a certain degree of structure in their lives, but they also require enough latitude to express themselves creatively. Otherwise they'll start behaving like that penned-in cow.

7. THE KEY TO SUCCESS IS COMPASSION

In his new adaptation of the Chinese sacred text *Tao Te Ching*, Stephen Mitchell offers a provocative take on Lao-tzu's approach to leadership:

> *I have just three things to teach:*
> *simplicity, patience, compassion.*
> *These three are the greatest treasures.*
> *Simple in actions and thoughts,*
> *you return to the source of being.*
> *Patient with both friends and enemies,*
> *you accord with the way things are.*

Compassionate toward yourself,
you reconcile all beings in the world.

All of these "treasures" have been integral to my coaching, but compassion has been the most important. In the West we tend to think of compassion as a form of charity, but I share Lao-tzu's view that compassion for all beings—not least of all oneself—is the key to breaking down barriers among people.

Now, "compassion" is a word not often bandied about in locker rooms. But I've found that a few kind, thoughtful words can have a strong transformative effect on relationships, even with the toughest men on the team.

Because I started as a player, I've always been able to empathize with young men facing the harsh realities of life in the NBA. Most players live in a state of constant anxiety, worrying about whether they're going to be hurt or humiliated, cut or traded, or, worst of all, make a foolish mistake that will haunt them for the rest of their lives. When I was with the Knicks, I was sidelined for more than a year with a debilitating back injury. That experience allowed me to talk with players I've coached from personal experience about how it feels when your body gives out and you have to ice every joint after a game, or even sit on the bench for an entire season.

Beyond that, I think it's essential for athletes to learn to open their hearts so that they can collaborate with one another in a meaningful way. When Michael returned to the Bulls in 1995 after a year and a half of playing minor-league baseball, he didn't know most of the players and he felt completely out of sync with the team. It wasn't until he got into a fight with Steve Kerr at practice that he realized he needed to get to know his teammates more intimately. He had to understand what made them tick, so that he could work with them more productively. That moment of awakening helped Michael become a compassionate leader and ultimately helped transform the team into one of the greatest of all time.

8. KEEP YOUR EYE ON THE SPIRIT, NOT ON THE SCOREBOARD

Management guru Stephen Covey tells this old Japanese tale about a samurai warrior and his three sons: The samurai wanted to teach his sons about the power of teamwork. So he gave each of them an arrow and asked them to break it. No problem. Each son did it easily. Then the samurai gave them a bundle of three arrows bound together and asked them to repeat the process. But none of them could. "That's your lesson," the samurai said. "If you three stick together, you will never be defeated."

This story reflects just how strong a team can be when each of its members surrenders his self-interest for the greater good. When a player isn't forcing a shot or trying to impose his personality on the team, his gifts as an athlete most fully manifest. Paradoxically, by playing within his natural abilities, he activates a higher potential for the team that transcends his own limitations and helps his teammates transcend theirs. When this happens, the whole begins to add up to more than the sum of its parts.

Example: We had a player on the Lakers who loved to chase down balls on defense. If his mind was focused on scoring points at the other end of the floor instead of on making steals, he wouldn't be able to perform either task very well. But when he committed himself to playing defense, his teammates covered for him on the other end, because they knew intuitively what he was going to do. Then, all of a sudden, everybody was able to hit their rhythm, and good things began to happen.

Interestingly, the other players weren't consciously aware that they were anticipating their teammate's behavior. It wasn't an out-of-body experience or anything like that. But somehow, mysteriously, they just sensed what was going to happen next and made their moves accordingly.

Most coaches get tied up in knots worrying about tactics, but I preferred to focus my attention on whether the players were moving together in a spirited way. Michael Jordan used to say that what he liked about my coaching style was how patient I remained during the final minutes of a game, much like his college coach, Dean Smith.

This wasn't an act. My confidence grew out of knowing that when the spirit was right and the players were attuned to one another, the game was likely to unfold in our favor.

9. SOMETIMES YOU HAVE TO PULL OUT THE BIG STICK

In the strictest form of Zen, monitors roam the meditation hall, striking sleeping or listless meditators with a flat wooden stick, called a *keisaku*, to get them to pay attention. This is not intended as punishment. In fact, the *keisaku* is sometimes referred to as a "compassionate stick." The purpose of the blow is to reinvigorate the meditator and make him or her more awake in the moment.

I haven't wielded a *keisaku* stick in practice, though there were times when I wished I'd had one handy. Still, I've pulled out some other tricks to wake players up and raise their level of consciousness. Once I had the Bulls practice in silence; on another occasion I made them scrimmage with the lights out. I like to shake things up and keep the players guessing. Not because I want to make their lives miserable but because I want to prepare them for the inevitable chaos that occurs the minute they step onto a basketball court.

One of my favorite ploys was to divide the players into two lopsided teams for a scrimmage, then not call any fouls on the weaker of the two. I liked to see how the players on the stronger team would

respond when all the calls were going against them and their opponents were running up 30-point leads. This scheme used to drive Michael nuts because he couldn't stand losing, even though he knew the
game was rigged.

One of the players I came down especially hard on was Lakers forward Luke Walton. I sometimes played mind games with him so that
he would know what it felt like to be stressed out under pressure. Once
I put him through a particularly frustrating series of exercises, and I
could tell by his reaction that I'd pushed him too far. Afterward I sat
down with him and said, "I know you're thinking about becoming a
coach someday. I think that's a good idea, but coaching isn't all fun
and games. Sometimes no matter how nice a guy you are, you're going
to have to be an asshole. You can't be a coach if you need to be liked."

10. WHEN IN DOUBT, DO NOTHING

Basketball is an action sport, and most people involved in it are high-
energy individuals who love to do something—*anything*—to solve
problems. However, there are occasions when the best solution is to
do absolutely nothing.

This is especially true when the media is involved. Reporters often
made fun of me for not directly confronting my players when they
acted immaturely or said something dumb in the press. The *Los Angeles Times*'s T. J. Simers wrote a funny column once about my pro-
pensity for inactivity and concluded wryly that "no one does nothing
better than Phil." I get the joke. But I've always been wary of asserting my ego frivolously just to give reporters something to write about.

On a deeper level, I believe that focusing on something other than
the business at hand can be the most effective way to solve complex
problems. When the mind is allowed to relax, inspiration often follows. Research is beginning to prove the point. In a commentary on
CNNMoney.com, *Fortune* senior writer Anne Fisher reported that

scientists have begun to realize "that people may do their best thinking when they are not concentrating on work at all." She cites studies
published in the journal *Science* by Dutch psychologists who concluded, "The unconscious mind is a terrific solver of complex problems when the conscious mind is busy elsewhere or, perhaps better
yet, not overtaxed at all."

That's why I subscribe to the philosophy of the late Satchel Paige,
who said, "Sometimes I sits and thinks, and sometimes I just sits."

11. FORGET THE RING

I hate losing. I always have. When I was a kid, I was so competitive I
frequently burst into tears and broke the board into pieces if one of
my older brothers, Charles or Joe, trounced me in a game. They loved
teasing me when I threw a sore loser's tantrum, which made me even
more determined to win the next time. I'd practice and practice until
I figured out a way to beat them and wipe the smug smiles off their
faces.

Even as an adult, I've been known to act out on occasion. Once,
after a particularly embarrassing loss to Orlando in the playoffs, I
shaved off most of my hair and stomped around the room for nearly
an hour until the anger subsided.

And yet as a coach, I know that being fixated on winning (or more
likely, not losing) is counterproductive, especially when it causes you
to lose control of your emotions. What's more, obsessing about winning is a loser's game: The most we can hope for is to create the best
possible conditions for success, then let go of the outcome. The ride is
a lot more fun that way. Bill Russell, the Boston Celtics great who
won more championship rings as a player than anyone else (eleven),
revealed in his memoir, *Second Wind*, that he sometimes secretly
rooted for the opposing team during big games because if they were
doing well, it meant he would have a more heightened experience.

Lao-tzu saw it another way. He believed that being too competitive could throw you out of whack spiritually:

> *The best athlete*
> *wants his opponent at his best.*
> *The best general*
> *enters the mind of his enemy . . .*
> *All of them embody*
> *the virtue of non-competition.*
> *Not that they don't love to compete,*
> *but they do it in the spirit of play.*

That's why at the start of every season I always encouraged players to focus on the journey rather than the goal. What matters most is playing the game the right way and having the courage to grow, as human beings as well as basketball players. When you do that, the ring takes care of itself.

3

RED

The greatest carver does the least cutting.

LAO-TZU

My first impression of the NBA was that it was an unstructured mess.

When Red Holzman recruited me for the New York Knicks in 1967, I'd never seen an NBA game before, except for a few playoff games on TV between the Boston Celtics and the Philadelphia Warriors. So Red sent me a film of a 1966 game between the Knicks and the Lakers, and I invited a bunch of my college teammates over to watch it on a big screen.

I was stunned by how sloppy and undisciplined both teams were. At the University of North Dakota, we prided ourselves on playing the game in a systematic way. In fact, in my senior year coach Bill Fitch had implemented a system of ball movement that I really liked, which I later learned was a version of the triangle that he'd picked up from Tex Winter.

There seemed to be no logic to the Knicks game we were watching. To me it looked like nothing more than a bunch of talented players running up and down the floor looking for shots.

Then the fight broke out.

Willis Reed, the Knicks' imposing six-nine, 235-pound power forward got tangled up with forward Rudy LaRusso near the Lakers' bench. Then there was a pause in the film, and when it started up again, Willis was shrugging several Lakers players off his back, before leveling center Darrall Imhoff and slugging LaRusso twice in the face. By the time they finally subdued him, Willis had also broken forward John Block's nose and thrown center Hank Finkel to the ground.

Wow. We all jumped up in unison and shouted, "Run that back again!" Meanwhile, I'm thinking, *What have I gotten myself into? This is the guy I'm going to be going up against day in and day out in practice!*

Actually, when I met Willis that summer, I found him to be a warm and friendly guy, who was dignified, bighearted, and a natural leader whom everyone respected. He had a commanding presence on the floor and he felt instinctively that his job was to protect his teammates. The Knicks expected Willis to be suspended for that incident in the game against L.A., but the league was more tolerant about fighting in those days and let it go. From that point on, big men around the league started thinking twice before getting into a tussle with Willis on the floor.

Reed wasn't the only great leader on the Knicks. In fact, playing for New York during the championship years was like going to grad school in leadership. Forward Dave DeBusschere, who had been a player/coach for the Detroit Pistons before joining the Knicks, was an astute floor general. Forward Bill Bradley, the future U.S. senator, was gifted at building consensus among the players and helping them meld together into a team. Shooting guard Dick Barnett, who later earned a Ph.D. in education, used his biting wit to keep everyone from taking themselves too seriously. And Walt Frazier, my roommate during the first season, was a masterful point guard who served as the team's quarterback on the floor.

But the man who taught me the most about leadership was the most unassuming of them all: Holzman himself.

The first time Red saw me play was during one of the worst games of my college career. I got into foul trouble early and never found my rhythm, as Louisiana Tech knocked us out in the first round of the NCAA small-college tournament. I scored 51 points in the consolation game against Parsons, but Red missed that one.

Nevertheless, Red must have seen something he liked because he grabbed Bill Fitch after the Louisiana Tech game and asked him, "Do you think Jackson can play for me?" Fitch didn't hesitate. "Sure he can play for you," he said, thinking that Red was looking for players who could handle full-court defense. It was only afterward that he realized that what Red really wanted to know was: Can this hick from North Dakota handle life in the Big Apple? Either way, Fitch says, his answer would have been the same.

Fitch was a hard-nosed coach—and ex-Marine—who ran practices as if they were Parris Island drills. He was a far cry from my mild-mannered Williston (North Dakota) high school coach, Bob Peterson, but I liked playing for him because he was tough, honest, and always pushing me to do better. Once, in my junior year, I got drunk during pledge week and made a fool of myself trying to lead a bunch of students in school cheers. When Fitch heard the story, he told me I would have to do push-ups every time I saw him on campus.

Still, I flourished in Fitch's system. We played full-court pressure defense, and I loved it. At six-eight I was big enough to play center, but I was also quick and energetic and had a large wingspan, which made it easy for me to harass playmakers and pick off steals. My arms were so long, in fact, that I could sit in the backseat of a car and open both front doors at the same time without leaning forward. In college, my nickname was "the Mop" because I was always falling on the floor, chasing after loose balls.

During my junior year, I came into my own, averaging 21.8 points and 12.9 rebounds per game, and was named first team All-American. We won the conference title that year and made the small-college Final Four for the second year in a row, losing in a tight semifinal game to Southern Illinois. The next year I averaged 27.4 points and 14.4 rebounds and scored 50 points twice on the way to making the All-American first team again.

At first I thought that if I was going to be drafted by the NBA, I would be picked by the Baltimore Bullets, whose head scout, my future boss, Jerry Krause, had been eyeing me. But the Bullets were outmaneuvered by the Knicks, who picked me early in the second round (seventeenth overall), leaving Krause, who'd gambled that I wouldn't go until the third round, kicking himself for years.

I was also drafted by the Minnesota Muskies in the American Basketball Association, which was attractive to me because it was closer to home. But Holzman wasn't going to let the Muskies win. He visited me that summer in Fargo, North Dakota, where I was working as a camp counselor, and made me a better offer. He asked me if I had any reservations about signing with the Knicks, and I replied that I was thinking about going to graduate school to become a minister. He said that there would be plenty of time after I finished my pro career to pursue whatever else I wanted to do. He also reassured me that I could turn to him if I had difficulty dealing with New York City.

As it turned out, John Lindsay, New York's mayor at the time, was in Fargo giving a speech at the organization where I was working. Red found the synchronicity of it all amusing. While I signed the contract that day, he said, "Can you imagine? The mayor of New York is here and everybody knows it. And you're here getting signed and nobody knows it."

That's when I knew I'd found my mentor.

When I arrived at training camp in October, the Knicks were in a holding pattern. We were still waiting for our new star forward, Bill Bradley, to show up after finishing Air Force Reserve boot camp. In fact, we were conducting training camp at McGuire Air Force Base in the hope that he would be able to break away at some point and start practicing with the team.

Although our roster was loaded with talent, the leadership structure hadn't yet been established. The putative top man was Walt Bellamy, a high-scoring center and future Hall of Famer. But Walt was constantly battling with Willis, who was much better suited for the lead role. At one point in the previous season, the two of them had run into each other and literally knocked themselves out fighting to establish position in the post. Dick Van Arsdale was the starting small forward, but many thought that Cazzie Russell was more talented. Meanwhile, Dick Barnett and Howard Komives made up a solid backcourt, but Barnett was still recovering from a torn Achilles tendon the year before.

On top of all that, it was clear that the players had lost confidence in coach Dick McGuire, whose nickname, "Mumbles," said a lot about his inability to communicate with the team. So it wasn't surprising when Ned Irish, president of the Knicks, moved McGuire to a scouting position in December and appointed Red head coach. Holzman was a tough, reserved New Yorker with a wry sense of humor and a strong basketball pedigree. A two-time All-American guard at City College of New York, he played for the Rochester Royals as a pro, winning two league championships, before becoming head coach of the Milwaukee/St. Louis Hawks.

Red was a master of simplicity. He didn't espouse any particular system, nor did he stay up all night inventing plays. What he believed in was playing the game the right way, which to him meant moving the ball on offense and playing intense team defense. Red learned the game in the pre–jump shot era when five-man ball movement was far more prevalent than one-on-one creativity. He had two simple rules, which he shouted from the sidelines during every game:

See the ball. Red focused much more attention on defense in practice because he believed that a strong defense was the key to everything. During one practice, Red, who could be extremely graphic when he needed to be, took copies of our plays and pretended to wipe his butt with them. "This is about how much good these things are," he said, dropping the pages on the floor. That's why he wanted us to learn to play defense together better, because once you did that, he believed, the offense would take care of itself.

In Red's view, awareness was the secret to good defense. He stressed keeping your eye on the ball at all times and being acutely attuned to what was happening on the floor. The Knicks weren't as big as other teams; nor did we have an overpowering shot blocker like the Celtics' Bill Russell. So under Red's direction, we developed a highly integrated style of defense that relied on the collective awareness of all five players rather than one man's brilliant moves under the basket. With all five men working as one, it was easier to trap ball handlers, cut off passing lanes, exploit mistakes, and launch fast breaks before the other team could figure out what was going on.

Red loved using full-court pressure to throw opponents off their games. In fact, in my very first practice, we implemented a full-court press for the whole scrimmage. That was perfect for Walt Frazier, Emmett Bryant, and me, because we'd played full-court defense in college. My teammates dubbed me "Coat Hanger" and "Head and Shoulders" because of my physique, but I much preferred the name broadcaster Marv Albert gave me: "Action Jackson." I knew that by playing forward instead of center, I was giving up my biggest strength—post play—but I could help the team out and get more time on the court by concentrating on defense. Besides, I didn't possess a fifteen-foot jumper yet and my ball-handling skills were so sketchy that Red later gave me a two-dribble rule.

Hit the open man. If Red were coaching today, he would be appalled at how self-absorbed the game has become. For him, selflessness was the holy grail of basketball. "This isn't rocket science," he would proclaim, adding that the best offensive strategy was to keep the ball moving among all five players to create shooting opportunities and make it hard for the other team to focus on one or two shooters. Even though we had some of the best shot creators in the game—notably Frazier and Earl "the Pearl" Monroe—Red insisted that everybody work together in unison to get the ball to the player with the best shot. If you decided to go solo, which few players ever attempted, you'd soon find yourself exiled to the end bench.

"On a good team there are no superstars," Red insisted. "There are great players who show they are great players by being able to play with others as a team. They have the ability to be superstars, but if they fit into a good team, they make sacrifices, they do things necessary to help the team win. What the numbers are in salaries or statistics don't matter; how they play together does."

Few teams in the NBA have ever been as balanced offensively as the 1969–70 Knicks. We had six players who consistently scored in double figures and none who averaged much higher than 20 points a game. What made the team so hard to defend was that all five starters were clutch shooters, so if you double-teamed one man who happened to be hot, it would open up opportunities for the other four—all of whom could hit big shots.

One thing that fascinated me about Red was how much of the offense he turned over to the players. He let us design many of the plays and actively sought out our thinking about what moves to make in critical games. Many coaches have a hard time giving over power to their players, but Red listened intently to what the players had to say because he knew we had more intimate knowledge of what was happening on the floor than he did.

Red's singular gift, however, was his uncanny ability to manage grown men and get them to come together with a common mission. He didn't use sophisticated motivational techniques; he was just straightforward and honest. Unlike many coaches, he didn't interfere in players' personal lives unless they were up to something that would have a negative effect on the team.

When Red took over as coach, practices were laughably chaotic. Players often arrived late and brought their friends and relatives as spectators. The facilities had broken floors, warped wooden backboards, and showers without any hot water, and the practices themselves were largely uncontrolled scrimmages without any drills or exercises. Red put a stop to all that. He instituted what he called "silly fines" for tardiness and banished from practices everybody who wasn't on the team, including the press. He ran tough, disciplined practices focused primarily on defense. "Practice doesn't make perfect," he used to say. "Perfect practice does."

On the road, there were no curfews or bed checks. Red had only one rule: The hotel bar belonged to him. He didn't care where you went or what you did as long as you didn't interrupt his late-night scotch with trainer Danny Whelan and the beat writers. Although he was more accessible than other coaches, he felt it was important to maintain a certain distance from the players because he knew that someday he might have to cut or trade one of us.

If he needed to discipline you, he rarely did it in front of the team, unless it was related to your basketball play. Instead he would invite you to his "private office": the locker-room toilet. He usually called me in to the toilet when I'd said something critical in the press about the team. I had good rapport with the reporters after years of playing cards together, and sometimes I had a tendency to be overly glib. Red was more circumspect. "Don't you realize," he'd say, "that these newspapers are going to be lining somebody's birdcage tomorrow?"

Red was notoriously sphinxlike with the media. He often took reporters out to dinner and talked for hours, but he rarely gave them anything they could use. He never criticized the players or any of our opponents. Instead he often toyed with reporters to see what kind of nonsense he could get them to print. Once after a particularly hard defeat, a reporter asked him how he managed to be so calm, and Red replied, "Because I realize that the only real catastrophe is coming home and finding out there's no more scotch in the house." Of course, the quote made the papers the next day.

What I loved about Red was his ability to put basketball in perspective. Early in the 1969–70 season, we went on an eighteen-game winning streak and pulled away from the rest of the pack. When the streak ended with a disappointing loss at home, reporters asked Red what he would have done if the Knicks had won, and he replied, "I'd go home, drink a scotch, and eat the great meal that [his wife] Selma is cooking." And what would he do now that we had lost? "Go home, drink a scotch, and eat the great meal Selma is cooking."

The turning point for the Knicks was another brawl, this time during a televised game against the Hawks in Atlanta in November 1968. The fight was ignited by Atlanta's Lou Hudson in the second half when he tried to dodge around Willis Reed's hard pick and ended up slugging him in the face. All of the Knicks got up and joined the battle (or at least pretended to), except for one player, Walt Bellamy.

The next day we had a team meeting to discuss the incident. The conversation revolved around Bellamy's no-show, and the consensus among the players was that he wasn't doing his job. When Red asked Walt why he hadn't supported his teammates on the floor, he said, "I don't think fighting is appropriate in basketball." Many of us may have agreed with him in the abstract, but fighting was an everyday reality in the NBA, and it didn't give any of us comfort to hear that our big man didn't have our backs.

A few weeks later the Knicks traded Bellamy and Komives to the Pistons for Dave DeBusschere—a move that solidified the starting lineup and gave us the flexibility and depth to win two world championships. Willis took over as center and established himself as team leader and Red's sergeant at arms. DeBusschere, a hard-driving, six-six, 220-pound player with great court sense and a smooth outside shot, stepped into the power forward position. Walt Frazier replaced Komives at point guard, teaming with Barnett, a gifted one-on-one player. Bill Bradley and Cazzie Russell shared the final position—small forward—because our starter, Dick Van Arsdale, had been picked up by the Phoenix Suns in that year's expansion draft. But Bill got the upper hand when Cazzie broke his ankle two months after the DeBusschere trade.

It was interesting to watch Bill and Cazzie compete for that position when Russell returned the next year. Both of them had been stars in college and prized picks in the draft. (Bill was a territorial selection in 1965, and Cazzie was the number one pick overall in 1966.) Bradley, who was nicknamed "Dollar Bill" because of his impressive (for that time) four-year, $500,000 contract, had averaged more than 30 points a game three years in a row at Princeton and led the Tigers to the NCAA Final Four, where he was named the tournament's most valuable player. After being drafted by the Knicks in 1965, he had decided to attend Oxford for two years as a Rhodes scholar before joining the team. There was so much hype about him that Barnett started referring to him sarcastically as "the man who could leap tall buildings with a single bound."

Cazzie got a lot of teasing as well. He too had scored a big contract ($200,000 for two years) and had been such a dynamic scorer at Michigan that the school's gym was dubbed "the House that Cazzie Built." Nobody questioned his skill: Cazzie was an excellent shooter who had led the Wolverines to three consecutive Big Ten titles. What amused the players was his obsession with health food and alternative therapies. For once, there was someone on my team who had more nicknames than I did. He was called "Wonder Boy," "Muscles Russell," "Cockles 'n' Muscles," and my favorite, "Max Factor," because he loved slathering massage oil on his body after workouts. His room was filled with so many vitamins and supplements that Barnett, his roommate, joked that you had to get a signed pharmaceutical note if you wanted to visit.

What impressed me about Bill and Cazzie was how intensely they were able to compete with each other without getting caught in a battle of egos. At first Bill had a hard time adjusting to the pro game because of his lack of foot speed and leaping ability, but he made up for those limitations by learning to move quickly without the ball and outsmart defenders on the run. Defending him in practice—which I often had to do—was nerve-racking. Just when you thought you had trapped him in a corner, he would skitter away and show up on the other side of the floor with an open shot.

Cazzie had a different problem. He was a great driver with a strong move to the basket, but the starting team worked better when Bradley was on the floor. So Red made Cazzie a sixth man who could come off the bench and ignite a game-turning scoring spree. Over time, Cazzie adjusted to the role and took pride in leading the second unit, which, in 1969–70, included center Nate Bowman, guard Mike Riordan, and forward Dave Stallworth (who had been sidelined for a year and a half recovering from a stroke), plus backup players John Warren, Donnie May, and Bill Hosket. Cazzie gave the unit a nickname: "the Minutemen."

Not too long ago, Bill attended a Knicks reunion and was surprised when Cazzie, who is now a minister, came up to him and apologized for his selfish behavior when they were competing for the same job. Bill told Cazzie that there was no need to apologize because he knew that, no matter how driven Cazzie was, he never put his own ambition above that of the team.

Unfortunately I couldn't be one of Cazzie's Minutemen in 1969–70. In December 1968 I had a serious back injury that required spinal fusion surgery and took me out of the game for about a year and a half. The recovery was horrendous: I had to wear a body brace for six months and was told that I had to limit physical activity, including sex, during that period. My teammates asked if I was planning to have my wife wear a chastity belt. I laughed, but it wasn't funny.

I probably could have returned to action in the 1969–70 season, but the team had gotten off to a great start and the front office decided to put me on the injured list for the whole year to protect me from being picked up in the expansion draft.

I wasn't worried about money because I had signed a two-year extension deal with the club after my rookie year. But I needed something to keep me occupied, so I did some TV commentary, worked on a book about the Knicks called *Take It All!* with team photographer George Kalinsky, and traveled with the team as Red's informal assistant coach. In those days most coaches didn't have assistants, but Red knew that I had an interest in learning more about the game, and he was looking for someone to bounce new ideas around with.

The assignment gave me an opportunity to look at the game the way a coach does.

Red was a strong verbal communicator, but he wasn't that visually oriented and rarely drew diagrams of plays on the board during pregame talks. Every now and then, to keep the players focused, he would ask them to nod their heads if they heard the word "defense" while he was talking—which happened about every fourth word. Still, the players drifted off when he was talking, so he asked me to break down the strengths and weaknesses of the teams we were facing and draw pictures of their key plays on the board. This forced me to start thinking of the game as a strategic problem rather than a tactical one. As a young player, you tend to focus most of your attention on how you're going beat your man in any given game. But now I began to see basketball as a dynamic game of chess in which all the pieces were in motion. It was exhilarating.

Another lesson I learned was about the importance of pregame rituals. The shootaround had yet to be invented, so most coaches tried to squeeze in whatever pregame instructions they had during the fifteen or twenty minutes before the players stepped out on the floor. But there's only so much a player can absorb when his body is pulsing with adrenaline. This is not a good time for deep left-brain discussions. It's the moment to calm the players' minds and strengthen their spiritual connection with one another before they head into battle.

Red paid a great deal of attention to the bench players because they played such a vital role on our team, which was often weakened by injuries. In Red's mind, it was just as important for the bench players to be actively engaged in the game as it was for the starters. To make sure the subs were prepared mentally, he'd usually give them several minutes' warning before putting them in the game. He also constantly goaded them to pay attention to the twenty-four-second clock, so they could jump in at any moment without missing a beat. Red made each player feel as if he had an important role on the team, whether he played four minutes a game or forty—and this helped turn the Knicks into a fast-moving, cohesive team.

As the playoffs arrived in 1969–70, the Knicks looked unstoppable. We finished the season with a league-leading 60-22 record and muscled our way past Baltimore and Milwaukee in the early rounds. Fortunately, we didn't have to worry about the Celtics, because Bill Russell had retired and Boston was in retrenching mode.

Our opponents in the championship finals were the Lakers, a star-studded team led by Wilt Chamberlain, Elgin Baylor, and Jerry West, who had a gnawing desire to win a ring after losing to Boston in six of the past eight NBA finals. But they weren't nearly as quick or mobile as we were, and their biggest weapon, Chamberlain, had spent most of the season recovering from knee surgery.

With the series tied 2–2, Willis went down with a torn thigh muscle in game 5 in New York, and we had to resort to a small, no-center lineup for the rest of the game. That meant DeBusschere and Stallworth—a six-six and six-seven tandem—had to use stealth and trickery to handle the seven-one, 275-pound Chamberlain, probably the most overpowering center ever to play the game. In those days it was illegal to move more than two steps off your man to double-team another player, so we had to institute a zone defense, which was also illegal but less likely to get called in front of a raging Knicks home crowd. On the offensive end, DeBusschere lured Chamberlain away from the basket with his pinpoint fifteen-footers, freeing the rest of the team to move more freely inside. That led to a decisive 107–100 win.

The Lakers returned home and tied up the series in game 6, setting up one of the most dramatic moments in NBA history. The big question was whether Willis would be able to return for game 7 in Madison Square Garden. The doctors kept us in the dark until the last minute. Willis couldn't flex his leg because of the muscle tear, and jumping was out of the question, but he dressed up for the game and took a few warm-up shots before retreating to the trainer's room for more treatments. I followed with my camera and took a great shot of him being injected in the hip with a giant shot of Carbocaine, but Red refused to let me publish it because he said that would be unfair to the press photographers, who had been denied access to the room.

As the game was about to start, Willis hobbled down the center aisle and onto the court, and the crowd went berserk. Future broadcaster Steve Albert, who was the honorary ball boy for the game, said he was looking at the Lakers when Willis appeared on the floor and "they all, to a man, turned around and stopped shooting and looked at Willis. And their jaws dropped. The game was over before it started."

Frazier moved the ball up court at the start of the game and hit Willis near the basket, and he knocked in a short jump shot. Then he scored again the next time up the floor, and all of a sudden the Knicks jumped out to a 7–2 lead, which usually doesn't mean much in the NBA, but in this case it did. Willis's commanding presence in the early going knocked the Lakers off their game and they never recovered.

Of course, it didn't hurt that Frazier had one of the greatest unsung performances in playoff history, scoring 36 points, with 19 assists and 7 rebounds. Though Walt was disappointed about being overshadowed by Willis, he too tipped his hat to the captain. "Now a lot of people say to me, 'Wow, I didn't know you had a game like that,'" said Frazier later. "But I know if Willis didn't do what he did, I wouldn't have been able to have the game I had. He got the fans involved and gave us confidence just by his coming out onto the floor."

The Knicks won 113–99 and we all became celebrities overnight. It was a bittersweet victory for me, however. I was grateful that my teammates voted me a full share of the playoff earnings and my first championship ring. But once the champagne stopped flowing, I felt guilty about not having been able to contribute more to the championship push. I was dying to get back in the game.

4

THE QUEST

The privilege of a lifetime is being who you are.
JOSEPH CAMPBELL

In the summer of 1972, my brother Joe and I took a motorcycle trip through the West that shifted the direction of my life.

I had returned to basketball two years earlier, but I still felt tentative on court and hadn't found my rhythm yet. And my marriage to Maxine, my college sweetheart, was foundering. The six-month rehabilitation I had undergone after surgery hadn't helped matters, and we had gone our separate ways—informally—earlier that year. Joe, who was a psychology professor at the State University of New York at Buffalo, had also separated from his wife. It seemed like a good time for us to hit the road.

I bought a used BMW 750 and met Joe in Great Falls, Montana, not far from my parents' parsonage. We set out on a journey across the Great Divide to British Columbia that lasted about a month. Joe and I took it slow, traveling about five to six hours in the morning and setting up camp in the afternoon. At night we'd sit around a campfire with a couple of beers and talk.

Joe didn't mince words. "When I watch you play," he said, "I get the impression that you're scared. It looks like you're afraid of getting hurt again and you're not throwing yourself into the game the way you used to. Do you think you've fully recovered?"

"Yes, but there's a difference," I replied. "I can't play at the same level. I still have some quickness, but I don't have as much power in my legs."

"Well," said Joe, "you're going to have to get that back."

As for the marriage, I said that Maxine and I had grown apart. She had no interest in the basketball world I inhabited, and I wasn't ready to settle down and become a family man in the suburbs. Plus she was ready to move on and pursue a career as a lawyer.

Joe was blunt. He said that for the past two years I hadn't put myself into my marriage, my career, or anything else. "Because you've been too afraid to really make an honest effort," he added, "you've lost the one love relationship you've always had—basketball. You need to be more aggressive about your life."

This was the message I needed to hear. When I returned to New York, I resolved to refocus my energy on my career, and for the next three seasons I played the best basketball of my life. Maxine and I made the split official and filed for divorce. I moved into a loft above an auto repair shop in the Chelsea district of Manhattan; Maxine settled with our four-year-old daughter, Elizabeth, in an apartment on the Upper West Side.

This was a wild, eye-opening time for me, and I lived the life of a sixties Renaissance man, complete with long hair and jeans, and a fascination with exploring new ways of looking at the world. I loved the freedom and idealism, not to mention the great music, of the countercultural wave that was sweeping through New York and the rest of country. I bought a bicycle and pedaled all over town, trying to connect with the *real* New York City. But no matter how much time I spent in Central Park, to me living in the city felt like living indoors. I needed to be someplace where I could feel a strong connection to the earth.

I also had a longing to reconnect with my spiritual core, which I'd been ignoring. During college, I'd studied other religions and been intrigued by the broad range of spiritual traditions from around the world. But that had been primarily an intellectual exercise, not a spiritually meaningful one. Now I felt compelled to go deeper.

My journey of self-discovery was filled with uncertainty but also alive with promise. Although I knew my parents' regimented approach to spirituality wasn't right for me, I was still intrigued with the idea of tapping into the power of the human spirit.

When I was a child, I had a number of curious health issues. At age two or so, I developed a large growth on my throat that baffled doctors and caused my parents great concern. They treated it with penicillin and it eventually went away, but I grew up feeling that there was something about me that wasn't quite right. Then, when I entered first grade, I was diagnosed with a heart murmur and was told to avoid physical activity for a whole year, which was pure torture for me because I was such an active kid.

One night when I was about eleven or twelve, I was sick and battling a high fever. I was sleeping fitfully, when all of a sudden I heard a roar, like the sound of a railroad train, building and building until it grew so loud I thought the train was going to burst into my bedroom. The sensation was completely overpowering, but for some reason I wasn't frightened. As the noise kept getting louder, I felt a powerful surge of energy radiating through my body that was much stronger and more all consuming than anything I'd ever experienced before.

I don't know where this power came from, but I awoke the next day feeling strong and confident and brimming with energy. The fever was gone, and after that my health improved dramatically and I rarely got colds or flus.

However, the primary impact of this spontaneous experience was psychological, not physical. After that night I had a greater belief in myself and a quiet faith that everything was going to work out for the best. I also seemed to be able to tap into a new source of energy within myself that I hadn't sensed before. From that point on, I felt confident enough to throw my whole mind, body, and soul into what I loved—and that, as much as anything, has been the secret of my success in sports.

I've always wondered where that power came from and whether I could learn how to tap into it on my own, not just on the basketball court but in the rest of my life as well.

That's one of the things I was searching for as I set out on my journey of self-discovery. I didn't know where I was going or what pitfalls I might stumble upon along the way. But I was encouraged by these lines from the Grateful Dead song "Ripple."

> *There is a road, no simple highway,*
> *Between the dawn and dark of night,*
> *And if you go no one may follow,*
> *That path is for your steps alone.*

To be honest, I'd already been on quite a ride. Because my parents were both ministers, my siblings and I had to be doubly perfect. We attended church twice on Sunday, in the morning to hear my father's sermon and in the evening to listen to my mother's. We also had to go to another service midweek and be star students in Sunday school, which was taught by Mom. Every morning we did devotions before breakfast, and at night we often memorized passages from the Bible.

Mom and Dad met while studying for the ministry at a Bible college in Winnipeg. They had taken different paths to get there. My father, Charles, was a tall, handsome man with curly hair, dark eyes, and a quiet, understated demeanor. Our Tory ancestors had picked the wrong side in the American Revolution and after the war moved to Ontario, where they received a land grant from King George III that became the Jackson family farm. My dad always thought he would go to college, but after he failed the qualifying exams—in large part because of ill health—he left school in eighth grade and worked the farm. Along the way he also spent some time as a lumberjack in Hudson Bay. Then one day, while milking cows in the barn, he suddenly got the call to join the ministry.

My mother, Elisabeth, was a striking, charismatic woman, with crystal blue eyes, blond hair, and strong Germanic features. She grew up in Wolf Point, Montana, where Grandfather Funk had moved the family after World War I to avoid strong anti-German sentiment in Canada. All of her siblings were valedictorians in high school, but Mom missed out by two tenths of a point because she had to skip six weeks of school to work on the fall harvest. Later she was teaching in a one-room schoolhouse when she attended a Pentecostal revival meeting and was swept away. By her early thirties, Mom had established herself as a traveling preacher in the small towns of eastern Montana.

My father was a widower when they started dating. His first wife had died a few years earlier while pregnant with their second child. (Their first child was my half sister, Joan.) My parents were drawn together more by a profound spiritual connection than by a romantic one. They were both captivated by the Pentecostal movement, which had spread quickly in rural areas during the 1920s and 1930s, and its fundamental idea that one could find salvation by connecting directly with the Holy Spirit. They were also taken by the prophecy in the Book of Revelations about the second coming of Christ and talked about how important it was to prepare spiritually for His arrival because it might come at any moment. Their deepest fear was not being right with God. "If you died today," my mother often asked, "would you meet your maker in heaven?" That was the big issue in our house.

My parents also strongly abided by St. Paul's teachings about separating yourself from materialistic society by being *in* this world but not *of* it. We weren't allowed to watch TV or movies or read comic books or go to dances—or even socialize with our school friends at the local canteen. Joan wasn't allowed to wear shorts or a swimsuit, and my brothers and I wore white shirts everywhere, except when we were playing sports. When I asked Joe recently what scared him as a child, he said being laughed at in school when he made mistakes. The other kids teased us relentlessly, calling us "holy rollers" and making fun of what appeared to them to be a strange, antiquated way of life.

When I was about eleven, my mother told me it was time for me to "seek the infilling of the Holy Spirit." My brothers and sister had already been "baptized" in the Holy Spirit and spoke in tongues. This was an important aspect of the Pentecostal faith. For years I'd watched other people go through this ritual, but it was never something I wanted to experience myself. But my parents really wanted me to do it, and they prayed with me every Sunday night after services, when I was actively seeking the gift of tongues.

After a couple years of devoted prayer and supplication, I decided that this wasn't going to be my thing. I started desperately searching for school activities that would take me away from my nearly 24-7 life at church. I acted in plays, sang in the choir, worked on a class float, and was a sports announcer on the school's radio program. When I was a senior in high school, my brother Joe snuck me out to my first movie, *Seven Brides for Seven Brothers*, when my parents were away at a conference.

But my real savior was basketball. In my junior year I grew four inches to six feet five and 160 pounds and started to really improve as a player. My height and long arms gave me a huge advantage, and I averaged 21.3 points a game that year, which helped my team, Williston High, make it to the final of the North Dakota state championship. But we had lost two times to our opponent, Rugby, during the regular season. I'd gotten into foul trouble in both games, so Coach Bob Peterson played a zone in the final game. We contained my high school rival, Paul Presthus, but Rugby shot the ball well enough to win by 12 points.

What I liked about basketball was how interconnected everything was. The game was a complex dance of moves and countermoves that made it much more alive than other sports I played. In addition, basketball demanded a high level of synergy. To succeed, you needed to rely upon everybody else on the floor, not just yourself. That gave the sport a certain transcendent beauty that I found deeply satisfying.

Basketball also saved me from having to go to church services most weekends. Our closest rival was 125 miles away, and we often took long overnight trips on the weekends to distant parts of the state. That meant I'd usually miss Friday-night and Sunday-morning services.

In my senior year I became a mini celebrity in the state. I averaged 23 points a game, and once again we made the state final, even though we didn't have as strong a record as the previous year. The final game against Grand Forks Red River was televised, and midway through the first half, I stole the ball and raced down the floor for a dunk. It made me kind of a folk hero in the state because most viewers had never seen a dunk before. I went on to finish with 35 points and was named MVP on our way to winning the championship.

After the game I met Bill Fitch, who had just been hired as the coach of the University of North Dakota, and he promised to save a place for me on his team if I was interested. A few weeks later he showed up in Williston to give the keynote address at the team's annual awards ceremony. At the end of his talk, he called one of my teammates and me up to the stage and handcuffed us together. "As soon as I finish this speech," he joked, "I'm going to take these boys back with me to UND."

Eventually my mother, who never attended any of my high school games, asked me how my spiritual life was progressing, and I had to tell her that I was struggling with my faith. This was a heartbreaking moment for her because she had already seen her older sons "stray" from the church. When I was a baby, my parents had made a pledge to their congregation that I would be brought up as a servant of the Lord, just like Charles and Joe before me. It must have been painful for them that none of us had lived up to their expectations. That's why, I think, they never abandoned hope that someday one of us might return to our true calling, the ministry.

When I was in college, I had another rude spiritual awakening. I had been raised on the literal reading of the Bible. So when I was studying Darwin's theory of evolution in biology class, it was disconcerting to learn that, according to the best estimates, humans had been walking upright on the planet for more than four million years. This revelation made me question a lot of what I'd been taught as a child and inspired me to try to resolve—in my own mind, at least—some of the inherent contradictions between religious dogma and scientific inquiry.

I decided to shift my major from political science to a combination of psychology, religion, and philosophy. That gave me the opportunity to explore a wide range of spiritual approaches from both East and West. I was especially taken by Nikos Kazantzakis's humanistic vision of Jesus in *The Last Temptation of Christ*, which paralleled much of what I had been reading about the Buddha. I was also moved by William James's *The Varieties of Religious Experience*, which not only helped me put my childhood experience in perspective but also showed me how my search to find a new, more authentic spiritual identity fit within the vast landscape of American culture.

I put that search on a back burner during my early years in the NBA. But when I moved to Chelsea, I befriended a psychology grad student and devout Muslim named Hakim who reignited my interest in spirituality and inspired me to explore meditation.

One summer in Montana I recruited a neighbor, Ron Fetveit, who was an observant Christian, to help me fix my leaky roof. While we were repairing shingles, we got into a long conversation about spiritual matters, and I confessed that I had a difficult time relating to his faith because of my childhood experience. "I know where you're coming from," he said, "but you know, there is no such thing as a grandchild of God. You are not your parents. You need to develop your own personal relationship with God."

At that point, I began quietly searching for spiritual practices that might work for me. One of my early discoveries was Joel S. Goldsmith, an innovative author, mystic, and former Christian Science healer who had founded his own movement, known as the Infinite Way. What attracted me to his work was his wholesale rejection of organization, ritual, and dogma. In his view, spirituality was a personal journey, period, and he designed his talks so that they could be interpreted from a wide range of perspectives. I was especially intrigued by Goldsmith's take on meditation, which he saw as a way to experience inner silence and plug into your intuitive wisdom. I'd always thought of meditation as a therapeutic technique for quieting the mind and feeling more balanced. But Goldsmith showed me that it could also be a substitute for prayer, a doorway to the divine.

Over time I moved on to other practices, but the Infinite Way was eye-opening for me. It was a stepping-stone from the rigid spirituality I'd been raised on to a broader vision of spiritual practice. When I was young, my mother used to cram my head with biblical scriptures every day because she believed that an idle mind was the devil's playground. But I thought that just the opposite was true. I wasn't interested in filling my head with more noise. I wanted to rest my mind and allow myself to just be.

Around this time I met my future wife, June, at my regular pinochle game in New York. She was a warm, fun-loving woman who had graduated from the University of Connecticut with a social-work degree. Our romance blossomed during a summer motorcycle trip around the Northwest, and we were married in 1974. Our first child, Chelsea, was born the next year, and our daughter Brooke, and twin sons, Charley and Ben, followed soon after.

One summer shortly after Chelsea was born, June and I went to visit my brother Joe and his new partner—June's sister, Deborah—who were living together in a commune in Taos, New Mexico. Joe had been a practicing Sufi for years and had recently left his teaching job in Buffalo to live at the Lama Foundation, a community dedicated to integrating spiritual practices from a wide range of traditions.

Sufism is a form of Islamic mysticism that focuses primarily on shifting consciousness from the personal to the divine. Sufis believe that you can't free yourself from identifying with the small, individual self unless you give yourself over to the power of the sacred. That means surrendering to what Sufi master Pir Vilayat Inayat Khan calls "the magical spell of unconditional love—that ecstatic embrace that bridges the separation between lover and beloved."

The Sufis at the Lama Foundation spent a good part of the day trying to connect with the divine through meditation, devotions, and an ecstatic form of chanting and bowing called *zikers*. Joe was attracted by the physicality of the practice, with its repetitive, dancelike movements designed to shift consciousness.

But after taking part in the rituals for several weeks, I decided that Sufism wasn't the right path for me. I was looking for a practice that would help me control my hyperactive mind.

A few years later I hired Joe to help me build a new house on Flathead Lake in Montana. After completing the frame, we brought in a construction worker to help us finish the job. He'd been studying Zen at the Mount Shasta monastery in northern California and had a calm, focused manner, along with a no-nonsense approach to work. I'd been interested in learning more about Zen ever since I'd read Shunryu Suzuki's classic, *Zen Mind, Beginner's Mind*. Suzuki, a Japanese teacher who played a key role in bringing Zen Buddhism to the West, talked about learning to approach each moment with a curious mind that is free of judgment. "If your mind is empty," he writes, "it is always ready for anything; it is open to everything. In the beginner's mind there are many possibilities; in the expert's mind there are few."

Joe and I joined our friend's group that summer and started sitting *zazen*—a form of meditation—with a group once a week. What appealed to me about Zen practice was its inherent simplicity. It didn't involve chanting mantras or visualizing complex images, as had other practices I'd tried. Zen is pragmatic, down to earth, and open to exploration. It doesn't require you to subscribe to a certain set of principles or take anything on faith; in fact, Zen encourages practitioners to question *everything*. Zen teacher Steve Hagen writes, "Buddhism is about *seeing*. It's about knowing rather than believing or hoping or wishing. It's also about not being afraid to examine anything and everything, including your own personal agendas."

Shunryu Suzuki's instructions on how to meditate are simple:

1. Sit with your spine straight, your shoulders relaxed, and
   your chin pulled in, "as if you were supporting the sky with
   your head."
2. Follow your breath with your mind as it moves in and out
   like a swinging door.
3. Don't try to stop your thinking. If a thought arises, let it
   come, then let it go and return to watching your breath.
   The idea is not to try to control your mind but to let
   thoughts rise and fall naturally over and over again. After
   some practice, the thoughts will start to float by like passing
   clouds and their power to dominate consciousness will
   diminish.

According to Suzuki, meditation helps you do things "with a quite
simple, clear mind" with "no notion or shadows." Most people have
two or three ideas running in their heads whenever they do something, and that leaves "traces" of thoughts that cause confusion and
are difficult to let go of. "In order not to leave any traces, when you
do something," he writes, "you should do it with your whole body
and mind, you should be concentrated on what you do. You should
do it completely, like a good bonfire."

It took me years of practice to still my busy mind, but in the process I discovered that the more aware I became of what was going on
inside me, the more connected I became to the world outside. I became more patient with others and calmer under pressure—qualities
that helped me immensely when I became a coach.

Three aspects of Zen have been critical to me as a leader:

1. GIVING UP CONTROL

Suzuki writes, "If you want to obtain perfect calmness in your zazen,
you should not be bothered by the various images you find in your

mind. Let them come and let them go. Then they will be under control."

The best way to control people, he adds, is to give them a lot of room and encourage them to be mischievous, then watch them. "To ignore them is not good; that is the worst policy," he writes. "The second worst is trying to control them. The best one is to watch them, just to watch them, without trying to control them."

This piece of advice came in handy later when I was dealing with Dennis Rodman.

2. TRUSTING THE MOMENT

Most of us spend the bulk of our time caught up in thoughts of the past or the future—which can be dangerous if your job is winning basketball games. Basketball takes place at such a lightning pace that it's easy to make mistakes and get obsessed with what just happened or what might happen next, which distracts you from the only thing that really matters—*this* very moment.

Practicing Zen not only helped me become more acutely aware of what was happening in the present moment but also slowed down my experience of time because it diminished my tendency to rush into the future or get lost in the past. Vietnamese Zen teacher Thich Nhat Hanh talks about "dwelling happily in the present moment," because that's where everything you need is available. "Life can be found only in the present moment," he writes. "The past is gone, and the future is not yet here, and if we do not go back to ourselves in the present moment, we cannot be in touch with life."

3. LIVING WITH COMPASSION

One aspect of Buddhism that I found to be especially compelling was the teachings on compassion. The Buddha was known as the "compassionate one," and according to religion scholars, his moral teachings bear a close resemblance to those of Jesus, who told his followers at the Last Supper: "This is my commandment, that you love one another as I have loved you. No one has greater love than this, to lay down one's life for one's friends." In a similar vein, the Buddha said, "Just as a mother would protect her only child at the risk of her own life, even so, cultivate a boundless heart towards all beings. Let your thoughts of boundless love pervade the whole world."

In the Buddhist view, the best way to cultivate compassion is to be fully present in the moment. "To meditate," said the Buddha, "is to listen with a receptive heart." In her book *Start Where You Are*, Buddhist teacher Pema Chodron contends that meditation practice blurs the traditional boundaries between self and others. "What you do for yourself—any gesture of kindness, any gesture of gentleness, any gesture of honesty and clear seeing toward yourself—will affect how you experience the world," she writes. "What you do for yourself, you're doing for others, and what you do for others, you're doing for yourself."

This idea would later become a key building block in my work as a coach.

In the meantime I still had a job to do as a player.

In the 1971–72 season Red Holzman, who was then general manager as well as head coach, made a number of moves that transformed the Knicks. First he traded Cazzie Russell to the San Francisco Warriors for Jerry Lucas, a strong, active big man who had a good twenty-five-foot shot but could also handle powerful centers like Dave Cowens and Kareem Abdul-Jabbar. Next, Red shipped Mike Riordan and Dave Stallworth to Baltimore for Earl "the Pearl" Monroe, probably the most creative ball handler in the game at that time.

Red also drafted Dean "the Dream" Meminger, a quick, long-legged guard from Marquette who was a terror on defense.

With this new infusion of talent, we morphed into a more versatile team than we'd ever been before. We had more size and depth, a broader array of scoring options than the 1969–70 team, plus the perfect blend of individual skill and team consciousness. Some of us worried that Monroe might try to upstage Frazier in the backcourt, but Earl adapted himself to Walt's game and added a dazzling new dimension to the offense. With Lucas, a passing magician, at center, we transformed from a power team into a multifaceted perimeter team, keying on fifteen-foot jump shots as well as layups. Red made me the prime backup to Dave DeBusschere and Bill Bradley—and I was energized in my new role. This was pure basketball at its finest, and I fit right in.

The only team we worried about in 1972–73 was the Celtics, who had dominated the Eastern Conference with a 68-14 record. In the four years since Bill Russell's departure, GM Red Auerbach had re-created the team in the classic Celtics tradition, with a strong, active center (Dave Cowens), a sly outside shooter (Jo Jo White), and one of the best all-around players in the game (John Havlicek).

Holzman wasn't a huge fan of Auerbach's because he used every trick he could to give his team an edge. Auerbach was a master of gamesmanship. One of his trademark ploys was to light a cigar when he thought his team had won the game, which infuriated his opponents, especially when the score was still close.

But Auerbach outdid himself in the 1973 playoffs, and it ultimately backfired on him. We met the Celtics in the Eastern Conference finals after beating Baltimore 4–1 in the first round. Boston had the home-court advantage in the series, and Auerbach took full advantage of it. Whenever we played in Boston, Auerbach made our lives miserable: He'd put us in locker rooms where the keys didn't work, the towels were missing, and the heat was set at over one hundred degrees and we couldn't open the windows. For this series, he put us in a different locker room for every game, and the last one—for game 7—was a cramped janitor's closet with no lockers and a ceiling so low many of us had to stoop to get dressed. Rather than demoralize us, as Auerbach no doubt expected, the locker-room gambit made us so angry it galvanized us even more.

No one had ever beaten the Celtics at home in a game 7 before, but we were still confident, because we had dominated Boston with our full-court press early in the series. The night before the big game, we were watching film of game 6 and noticed that Jo Jo White was killing us coming off high screens. Meminger, who was covering Jo Jo, started to get defensive, and Holzman snapped back. "I don't give a damn about the screen," he said. "Find a way to get through the screen and stop this guy. Don't bitch about the screen, just get the job done."

The next day Dean was a man possessed. He went at Jo Jo early and shut him down, effectively short-circuiting the Celtics' offensive game plan. Then Dean came alive on the other end, breaking through the Celtics' press and igniting a decisive 37–22 run in the second half. After that, Boston never recovered. The final score was Knicks 94, Celtics 78.

I've never seen Red Holzman happier than he was that night in the Boston janitor's closet. It meant a great deal to him to beat his nemesis, Auerbach, on his own turf. Beaming with joy, he came over to me and said with a wry smile, "You know, Phil, sometimes life is a mystery and you can't tell the difference between good and evil that clearly. But this is one of those times when good definitely triumphed over evil."

The championship series against the Lakers was anticlimactic. They surprised us in the first game, but we closed down their run-

ning game after that and won in five. The postgame celebration in
L.A. was a fizzle: just a handful of reporters standing around looking
for quotes. But I didn't care. I finally had a ring I could call my own.

The next season—1973–74—was one the best of my career. I settled
into my role as sixth man and averaged 11.1 points and 5.8 rebounds
per game. But the team was going through a transformation that
worried me.

The hallmark of the championship Knicks was the extraordinary
bond among the players and the selfless way we worked together as a
team. That bond was particularly strong during our advance to the
first championship in 1970. After the arrival of Earl Monroe, Jerry
Lucas, and Dean Meminger in 1971, the team chemistry shifted, but
a new bond formed that was more strictly professional in nature yet
no less effective. We didn't spend a lot of time with one another off
the court, but we meshed brilliantly on the floor. Now the team was
going through another sea change, but this time the effect would be
more disruptive.

We struggled to hold things together during the 1973–74 season
with Reed, Lucas, and DeBusschere hobbled by injuries, and we
limped into the Eastern Conference finals against the Celtics after
barely surviving a tough seven-game series with the Bullets. The pivotal moment came in game 4 in Madison Square Garden, with the
Celtics up 2–1 in the series and young backup center John Gianelli
and me trying to make up for our diminished big men. But this time
there would be no magical Willis Reed epiphany. Boston's Dave
Cowens and John Havlicek knew how to take advantage of our lack
of strong front-court leadership and outmaneuvered us at every critical turn in the second half. Boston won 98–91.

The Celtics finished us off three days later in Boston en route to another successful championship run against the Milwaukee Bucks. I remember sitting in Logan Airport with my teammates after that loss and feeling as if our once-glorious dynasty had come to an end. Lucas and DeBusschere had already announced that they were planning to retire. By the time the next season got under way, Reed and Barnett had also moved on and Meminger had been picked up by New Orleans in the expansion draft and traded to Atlanta.

Nothing was the same after that. I stepped in as a starter the next year to replace DeBusschere and played pretty well, but only three other members of the core team remained—Walt Frazier, Bill Bradley, and Earl Monroe—and it was difficult to forge the kind of unity we'd had before. Times were changing, and the new players flooding into the NBA were more interested in showing off their flashy skills and living the NBA high life than in doing the hard work of creating a unified team.

Over the next two years, we added some talented players to the roster, including All-NBA star Spencer Haywood and three-time NBA scoring champion Bob McAdoo, but neither of them seemed to be that interested in mastering the Knicks' traditional combination of intense defense and selfless teamwork.

Every day the gap between generations became more apparent. The new players, who were accustomed to being pampered in college, started complaining that nobody was taking care of their laundry or that the trainer wasn't doing good enough tape jobs. The old Knicks were used to taking responsibility for our own laundry because there was no equipment manager then, and strange as it may sound, washing our own uniforms had a unifying effect on the team. If the newcomers weren't willing to wash their own gear, we wondered whether they would take responsibility for what they had to do on court.

It didn't take long to find out. Within a remarkably short time, the Knicks transitioned into a dual-personality team that could run up

15-point leads, then collapse at the end because we couldn't marshal a coordinated attack. We held several team meetings to discuss the problem, but we couldn't agree on how to bridge the gap. Nothing Red did to stimulate team play worked.

In 1976 the Knicks failed to make the playoffs for the first time in nine years. A year later Bradley retired and Frazier was traded to the Cleveland Cavaliers. Then Red stepped down and was replaced by Willis Reed.

I thought the 1977–78 season would be my last, but in the off-season the Knicks made a deal to send me to the New Jersey Nets. I was reluctant at first, but I agreed to come on board when coach Kevin Loughery called and told me that he needed my help to work with the younger players. "I know you're at the end of your career," he said, "but coming to New Jersey could be a good bridge between playing and coaching."

I wasn't that interested in becoming a coach, but I was intrigued by Loughery's maverick style of leadership. After training camp, Loughery said he wanted to move me over to assistant coach, but before that could happen forward Bob Elliott got injured and I was activated as a player. Nevertheless, I got a chance that year to work with the big men as a part-time assistant coach and take over for Kevin as head coach when he was thrown out of games by the refs, which happened fourteen times that season.

Loughery, who had won two ABA championships, had an exceptional eye for the game and was gifted at exploiting mismatches. But what I learned from him was how to push the envelope and get away with it. Loughery was the first coach I knew who had his players double-team inbound passers at half-court, a high-risk move that often paid off. He also adopted Hubie Brown's ploy of double-teaming the ball handler and made it a regular part of the defense, even though it wasn't strictly legal. One of his biggest innovations was developing out-of-the-box isolation plays for our best shooters. That tactic didn't exactly align with Holzman's model of five-man offense, but it fit the Nets lineup, which was loaded with good shooters, and opened the way for new forms of creativity to flower in the years to come.

Our star player was Bernard King, an explosive small forward with a superquick release who had averaged 24.2 points and 9.5 rebounds per game as a rookie the year before. Unfortunately, he also had a substance-abuse problem. One night that season he was found asleep at the wheel at a stop sign and was arrested for drunk driving and cocaine possession. (The charges were later dropped.) This incident pushed Loughery over the edge. He was known for being good at managing self-absorbed stars, but he felt he wasn't getting through to King and was losing control of the team. So he threatened to quit. When general manager Charlie Theokas asked Loughery to suggest a replacement, he put my name forward. I was a little stunned when I heard this, but it felt good to know that someone of Kevin's stature thought I could handle the job. Eventually Loughery backed down. Several months later, the Nets traded King to the Utah Jazz, where he spent most of the season in rehab.

At the start of the 1979–80 season, Loughery told me that he was going to cut me from the active roster but offered me a job as a full-time assistant coach at a substantial pay cut. This was the moment I had always dreaded. I remember driving my car to the Nets' training center in Piscataway, New Jersey, and thinking that I was never going to feel the thrill of battle again. Sure, I said to myself, I might have some high moments in the future, but unless I had to go through a life-and-death crisis of some kind, I'd probably never have another experience quite like the one I'd had as a player in the NBA.

Being a coach was not the same, or at least that was how I felt at the time. Win or lose, I'd always be one step removed from the action.

Somewhere on the outskirts of Piscataway, I found myself having an imaginary conversation with my father, who had died a few months earlier.

"What am I going to do, Dad?" I said. "Is the rest of my life going to be total drudgery, just going through the motions?"

Pause.

"How can anything else ever be as meaningful to me as playing basketball? Where am I going to find my new purpose in life?"

It would take several years for me to find the answer.

5

DANCES WITH BULLS

Don't play the saxophone. Let it play you.
CHARLIE PARKER

This wasn't the first time that Jerry Krause had called me about a job with the Bulls. Three years earlier, when Stan Albeck was head coach, Jerry had invited me to interview for an assistant-coach slot. I was coaching in Puerto Rico at the time and arrived in Chicago sporting a beard and dressed for the tropics. Atop my head was an Ecuadorian straw hat with a blue parrot feather sticking out of it—very fashionable (and practical) down in the islands. Albeck took one look at me and invoked his veto power. Jerry had already rejected Stan's first choice for assistant coach, so Stan's veto may have been payback. In any case, I didn't get the job.

The second time around Krause advised me to lose the beard and wear a sport jacket and tie. The new head coach was Doug Collins, whom I'd played against when he was a star shooting guard for the Philadelphia 76ers. He was a smart, energetic coach whom Krause had hired to replace Albeck in 1986. Krause was looking for someone who could galvanize the Bulls' young players into a championship-contending team—which Doug did. Johnny Bach, who knew Collins from their days with the 1972 Olympics team, said Doug reminded him of coach Adolph Rupp's famous pronouncement that there are only two kinds of coaches: those who lead teams to victory and those who *drive* them. Doug was definitely in the second category. Although he didn't have a deep coaching background, he had boundless energy, which he used to rev up the players for big games.

Doug and I hit it off immediately. On the ride back to my hotel after dinner with Jerry, Doug said he was looking for someone with a history of winning championships to inspire the players. Two days later Jerry offered me a job as assistant coach and gave me one more piece of fashion advice. The next time you come back to Chicago, he said, bring along your championship rings.

The Bulls were a team that was about to break loose. They still had a few holes in their lineup: Their center, Dave Corzine, was not that quick or skilled on the boards, and their six-eleven forward, Brad Sellers, had chronic injury problems. But they had a strong power forward, Charles Oakley, a solid outside shooter, John Paxson, and two promising rookie forwards, Scottie Pippen and Horace Grant, whom Bach called "the Dobermans" because they were fast and aggressive enough to play smothering pressure defense.

The star, of course, was Michael Jordan, who had blossomed the previous year into the most transcendent player in the game. Not only did he win the scoring title, averaging 37.1 points per game, he also tested the limits of human performance, creating breathtaking moves in midair. The only player I knew who came close to Michael's leaps was Julius Erving, but Dr. J didn't have Jordan's remarkable energy. Michael would have a great game one night and follow it with an even more mind-boggling performance the next day, then come back two days later and do it all over again.

The Bulls' chief rivals were the Detroit Pistons, a rough, physical team that proudly referred to themselves as "the Bad Boys." Led by point guard Isiah Thomas, the Pistons were always spoiling for a fight, and they had a team full of bruisers, including Bill Laimbeer, Rick Mahorn, Dennis Rodman, and John Salley. Early in my first season a fight broke out between Mahorn and the Bulls' Charles Oakley that erupted into a melee. Doug Collins rushed on court to calm things down and was hurled over the scorers' table. Johnny Bach also sprained his wrist trying to be a peacemaker. Thomas boasted later that the Pistons were "the last of the gladiator teams."

The Pistons were a shrewd veteran team skilled at exploiting opponents' weaknesses. With the Bulls, that meant using physical intimidation and cheap shots to get the younger, less experienced players to lose it emotionally. But that tactic didn't work with Jordan, who wasn't easily intimidated. To contain him, coach Chuck Daly devised a strategy called "the Jordan Rules" designed to wear Michael down by slamming him with multiple bodies whenever he had the ball. Michael was an incredibly resilient player who would often make shots with two or three players hanging on him, but the Pistons' strategy was effective—initially, anyway—because the Bulls didn't have many other options on offense.

My job was to travel around the country and scout the teams the Bulls would be facing in the coming weeks. This gave me a chance to see firsthand how dramatically the rivalry of Magic Johnson's Lakers and Larry Bird's Celtics had transformed the NBA. Only a few years earlier the league had been in serious trouble, weighed down by drug abuse and out-of-control egos. But now it was soaring again with charismatic young stars and two of the league's most storied franchises playing an exciting new brand of team-oriented basketball that was fun to watch.

Even more important, this job was a chance for me to go to graduate school in basketball, with two of the best minds in the game: Johnny Bach and Tex Winter. I had just spent the past five years as head coach of the Albany Patroons and had experimented with all kinds of ideas about how to make the game more equitable and collaborative, including paying all the players the same salaries one year. We won the league championship during my first season as coach, and I discovered that I had a gift for making adjustments during games and getting the most out of the talent on the roster. But after a while I realized that my biggest weakness as a coach was my lack of formal training. I hadn't gone to Hoops U or any of the summer clinics where coaches share trade secrets. Working with Johnny and Tex was my chance to play catch-up. In the process I realized that some of the long-forgotten strategies of the past could be revitalized and made relevant for today's game.

Bach was a master of Eastern-style basketball, the aggressive, in-your-face version of the game played east of the Mississippi. He grew up in Brooklyn and played basketball and baseball at Fordham and Brown before joining the navy and serving in the Pacific during World War II. After brief stints with the Boston Celtics and New York Yankees, he was named one of the youngest head coaches of a major college basketball team, at Fordham in 1950. Later he was successful coaching Penn State for ten years. Then he moved over to the NBA as an assistant coach and briefly served as head coach for the Golden State Warriors. In 1972, while he was an assistant coach of the U.S. Olympic team, Johnny hit it off with Collins, who played a pivotal role in the controversial gold-medal game. Doug scored the two free throws that would have won the game if an IOC official hadn't inexplicably decided to put three seconds back on the clock after the buzzer had sounded.

Unlike Tex, Johnny didn't subscribe to any particular system of play. He was a walking encyclopedia of basketball strategy who relied on his quick wits and photographic memory to devise creative ways to win games. When I was in the office, Johnny would often show up at my desk with dog-eared books by coaching geniuses I'd never heard of and videotapes of current NBA teams using moves invented years ago.

Once I was sitting at my VCR trying to decipher what kind of offense the Milwaukee Bucks were running, and I called Johnny over to look at the tape. He took one glance and said, "Oh, that's Garland Pinholster's pinwheel offense." Then he proceeded to explain that Pinholster was one of the nation's most innovative coaches in the fifties and sixties. He was a coach at small Oglethorpe College in Georgia and amassed a 180-68 record using the continuous-motion offense he'd invented before losing interest in basketball and going into the grocery business and state politics.

Bach, who focused primarily on defense, had a fondness for using military images and playing clips from old war movies to get the players ready for battle. One of his favorite symbols was the ace of spades, which the Marines in World War II used, according to Johnny, to honor their fallen comrades. If Johnny drew an ace of spades on the board next to an opposing player's name, that meant the Bulls defenders were to "kill" that player whenever he had the ball.

I wasn't as thrilled with war imagery as Johnny was, so I started using music videos (and later movie clips) during my talks. I started off with Jimi Hendrix's rendition of "The Star-Spangled Banner," then moved over to David Byrne songs and Freddie Mercury's "We Are the Champions." Eventually I learned to use the videos to get subtle messages across. During one playoff run, I created a video with the Talking Heads' anthem "Once in a Lifetime"—a song about the dangers of wasting the present moment.

I've always felt that there is a strong connection between music and basketball. The game is inherently rhythmic in nature and requires the same kind of selfless, nonverbal communication you find in the best jazz combos. Once when John Coltrane was playing in

Miles Davis's band, he went off on an interminably long solo that made Miles furious. "What the fuck?" Miles shouted.

"My axe just wouldn't stop, brother," Coltrane replied. "It just kept on going."

"Well, then, put the motherfucker down."

Steve Lacy, who played with Thelonious Monk, set down a list of Monk's advice for the members of his combo. Here's a selection:

- Just because you're not a drummer, doesn't mean you don't have to keep time.
- Stop playing all those weird notes (that bullshit), play the melody!
- Make the drummer sound good.
- Don't play the piano part, I'm playing that.
- Don't play everything (or every time); let some things go by . . . What you don't play can be more important than what you do.
- When you're swinging, swing some more.
- Whatever you think can't be done, somebody will come along and do it. A genius is the one most like himself.
- You've got to dig it to dig it, you dig?

What I love about Monk's list is his basic message about the importance of awareness, collaboration, and having clearly defined roles, which apply as much to basketball as they do to jazz. I discovered early that the best way to get players to coordinate their actions was to have them play the game in 4/4 time. The basic rule was that the player with the ball had to do something with it before the third beat: either pass, shoot, or start to dribble. When everyone is keeping time, it makes it easier to harmonize with one another, beat by beat.

The man who understood this better than anyone was Tex Winter, the other great basketball mind on the Bulls staff. Tex, an expert
in free-flowing Western-style basketball, is best known for his work
with the triangle offense—or triple-post offense, as he called it—
which he learned playing for Coach Sam Barry at the University of
Southern California. Although he didn't invent the triangle offense,
Tex expanded it with several key innovations, including creating a
sequence of passes that led to coordinated movement among the players. Tex was also a gifted teacher who designed his own drills to make
the players proficient in the basic actions.

When Tex was twenty-nine years old, he landed the top job at
Marquette and became the youngest ever head coach of a Division I
college. Two years later he took over the men's program at Kansas
State, implemented the offense, and transformed the Wildcats into an
NCAA tournament regular. During that period, Jerry Krause, then a
scout, befriended Tex and spent a lot of time in Manhattan, Kansas,
learning basketball strategy from him. At one point Jerry told Tex
that if he ever became general manager of an NBA franchise, Tex
would be his first hire. Tex didn't think anything of it at the time.
Then, years later, when he was coaching at LSU, he saw a news story
on ESPN about Krause being named GM of the Bulls and said to his
wife, Nancy, that the next phone call he got would be from Jerry. He
was right.

Ever since I started coaching in the CBA, I'd been looking for a
system of offense that approximated the selfless ball movement we'd
used with the championship Knicks. I played around with the flex
system—a fast-moving, flowing offense popular in Argentina and
Europe—but it was limited. I didn't like the way the players had to
space themselves in relation to one another and there was no way to
disrupt the offense and do something else, if the situation demanded

it. In contrast, the triangle not only required a high level of selflessness, but was also flexible enough to allow players a great deal of individual creativity. That suited me perfectly.

The triangle gets its name from one of its key features—a sideline triangle formed by three players on the "strong" side of the floor. But I prefer to think of the triangle as "five-man tai chi" because it involves all the players moving together in response to the way the defense positions itself. The idea is not to go head to head against the defense but to read what the defense is doing and respond accordingly. For instance, if the defense swarms Michael Jordan on one side of the floor, that opens up a series of options for the other four players. But they all need to be acutely aware of what's happening and be coordinated enough to move together in unison so they can take advantage of the openings the defense offers. That's where the music comes in.

When everyone is moving in harmony, it's virtually impossible to stop them. One of the biggest converts to the triangle—eventually—was Kobe Bryant, who loved the unpredictability of the system. "Our teams were hard to play against," Kobe says, "because the opposition didn't know what we were going to do. Why? Because *we* didn't know what we were going to do from moment to moment. Everybody was reading and reacting to each other. It was a great orchestra."

There are all kinds of misconceptions about the triangle. Some critics believe that you need to have players of Michael and Kobe's caliber to make it work. Actually, the reverse is true. The triangle wasn't designed for the superstars, who will find ways to score no matter what system you use, but for all the other players on the team who aren't capable of creating their own shots. It also gives every player a vital role in the offense, whether they end up shooting or not.

Another misconception is that the triangle is far too complicated for most players to learn. In fact, once you master the fundamentals, it's far easier to learn the triangle than the more complex offenses prevalent today. The main thing you need to know is how to pass the ball and read defenses accurately. At one time most players learned these skills in high school or college, but that's not true with many of the young players coming into the NBA now. As a result, we had to spend a lot of time teaching them how to play the game, starting with the most basic skills, from dribbling with control to footwork and passing.

Tex was a master at this. He had developed a whole series of drills to teach players how to execute fundamentals. He trained them to create the right amount of spacing between one another on the floor and to coordinate their movements according to a basic set of rules. As far as Tex was concerned, the genius was in the details, and it didn't matter whether you were Michael Jordan or the lowest rookie on the team; Tex would badger you until you got it right.

Every year Tex, who loved inspirational sayings, would recite to the team his favorite proverb about the importance of learning the details:

> *For want of a nail the shoe was lost.*
> *For want of a shoe the horse was lost.*
> *For want of a horse the rider was lost.*
> *For want of a rider the message was lost.*
> *For want of a message the battle was lost.*
> *For want of a battle the kingdom was lost.*
> *And all for the want of a horseshoe nail.*

One thing I liked about Tex's system, from a leadership perspective, was that it *depersonalized criticism*. It gave me the ability to critique the players' performance without making them think I was attacking them personally. Pro basketball players are highly sensitive to criticism because almost everything they do is judged on a daily basis by coaches, the media, and just about anyone who owns a TV set. The beauty of the system—and this applies to all kinds of systems, not just the triangle—was that it turned the whole team into a *learning organization*. Everybody from Michael on down had something to learn, no matter how talented or untalented he was. So when I came down hard on a player in practice, he understood that I was merely trying to get him to understand how to work the triangle offense. As I said earlier, the road to freedom is a beautiful system.

Another aspect of the system I liked was its reliability; it gave the players something to fall back on when they were under stress. They didn't have to pretend to be like Mike and invent every move they made. All they had to do was play their part in the system, knowing that it would inevitably lead to good scoring opportunities.

The system also gave players a clear purpose as a group and established a high standard of performance for everyone. Even more important, it helped turn players into leaders as they began teaching one another how to master the system. When that happened, the group would bond together in ways that moments of individual glory, no matter how thrilling, could never foster.

Doug Collins wasn't as enamored with the system as I was. When he took over the Bulls in 1986, he made an effort to implement it, but he soon abandoned it because it didn't fit well with the defense he wanted to run. Collins was a strong believer in one of Hank Iba's cardinal rules: The guards should be on their way to half-court for defensive purposes when the ball is rebounded or inbounded. The challenge with the triangle offense is that it often requires guards to move into one of the corners to create a triangle with two other players. That makes it harder for them to get back on fast breaks.

So Doug moved away from the triangle but didn't replace it with another system. Instead he had the players learn a repertoire of forty to fifty plays that were constantly in flux. Then he would call plays from the sidelines as the game progressed, based on what he saw happening on the floor. This style of coaching, which is not uncommon in the NBA, was well suited to Doug. He had exceptional court vision and got energized by being actively involved in the game. The downside was that it made the players overly dependent on his minute-by-minute direction. It also turned everybody except Michael into a supporting actor, because many of the plays were designed to capitalize on his scoring genius. Too often the Bulls offense consisted of four players creating room for M.J. to work his magic, then watching him do it. The press had already started referring to the Bulls sarcastically as Jordan and the Jordanaires.

During training camp that first year, I told Doug I thought Michael was doing too much on his own and needed to emulate Magic and Bird in the way they worked with their teammates and transformed them into a team. I added that Red Holzman used to say that "the real mark of a star was how much better he made his teammates."

"That's great, Phil," Doug replied. "You've got to tell Michael that. Why don't you go tell him right now?"

I hesitated. "I've only been here a month, Doug. I'm not sure I know Michael well enough to tell him something Red told me." But Doug insisted that I go explain to Michael "the mark of a star."

So I went down to the media room where Michael was talking to reporters and pulled him aside. This was my first real conversation with Michael, and I was a little embarrassed. I told him Doug thought he should hear what Holzman had to say about being a star, and I repeated Red's famous line. Michael studied me for a few seconds, then said, "Okay, thanks," and walked away.

I'm not sure what Michael thought of my pronouncement at the time, but what I learned later was that he was much more coachable than other stars because he had such a deep respect for his college coach, Dean Smith. He also had a keen interest in doing whatever it took to win his first NBA championship.

The only other occasion when I had a personal exchange with M.J. while an assistant coach was at a season-ticket-holder luncheon in Chicago. My son, Ben, who was in grade school, was a huge Jordan fan. He had several pictures of Michael in his room and had told one of his teachers that his dream in life was to meet his idol. The year before, when we were living in Woodstock, I had taken Ben to see the Bulls play the Celtics in Boston and he had waited for a long time after the game to get Michael's autograph. But when M.J. finally emerged from the locker room, he'd walked by without stopping. So now that I was with the Bulls I decided to take Ben to the season ticket holders' luncheon and introduce him to Michael in person. When we were there, I told M.J. about Ben's long wait in the Boston Garden. Michael smiled and was very gracious toward Ben, but I felt a little uncomfortable about putting him on the spot.

After that, I made a point of not asking M.J. for any special favors. I wanted our relationship to be squeaky clean. I didn't want to be his tool. Later, when I took over as head coach, I made it a policy to give Michael a lot of space. I took care to create a protected environment for him where he could relate freely with his teammates and be himself without worrying about intrusions from the outside world. Even in those early days, the clamor of fans trying to get a little piece of Michael Jordan was mind-boggling. He couldn't go out to restaurants without being hounded, and the workers at most hotels would line up outside his room looking for autographs. One night after a game in Vancouver, we literally had to peel dozens of Jordan worshippers off the team bus before we could pull out of the parking lot.

One of the players I worked with closely during my tenure as an assistant coach was Scottie Pippen. We both started with the team the same year, and I spent a lot of time helping him learn how to pull up and shoot off the dribble. Scottie was a quick learner and devoted time to absorbing how the triangle worked. He had been a point guard in college before becoming a small forward, and he had an innate sense of how all the pieces fit together on the floor. Scottie had long arms and excellent court vision, which made him the perfect person to spearhead our defensive attack.

What impressed me most about Scottie, however, was his development over time as a leader—not by mimicking Michael but by teaching his teammates how to play within the system and always offering a compassionate ear when they ran into trouble. This was critical because Michael wasn't very accessible and many of the players were intimidated by his presence. Scottie was someone they could talk to, someone who would keep an eye out for them on court. As Steve Kerr says, "Scottie was the nurturer; Michael was the enforcer."

The Bulls started to take off during my first season with the team, 1987–88. We won fifty games and finished tied for second in the tough Central Division. Michael continued to soar, winning his second scoring title and his first MVP award. The best sign was the 3–2 victory over the Cleveland Cavaliers in the first round of the playoffs. But the Pistons rolled over the Bulls in five games in the conference finals, en route to the championship finals, against the Los Angeles Lakers.

During the off-season Jerry Krause traded Charles Oakley to the Knicks for Bill Cartwright, a move that infuriated Michael because he considered Oakley his protector on the floor. Jordan made fun of Cartwright's "butterfingers" and dubbed him "Medical Bill" because of his ongoing foot problems. But despite his small shoulders and narrow frame, Bill was a smart, rock-solid defender who could shut down Patrick Ewing and other big men. Once we ran a drill in practice that ended up pitting six-six Michael against seven-one Cartwright in a one-on-one battle of wills. Michael was determined to dunk over Cartwright, but Bill was equally determined not to let that happen. So they collided in midair and everyone held their breath while Bill slowly eased Michael to the floor. After that, Michael changed his tune on Cartwright.

Cartwright wasn't the only weapon the team needed to move to the next level. Collins was pushing hard for Krause to find a strong, playmaking point guard who could orchestrate the offense like Isiah Thomas did in Detroit. But the team had already gone through several point guards—including Sedale Threatt, Steve Colter, and Rory Sparrow—trying to find someone who would meet Jordan's expectations. The latest candidate was Sam Vincent, who had come over in a trade with Seattle, but he didn't last long. So Doug decided to make Jordan the point guard, which worked fairly well but reduced M.J.'s scoring options and wore him down physically during the regular season.

At one point, Doug got into a heated argument with Tex about the point-guard dilemma. Tex suggested that if Doug instituted a system of offense—not necessarily the triangle but any system—he wouldn't have to rely so heavily on a point guard to run the offense. By this time, Doug had grown weary of listening to Tex's constant stream of criticism, so he decided to banish him to the sidelines and reduce his role as a coach.

When Krause heard about this move, he began to lose faith in Collins's judgment. Why would anyone in his right mind exile Tex Winter to Siberia? The players seemed to be losing faith in Doug as well. He changed plays so frequently—often modifying them in the middle of games—that team members began to refer to the offense flippantly as "a play a day."

A critical point came during a game in Milwaukee right before Christmas. Doug got into a battle with the refs and was tossed out late in the first half. He turned the team over to me and handed me his play card. The Bulls were so far behind, I decided to run a full-court press and give the players a free hand running the offense, rather than calling Doug's plays. The team quickly turned the game around and we won handily.

What I didn't realize until later was that toward the end of the game the Chicago TV broadcast showed my wife, June, sitting next to Krause and his wife, Thelma, in the stands. That, as much as anything else, created a great deal of tension between Doug and me over the next few months.

A few weeks later, I was in Miami planning to scout a game when I got a call from Krause telling me that he didn't want me to be away from the team anymore. Doug and Michael, I learned later, had gotten in an argument of some kind, and Jerry wanted me available to step in if there was more friction on the team. Soon after, Jerry began to take me into his confidence.

Eventually things settled down, and the Bulls stumbled through the rest of the season, finishing fifth in the conference with three fewer wins than the previous year. But the addition of Cartwright and the rise of Pippen and Grant made the team much better positioned than before to make a strong run in the playoffs.

The first round against the Cavaliers went all five games, but Michael was bursting with confidence when he boarded the bus for the finale in Cleveland. He lit a cigar and said, "Don't worry, guys. We're going to win." Cleveland's Craig Ehlo almost made him eat his words when he put the Cavs ahead by one with seconds left. But Michael responded with a balletic double-clutch shot, with Ehlo draped all over him, to win the game, 101–100. Afterward Tex said to me, "I guess now they won't be changing coaches anytime soon." I had to smile. I didn't care, because we were on our way to the Eastern Conference finals. The Bulls had come a long way from their 40-42 record the year before I'd joined the team.

Next we faced the Pistons, and, as usual, it was an ugly affair. Chicago won the first game at the Silverdome, but after that the Pistons overpowered the Bulls with their intimidating defense and won the series, 4–2. Krause told me later that midway through that series he told owner Jerry Reinsdorf that the team needed to replace Collins with someone who could win a championship.

After the playoffs I attended the NBA's talent showcase in Chicago, an event organized by the league for draft-eligible players to show off their skills to coaches and scouts. While I was there, Dick McGuire, my first coach with the Knicks, asked me if I would be interested in replacing New York's head coach, Rick Pitino, who was leaving to coach the University of Kentucky. I said I would, and suddenly the wheels were in motion.

Shortly after that, Reinsdorf invited me to meet him at O'Hare Airport. I'd always liked Jerry because he had grown up in Brooklyn and was a big fan of the Knicks' selfless style of basketball. He'd gotten wind of my interest in the New York job and asked me if I could choose, which team I'd rather coach, the Bulls or the Knicks. I said I had a lot of affection for New York, having played there, but I also thought the Bulls were poised to win multiple championships, while the Knicks would be lucky to win one. In short, I said I'd rather stay with the Bulls.

A few weeks later Krause called me in Montana and asked me to go to a secure phone. So I drove my motorcycle into town and called him back from a pay phone. He told me that he and Reinsdorf had decided to make a coaching change, and he offered me the job.

I was thrilled, but the fans in Chicago were not so pleased. Collins was a popular figure in town and he'd taken the team to new heights during the past three years. When reporters asked Reinsdorf why he had made such a risky move, he said, "Doug brought us a long way from where we had been. You cannot say he wasn't productive. But now we have a man we feel can take us the rest of the way."

The pressure was on.

6

WARRIOR SPIRIT

I think lightly of yourself and think deeply of the world.

MIYAMOTO MUSASHI

As I sat by Flathead Lake in Montana that summer, contemplating the season ahead, I realized that this was a moment of truth for the Bulls. For the past six years we had been struggling to create a team around Michael Jordan. Now we had the talent in place to win a championship, but there was an important piece missing. In a word, the Bulls needed to become a tribe.

To succeed we had to get by the Detroit Pistons, but I didn't think we could outmuscle them unless we acquired a completely different lineup. They were just too good at fighting in the "alligator wrestling pond," as Johnny Bach called it. And when we tried to play the game their way, our players ended up getting frustrated and angry, which was just what the Pistons hoped would happen.

What our team could do, though, was outrun the Pistons—and outdefend them as well. Nobody on the Pistons, except perhaps Dennis Rodman, was quick enough to keep up with Michael, Scottie, and Horace on the fast break. And with Bill Cartwright's formidable presence under the basket, we had the makings of one of the best defensive teams in the league. M.J. had taken great pride in winning the

Defensive Player of the Year award the previous season, and Scottie and Horace were quickly developing into first-rate defenders. But in order to exploit those advantages, we needed to be more connected as a team and to embrace a more expansive vision of working together than simply getting the ball to Michael and hoping for the best.

When I was an assistant coach, I created a video for the players with clips from *The Mystic Warrior*, a television miniseries about Sioux culture based on the best-selling novel *Hanta Yo* by Ruth Beebe Hill. Ever since childhood I've been fascinated by the Sioux, some of whom lived in my grandfather's boardinghouse, which was near a reservation in Montana. When I was with the Knicks, a Lakota Sioux friend from college, Mike Her Many Horses, asked me to teach a series of basketball clinics at the Pine Ridge Indian Reservation in South Dakota. The purpose was to help heal the rift in his community caused by the 1973 standoff between police and American Indian movement activists at the site of the Wounded Knee massacre. I discovered during those clinics, which I taught with my teammates Bill Bradley and Willis Reed, that the Lakota loved the game and played it with an intense spirit of connectedness that was an integral part of their tribal tradition.

One of the things that intrigued me about Lakota culture was its view of the self. Lakota warriors had far more autonomy than their white counterparts, but their freedom came with a high degree of responsibility. As Native American scholar George W. Linden points out, the Lakota warrior was "the member of a tribe, and being a member, he never acted against, apart from, or *as* the whole without good reason." For the Sioux, freedom was not about being absent but about being present, adds Linden. It meant "freedom *for*, freedom for the realization of greater relationships."

The point I wanted to make by showing the players *The Mystic Warrior* video was that connecting to something beyond their individual goals could be a source of great power. The hero of the series, who was based loosely on Crazy Horse, goes into battle to save his tribe after experiencing a powerful vision. In our discussion after watching the video, the players seemed to resonate with the idea of bonding together as a tribe, and I thought I could build on that as we moved into the new season.

As I mentioned in the first chapter, management experts Dave Logan, John King, and Halee Fischer-Wright describe five stages of tribal development in their book, *Tribal Leadership*. My goal in my first year as head coach was to transform the Bulls from a stage 3 team of lone warriors committed to their own individual success ("*I'm* great and you're not") to a stage 4 team in which the dedication to the We overtakes the emphasis on the Me ("*We're* great and you're not").

But making that transition would take more than simply turning up the heat. I wanted to create a culture of selflessness and mindful awareness at the Bulls. To do that, I couldn't just rely on one or two innovative motivational techniques. I had to devise a multifaceted program that included the triangle offense but also incorporated the lessons I had learned over the years about bonding people together and awakening the spirit.

My first step was to talk with Michael.

I knew Michael wasn't a fan of the triangle. He referred to it sarcastically as "that equal-opportunity offense" that was designed for a generation of players who didn't have his creative one-on-one skills. But at the same time I knew that Michael longed to be part of a team that was more integrated and multidimensional than the current incarnation of the Bulls.

This was not going to be an easy conversation. Basically I was planning to ask Michael, who had won his third scoring title in a row the previous season with an average of 32.5 points per game, to reduce the number of shots he took so that other members of the team could get more involved in the offense. I knew this would be a challenge for him: Michael was only the second player to win both a scoring title and the league MVP award in the same year, the first being Kareem Abdul-Jabbar in 1971.

I told him that I was planning to implement the triangle and, as a result, he probably wouldn't be able to win another scoring title. "You've got to share the spotlight with your teammates," I said, "because if you don't, they won't grow."

Michael's reaction was surprisingly pragmatic. His main concern was that he didn't have much confidence in his teammates, especially Cartwright, who had difficulty holding onto passes, and Horace, who wasn't that skilled at thinking on his feet.

"The important thing," I replied, "is to let everybody touch the ball, so they won't feel like spectators. You can't beat a good defensive team with one man. It's got to be a team effort."

"Okay, I guess I could average thirty-two points," he said. "That's eight points a quarter. Nobody else is going to do that."

"Well, when you put it that way, maybe you *can* win the title," I said. "But how about scoring a few more of those points at the end of the game?"

Michael agreed to give my plan a try. Shortly after our conversation, I later learned, he told reporter Sam Smith, "I'll give it two games." But when he saw that I wasn't going to back down, Michael dedicated himself to learning the system and figuring out ways to use it to his advantage—which is exactly what I had hoped he would do.

It was fun watching Tex and Michael argue about the system. Tex admired Jordan's skill, but he was a purist about the triangle and wasn't shy about giving Michael a piece of his mind when he went off script. Meanwhile, Michael wasn't shy about creating variations on

Tex's beautiful machine. He thought the system was at best a three-quarter offense. After that the team needed to improvise and use its "think power" to win games.

It was a clash of visions. Tex believed it was foolhardy for a team to rely so heavily on one person, no matter how talented he was. Michael argued that his creativity was opening up exciting new possibilities for the game.

"There's no *I* in the word 'team,'" Tex would say.

"But there is in the word 'win,'" Michael would counter with a grin.

As far as I was concerned, they were both right—up to a point. I didn't believe the triangle alone was the answer for the Bulls. What I was looking for was the middle path between Tex's purity and Michael's creativity. It took time, but once the players had mastered the basics, we added some variations to the system that allowed the team to set certain plays in motion to avoid intense defensive pressure. Once that happened, the Bulls' game really took off.

Another change I introduced to make the Bulls less Jordan-centric was to shake up the team's pecking order. Michael had a powerful presence on the floor, but he had a different style of leadership than Larry Bird or Magic Johnson, who could galvanize a team with their magnetic personalities. As *Los Angeles Times* columnist Mark Heisler put it, Jordan wasn't "a natural leader, he was a natural doer." He drove the team with the sheer force of his will. It was as if he were saying, "I'm going out here, men, and I'm going to kick some ass. Are you coming with me?"

Michael also held his teammates to the same high standard of performance he expected of himself. "Michael was a demanding teammate," says John Paxson. "If you were on the floor, you had to do your job and do it the right way. He couldn't accept anyone not caring as much as he did."

I thought we needed another leader on the team to balance Michael's perfectionism, so I named Bill Cartwright cocaptain. Despite his soft-spoken demeanor, he could be deceptively forceful when he wanted to be, and he wasn't afraid to stand up to Michael, which Jordan respected. "Bill was a quiet, quiet leader," says Michael. "He didn't talk much, but when he did, everybody listened. He would challenge me when he felt I was out of place. Which was okay. We had that kind of relationship. We challenged each other."

The players called Cartwright "Teach" because he took other big men to school when they tried to get past him in the lane. "Bill was the physical rock of our team," says Paxson. "He didn't back down for anybody—and the game was much more physical then. He was like a big brother. If someone was picking on you, he was going to make sure you knew that he was there looking out for you."

At thirty-two, Bill was the oldest player on the team. He knew instinctively what we were trying to do with the Bulls and had a gift for explaining it to the players better than I could. One of my weaknesses is that sometimes I speak in broad generalizations. Bill brought the conversation back to earth.

Basketball is a great mystery. You can do everything right. You can have the perfect mix of talent and the best system of offense in the game. You can devise a foolproof defensive strategy and prepare your players for every possible eventuality. But if the players don't have a sense of oneness as a group, your efforts won't pay off. And the bond that unites a team can be so fragile, so elusive.

Oneness is not something you can turn on with a switch. You need to create the right environment for it to grow, then nurture it carefully every day. What the Bulls needed, I decided, was a sanctuary where they could bond together as a team, protected from all the

Behold the child: My mom and me at my dedication at the Bethel Tabernacle Church in Anaconda, Montana, 1945.

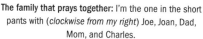

The family that prays together: I'm the one in the short pants with (*clockwise from my right*) Joe, Joan, Dad, Mom, and Charles.

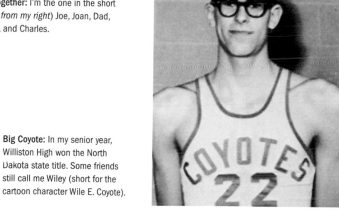

Big Coyote: In my senior year, Williston High won the North Dakota state title. Some friends still call me Wiley (short for the cartoon character Wile E. Coyote).

Role models: At UND I was schooled by two future NBA coaches: head coach Bill Fitch (*left*) and assistant coach Jimmy Rodgers.

Born to be wild: I could baffle batters with my curve in college, but sometimes, as Fitch liked to say, my fastball "couldn't find home plate with a Geiger counter."

Birth of a rivalry: Even as a player, I liked to dog Pat Riley.

One for all: Celebrating with (*from left*) Jerry Lucas, Walt Frazier, Willis Reed, and Bill Bradley after beating the Celtics in game 7 of the 1973 Eastern Conference finals in Boston.

Master class: Studying game film with (*from left*) Walt, Dick Barnett, Jerry, Dean Meminger, Willis, and Coach Red Holzman.

Down home in midtown: Dropping by the Knicks office with my favorite ride in 1974.

The Whopper: With sons Ben (*left*) and Charley (*right*) at Flathead Lake in Montana, after hauling in a Lake Mackinaw trout that was almost as big as they were.

All my children: (*from left*) Ben, Brooke, Elizabeth, Charley, and Chelsea at Avalanche Lake in Glacier National Park.

The family that plays together: A boys versus girls game with (*from left*) Charley, June, Chelsea, Brooke, and Ben at a schoolyard in Bannockburn, Illinois.

The architect: Not everyone loved Jerry Krause, but he was a master at building teams that won rings.

Here comes the future: A young Kobe Bryant (*center*) tries to break through Scottie Pippen (*left*) and Michael Jordan in 1998.

Mr. T: In the early days I often had to remind the Bulls not to stray from the triangle offense.

Elvis is in the building: Michael Jordan arrives on court
with John Paxson (*left*) and Horace Grant with his trademark glasses in 1991.

The Chicago brain trust: Jim Cleamons (*left*), Johnny Bach, and Tex Winter, who wrote the play-by-play for each game in his own version of hieroglyphics, in 1990.

To the victors goes the bling: Showing off the trophies in Chicago's Grant Park after winning our sixth NBA title, with (*from left*) Toni Kukoc, Ron Harper, Dennis Rodman, Pippen, Jordan, Mayor Richard M. Daley, and Governor James Edgar.

The way of the Worm (*left*): The fans were fascinated by Rodman's hair, but I admired his impeccable timing on the boards.

Bulls totems: (*left*) I had this group of portraits done by Chicago artist Tim Anderson after we won our first three-peat. It includes everyone who played on all three teams during that run, plus yours truly. (*From top*) Jordan, Bill Cartwright, Pippen, Grant, Paxson, B. J. Armstrong, Scott Williams, Stacey King, and Will Perdue.

These portraits (*right*), also done
by Anderson, feature the players
on all three teams of the second
three-peat run. (*From top*)
Jordan, Pippen, Rodman, Harper,
Luc Longley, Kukoc, Steve Kerr,
Bill Wennington, Jud Buechler,
and Randy Brown.

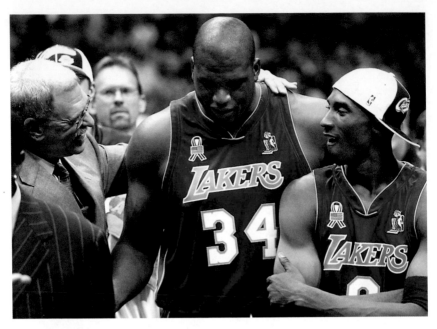

Three's the dream: With Shaquille O'Neal and Kobe after winning the Lakers' third consecutive title in 2002 against the Nets in East Rutherford, New Jersey.

The short goodbye: I invited (*from left*) Charley, Ben, Brooke, and Chelsea to this press conference after the 2004 finals because I thought it was going to be my last as the Lakers' coach. To my surprise, a year later I was back.

Passing fancy (*right*): Kobe dishes off to a surprised Shaq during game 1 of the 2001 championship finals against the Philadelphia 76ers in L.A.

Top chef: Preparing Christmas dinner with Brooke at my home in Playa del Rey, Calif.

My fiancee: Jeanie Buss and me at Chelsea's wedding in Montana in 2007.

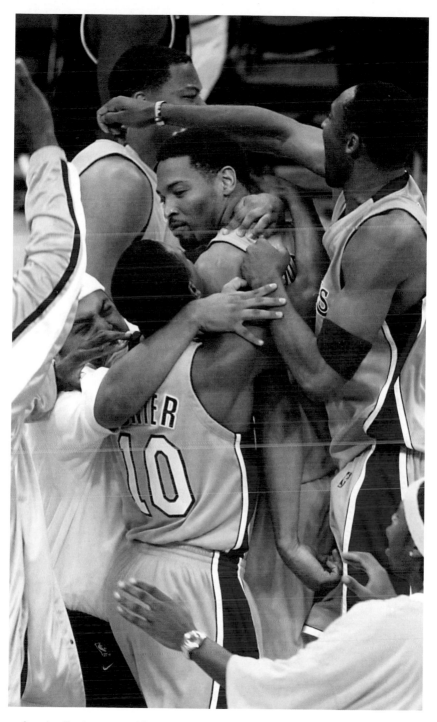

Group hug: The players surround Robert Horry (*center*) after he hit one of his "magic" three-pointers to win game 4 of the Western Conference finals against the Sacramento Kings in LA.

Pregame prep: Showing Pau Gasol and Adam Morrison a defensive assignment before game 4 of the Western Conference finals at Denver's Pepsi Center in 2009.

The LA brain trust: In my custom-designed chair with (*in front row, from left*) Brian Shaw, Kurt Rambis, Frank Hamblen, and Gary Vitti. *Back row:* Rasheed Hazzard (*left*), Dr. Steve Lombardo, Chip Schaefer, and Cleamons.

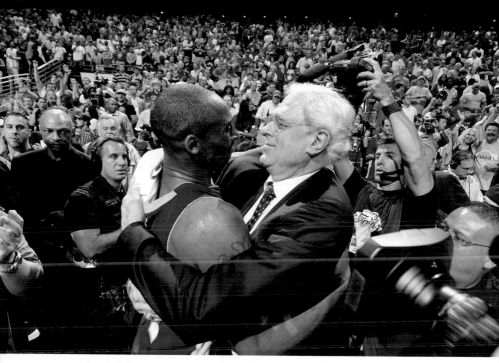

A **"knowing" moment:** Kobe and I embrace after winning the 2009 NBA title in Orlando.

The X factor: After the 2009 win in Orlando, my kids gave me this hat to commemorate my record-breaking tenth NBA title.

Sacred circle: Giving last-minute notes to the team before game 7 of the 2010 finals in LA. *(From left)* Andrew Bynum, Lamar Odom, Pau, Ron Artest, Derek Fisher, Shannon, Sasha, Jordan, and Josh Powell

Hard line: Pau, Kobe, Fish, and Lamar get ready to stop another Celtics drive in game 7 of the finals.

Tears of joy: Derek Fisher breaks down in the locker room after his inspiring performance in game 3 of the 2010 championship finals in Boston.

Happy ending: The fans shower Kobe with love after the 2010 win in the Staples Center.

"It's over!" Walking to the locker room with Charley (*left*), Brooke, and Chelsea after the longest half I've ever had to sit through finally ended, in game 4 of the 2011 Western Conference semi-finals in Dallas.

distractions of the outside world. I prohibited players from bringing family and friends to our training facility, except on special occasions. I also restricted the media from observing practices. I wanted the players to feel that they could act naturally during practice without having to worry about doing or saying something that might show up in the papers the next day.

As the season progressed, I slowly started to introduce the team to some of the tribal customs of the Lakota. Some of these were quite subtle. At the beginning of every practice, we had the core team—players, coaches, and training staff—convene in a circle at center court to discuss our objectives for that day. And we would end practice the same way.

Lakota warriors always gathered in circular formations because the circle was a symbol of the fundamental harmony of the universe. As Black Elk, the famed Lakota wise man, explained it:

Everything the Power of the World does is done in a circle. The sky is round, and I have heard that the earth is round like a ball, and so are the stars. . . . The sun comes forth and goes down again in a circle. The moon does the same and both are round. Even the seasons form a great circle in their changing and always come back again to where they were. The life of a man is a circle from childhood-to-childhood, and so it is in everything where power moves.

For the Lakota everything is sacred—including the enemy—because they believe in the fundamental interconnectedness of all life. That's why Lakota warriors didn't seek to conquer other tribes. They were far more interested in performing acts of bravery, such as counting coup (touching an enemy with a stick), taking part in a raiding

party to steal horses, or rescuing a fellow warrior who had been captured. For the Lakota going into battle was a joyful experience, much
like playing a game, though the stakes were obviously much higher.

Another Lakota practice I adopted was beating a drum when I
wanted the players to congregate in the tribal room for a meeting.
The tribal room—aka the video room—was decorated with several
Indian totems I'd been given over the years: a bear-claw necklace (for
power and wisdom), the middle feather of an owl (for balance and
harmony), a painting illustrating the story of Crazy Horse's journey,
and photos of a newborn white buffalo calf, a symbol of prosperity
and good fortune. Sometimes when the team lost a particularly lopsided game, I'd light a sage smudge stick—a Lakota tradition—and
playfully wave it through the air to purify the locker room. The first
time I did it, the players ribbed me: "What kind of weed you smokin'
there, Phil?"

The coaching staff also played a critical role in getting the players
to shift consciousness. When I was an assistant coach, Tex, Johnny,
and I used to sit around for hours talking about the history of the
game and the right way to play it. We didn't agree on everything, but
we did develop a high level of trust and a commitment to modeling
the sort of teamwork that we wanted the players to embrace.

Needless to say, the coaching profession attracts a lot of control
freaks who remind everyone constantly that they're the alpha dog in
the room. I've been known to do this myself. But what I've learned
over the years is that the most effective approach is to delegate authority as much as possible and to nurture everyone else's leadership
skills as well. When I'm able to do that, it not only builds team unity
and allows others to grow but also—paradoxically—strengthens my
role as leader.

Some coaches limit staff input because they want to be the dominant voice in the room. But I encouraged everyone to take part in the

discussion—coaches and players alike—to stimulate creativity and set a tone of inclusiveness. This is especially important for players who don't get a lot of playing time. My favorite poem about the power of inclusion is Edwin Markham's "Outwitted":

> *He drew the circle that shut me out—*
> *Heretic, rebel, a thing to flout.*
> *But love and I had the wit to win:*
> *We drew a circle that took him in!*

When I'm hiring coaches, my strategy is to surround myself with the strongest, most knowledgeable people I can find and give them a lot of room to express themselves. Shortly after I took over as head coach, I hired Jim Cleamons, one of my former Knicks teammates, to fill out the roster. He was one of the most skilled guards in the game, and I knew he could help nurture our young talent. But what endeared him to me most was that he had trained at Ohio State under coach Fred Taylor, one of the best system-oriented coaches in the history of the sport. Tex and Johnny couldn't wait to pick Jim's brain.

Each assistant coach had a clear role. Tex was in charge of teaching everyone offensive skills as well as the basic fundamentals of the triangle system. Johnny oversaw the defense and specialized in getting the players revved up for each new opponent. And Jim worked one on one with the players who needed more instruction. Every morning the coaching staff and I would meet for breakfast and discuss the fine points of the practice plan, as well as the latest scouting reports. That allowed us to share information with one another and make sure we were all on the same page in terms of day-to-day strategy. Each coach had a high level of autonomy, but when we talked to the players, we spoke as one.

The team got off to a slow start that first year. Most of the players were wary of the system. "It was frustrating," says Scottie. "We didn't have a good feel for each other. And late in games, we would go away from the offense because we didn't have confidence in it." But in the second half of the season, the team started to get more comfortable and we went on a 27-8 streak. Most opposing teams were confused about how to cover Michael now that he was moving more without the ball. They couldn't double- and triple-team him, as they did when he had possession. But they also couldn't afford to take their eyes off him, no matter where he was, and that created a lot of unexpected openings for other players.

We finished second in our division with a 55-27 record and breezed through the first two series of the playoffs, against Milwaukee and Philadelphia. But our next opponent, Detroit, was not as accommodating. Even though we'd beaten the Pistons during the regular season, memories of the mauling we had taken during the previous playoffs still haunted some of the players, especially Scottie, who had to leave game 6 with a concussion after being clocked from behind by center Bill Laimbeer. Scottie was also coping with a difficult personal issue. He'd missed most of the Philadelphia series in order to attend his father's funeral, and the stress of having to grieve in public was difficult for him to bear.

It was a brutal series that came down to a seventh game at the Pistons' new stadium in Auburn Hills, Michigan. We were struggling. Paxson had sprained his ankle in the previous game, and Scottie was suffering from a horrible migraine that blurred his vision so badly that he couldn't distinguish the colors of the jerseys. Both men tried to stumble through the game anyway, but the team fell apart in an embarrassing second period, and we never recovered. We lost by 19 points, and it felt like 100.

After the game, Jerry Krause showed up in the locker room and launched into a tirade, which was unusual. And Michael was so angry he burst into tears in the back of the team bus. "I made up my mind right then and there it would never happen again," he said later.

My reaction was more subdued. Yes, it was a difficult loss, one of the worst games I've ever had to coach. But once the noise died down, I noticed that the pain of humiliating defeat had galvanized the team in a way I'd never seen before. The Bulls were beginning to morph into a tribe.

7

HEARING THE UNHEARD

And above all, watch with glittering eyes the whole world around you because the greatest secrets are always hidden in the most unlikely places. Those who don't believe in magic will never find it.

ROALD DAHL

In the foyer of my home in Southern California hangs a tall totem-like painting of the core players who won the Bulls' first three championships. It's a series of portraits stacked vertically, starting with Michael Jordan at the top, followed by the other starters, then the backup players. With its elegant red border, subdued color palette, and dignified rendering of each player, the painting feels more like a sacred object than a collection of images. I like that the artist, Tim Anderson, made no distinction between the stars and the role players, except for the order in which they appear. Everyone's picture is the same size, and each possesses the same quiet poise. To me, the painting is a tribute to the concept of team.

After that wrenching loss to Detroit in the playoffs, we still had a long way to go before we reached that ideal. But we were definitely moving in the right direction. The players were beginning to embrace the system and show signs of becoming a more selfless, stage 4 team.

Over the summer I spent time reflecting on what we needed to do to accelerate the process. For starters, we needed to pace ourselves through the grueling eighty-two-game season as if we were running a marathon, not a series of sprints. To unseat the Pistons, we had to secure home-court advantage early and peak at the right time, both physically and psychologically. Second, we needed to use our swarming, high-pressure defense more effectively, especially in the playoffs, when defense usually makes the difference between success and failure. Third, it was important to make sure that each game was meaningful in terms of what we were trying to do as a team. I often reminded the players to focus on the journey rather than the endgame, because if you give the future all your attention, the present will pass you by.

The most important thing was to get the players to develop a strong group intelligence in order to work more harmoniously together. There's a section in Rudyard Kipling's *The Second Jungle Book* that sums up the kind of group dynamic I was looking for them to create. During the 1990–91 season that became our team motto:

> Now this is the Law of the Jungle—as old and true as
> the sky;
> And the Wolf that shall keep it may prosper, but the Wolf
> that shall break must die.
> As the creeper that girdles the tree-trunk, the Law runneth
> forward and back—
> For the strength of the Pack is the Wolf, and the strength of
> the Wolf is the Pack.

When I started playing for the Knicks, I spent a couple of summers as a grad student in psychology at the University of North Dakota. During that time, I studied the work of psychologist Carl Rogers, whose groundbreaking ideas on personal empowerment have had a strong influence on my approach to leadership. Rogers, one of the founders of humanistic psychology, was an innovative clinician who, after years of experimenting, developed several effective techniques for nurturing what he called the "real self" rather than the idealized self we think we're supposed to become. The key, he believed, was for the therapist to create a relationship with the client focused not on solving a problem but on nurturing personal growth.

For that to happen, Rogers said, the therapist had to be as honest and authentic as possible and regard the client as a person of unconditional worthiness, no matter what his or her condition. The paradox, he writes in his seminal work, *On Becoming a Person*, "is that the more I am simply willing to be myself, in all this complexity of life and the more I am willing to understand and accept the realities in myself and in the other person, the more change seems to be stirred up."

In Rogers's view, it's virtually impossible for anyone to change unless he thoroughly accepts who he is. Nor can he develop successful relationships with others unless he can discover the meaning of his own experience. He explains: "Each person is an island unto himself, in a very real sense, and he can only build bridges to other islands if he is first of all willing to be himself and permitted to be himself."

I don't pretend to be a therapist. But the process Rogers describes is not unlike what I've tried to do as a coach. Rather than squeeze everybody into preordained roles, my goal has always been to foster an environment where the players can grow as individuals and express themselves creatively within a team structure. I wasn't interested in becoming best friends with the players; in fact, I think it's important to maintain a certain distance. But I tried to develop genuine, caring relationships with each player, based on mutual respect, compassion, and trust.

Transparency is the key. The one thing players won't stand for is a coach who won't be honest and straightforward with them. During my first year coaching the Bulls, B.J. Armstrong lobbied to replace John Paxson as the starting point guard. B.J. argued that he was a better playmaker than John and could beat him off the dribble. But he had been a reluctant convert to the triangle offense because he thought it would hamper his ability to show off his stylish one-on-one moves. I told him that I appreciated his enthusiasm, but I wanted him to share minutes with Pax because John worked better with the starters and we needed B.J. to energize the second unit. What's more, the team flowed together more effectively when John was in the lineup. B.J. wasn't thrilled with my decision, but he got the message. A few years later, after he'd demonstrated that he could run the offense and play cooperatively, we made him a starter.

One of the hardest jobs of a coach is keeping the role players from undermining team chemistry. New York Yankees manager Casey Stengel used to say, "The secret of managing is to keep the guys who hate you away from the guys who are undecided." In basketball, the guys who hate you are usually the ones who aren't getting as much playing time as they think they deserve. Having been a backup myself, I know how aggravating it can be if you're languishing on the bench in the middle of a crucial game.

My strategy was to keep the backups as engaged as possible in the flow of the game. If the triangle offense was working right, Tex used to say, the team should play together as if they were "five fingers on a hand." So when backup players went into the game, they needed to be able to merge seamlessly with the players on the court. During those early years, I used a ten-man rotation—five starters and five backups—to make sure the nonstarters had enough time on court to get in sync with the rest of the team. Late in the season I would trim the rotation down to seven or eight players, but I tried to pull the other backups in whenever possible. Sometimes role players can have a surprising impact. Take Cliff Levingston, a backup power forward who played limited minutes during the 1990–91 season but flourished in the playoffs because he matched up well against the Detroit front line.

I'm not a big hugger or someone who doles out praise easily. In fact, some people find me aloof and enigmatic. My style is to show appreciation with subtle gestures—a nod of recognition here, a touch on the arm there. I learned this from Dick McGuire, my first coach on the Knicks, who used to come by my locker after games and quietly reassure me that he was looking out for me and would try to give me more time during the next game. As a coach, I tried to convey to each player that I cared for him as a person, not just as a basketball factotum.

The great gift my father gave me was showing me how to be genuinely compassionate while also commanding people's respect. Dad was a tall, majestic figure with a distinguished carriage, a warm smile, and a softness about the eyes that made him look trustworthy, caring, and a little mysterious. He resembled portraits I've seen of George Washington, a man who was soft-spoken and modest yet totally in control. As a child, I'd often stand next to my father and greet church members as they left services. Some said I looked like him in the dignified way I held my body. No question, I've benefited as a coach from having a large frame and a deep, resounding voice. When I talk to players, I don't have to look up at them; we can converse eye to eye.

Dad was a pastor in the true sense of the word. He was one of the few genuinely Christian men I've ever met. He lived by a simple set of rules dictated by the Bible and avoided lawsuits and animosity in general because they conflicted with his Christian ideals. While my mother often railed about fire and brimstone in her sermons, Dad focused primarily on benevolence and having a generous heart. He cared deeply for his parishioners and prayed for each one of them in his study after breakfast. The church members felt protected and re-assured by him, which helped bind the community together. This was a lesson I never forgot.

As a rule, pro basketball players are not forthcoming about their deepest yearnings. They prefer to communicate nonverbally or make jokes rather than reveal any vulnerability, particularly when they're talking to their coach. So it can be tricky trying to unearth what makes each player tick.

I was always looking for new ways to get inside the players' heads. When I started coaching the Bulls, I had the players create what I called a personal shield, a simple profile based on questions such as "What's your greatest aspiration?" "Who's influenced you the most?" and "What's something people don't know about you?" Later I asked them to fill out a more formal questionnaire and used their answers to probe more deeply during our one-on-one meetings midway through the season.

My favorite psychological tool was one June called a "social bull's-eye," which creates a picture of how people see themselves in relation to the group. On one of our long road trips, I'd give each of the play-ers a sheet of paper with a three-ring bull's-eye, representing the team's social structure, in the center. Then I'd ask them to position them-selves somewhere on the bull's-eye based on how connected they felt to the team. Not surprisingly, the starters usually placed themselves somewhere near the eye, and the backups scattered themselves in the second and third rings. One year backup forward Stacey King, a fast-talking, stylishly dressed player who made everyone laugh, drew him-self hovering far outside the third ring. When I asked him why, he said, "I don't get any playing time, Coach." Which wasn't true, but it was how he felt. On the surface, Stacey seemed confident and gre-garious, but inside he felt like an outsider struggling for recognition. I don't think I ever figured out how to heal that wound.

My intention was to give the players the freedom to figure out how to
fit themselves within the system, rather than dictating from on high
what I wanted them to do. Some players felt uncomfortable because
they'd never been given that kind of latitude before. Others felt completely liberated.

As the 1990–91 season opened, I decided to leave Michael alone. I
knew he needed time to figure out how to work within the system in
a way that made sense for him. During the off-season he had decided
that he needed to bulk up to fend off the physical beating he was
taking from the Pistons and other teams. He hired Tim Grover, a
physical-training specialist who put him through a grueling series of
workouts to increase his endurance and strengthen his upper and
lower body. As always, Michael was incredibly disciplined about the
workouts and arrived at training camp looking much bigger and
stronger, particularly in his shoulders and arms.

Michael loved challenges. So I challenged him to imagine a new
way of relating to his teammates. He expected his teammates to perform at his level, even though there were only a handful of players in
the league who could meet that standard. I encouraged him to take
a fresh look at his role on the team and try to envision ways he could
serve as a catalyst to get all the players to work together. I didn't dictate to him what I wanted; I simply pushed him to think about the
problem in a different way, mostly by asking him questions about
the impact that this or that strategy might have on the team. "How
do you think Scottie or Horace would feel if you did this?" I would
say. I treated him like a partner, and slowly he began to shift his way
of thinking. When I let him solve the problem himself, he was more
likely to buy into the solution and not repeat the same counterproductive behavior in the future.

Looking back, Michael says that he liked this approach because it "allowed me to be the person I needed to be." Sometimes I would tell him that he needed to be aggressive and set the tone for the team. Other times I'd say, "Why don't you try to get Scottie going so that the defenders will go after him and then you can attack?" In general, I tried to give Michael room to figure out how to integrate his personal ambitions with those of the team. "Phil knew that winning the scoring title was important to me," Michael says now, "but I wanted to do it in a way that didn't take away from what the team was doing."

Every now and then, Michael and I would have a dispute, usually when I criticized one of his ego-driven moves. But our run-ins never blew up into major fights. "It took me a while to calm down," says Michael. "Maybe I had to look at myself in the mirror and try to understand exactly what Phil was saying. And I imagine he did the same thing. Every time we had one of those encounters, our mutual respect grew." I agree.

Another player who made a significant leap that season was Scottie Pippen. Of course, he was used to making big leaps. He grew up, the youngest of twelve children, in Hamburg, Arkansas. His family didn't have much money, in part because his father had been disabled by a stroke while working at a paper mill. Still, Scottie was the golden boy in the family. Though he didn't get any scholarship offers, he enrolled at the University of Central Arkansas and worked his way through school, doing odd jobs and serving as varsity team manager. His debut as a walk-on for the freshman team was not spectacular: He averaged 4.3 points and 2.9 rebounds per game. But over the next year he grew four inches to six feet five and returned to school, after playing hard all summer, far better than anyone else on the team. "I was always a good ball handler," says Scottie. "And that was a big advantage when I grew because now you had to be a center to guard me. And there weren't that many big guys in the league."

Scottie, who hit six feet seven by the time he graduated, averaged 26.3 points and 10 rebounds a game and was named a consensus All-American in his senior year. Jerry Krause, who had spotted him early, made a few deft trades in order to draft him fifth overall in 1987. But Scottie was pegged as a traditional small forward and had a difficult time fitting into that role because he wasn't a strong outside shooter. But he did have the rare skill of being able to grab a rebound and drive all the way through traffic to attack the basket at the other end. Guarding Michael in practice also turned Scottie into a formidable defender. But what impressed me most when I first started working with him was his ability to read what was happening on the floor and react accordingly. He'd been a point guard in high school and still had that kind of share-the-ball mentality. While Michael was always looking to score, Scottie seemed to be more interested in making sure the offense succeeded as a whole. In that respect, he modeled himself more after Magic Johnson than after Michael Jordan.

So in my second year as head coach I created a new position for Scottie—"point forward"—and had him share the job of moving the ball up court with the guards—an experiment that worked out far better than I expected. That switch unleashed a side of Scottie that had never been tapped, and he blossomed into a gifted multidimensional player with the ability to break games wide open on the fly. As he puts it, the shift "made me the player I wanted to be in the NBA."

Scottie finished second on the team in scoring (17.8), rebounds (7.3), and steals (2.35) in 1990–91 and would be named to the All-Defense First Team the following year. The effect on the team was powerful. Shifting Scottie to point guard put the ball in his hands as much as in Michael's, and it allowed M.J. to move to the wing and play a number of different roles in the offense, including leading the attack on transition. The shift also opened up possibilities for other players because Scottie was more egalitarian than Michael in the way he distributed the ball. All of a sudden a new, more collaborative group dynamic was evolving.

At that time most coaches subscribed to the Knute Rockne theory of mental training. They tried to get their players revved up for the game with win-one-for-the-Gipper-style pep talks. That approach may work if you're a linebacker. But what I discovered playing for the Knicks is that when I got too excited mentally, it had a negative effect on my ability to stay focused under pressure. So I did the opposite. Instead of charging players up, I developed a number of strategies to help them quiet their minds and build awareness so they could go into battle poised and in control.

The first thing I did with the Bulls was to teach the players an abbreviated version of mindfulness meditation based on the Zen practice I'd been doing for years. I didn't make a big deal of it. We sat for about ten minutes or so during practice, usually before one of our video-viewing sessions. Some players thought it was weird; others used the time to take a nap. But they humored me because they knew that meditation was an important part of my life. From my point of view, getting the players to sit quietly together for ten minutes was a good start. And some players, notably B.J. Armstrong, took a serious interest in meditation and pursued it further on their own.

I wasn't trying to turn the Bulls into Buddhist monks. I was interested in getting them to take a more mindful approach to the game and to their relationships with one another. At its heart, mindfulness is about being present in the moment as much as possible, not weighed down by thoughts of the past or the future. According to Suzuki-roshi, when we do something with "a quite simple, clear mind . . . our activity is strong and straightforward. But when we do something with a complicated mind, in relation to other things or people, or society, our activity becomes very complex."

To be successful at basketball, as author John McPhee once pointed out, you need to have a finely tuned sense of where you are and what's happening around you at any given moment. A few players are born with this skill—Michael, Scottie, and Bill Bradley, to name a few—but most players have to learn it. What I discovered after years of meditation practice is that when you immerse yourself fully in the moment, you start developing a much deeper awareness of what's going on, right here, right now. And that awareness ultimately leads to a greater sense of oneness—the essence of teamwork.

John Paxson once sent me an article from the *Harvard Business Review* that he said reminded him of me. The article—"Parables of Leadership" by W. Chan Kim and Renée A. Mauborgne—was composed of a series of ancient parables that focused on what the authors called "the unseen space of leadership." The story that had caught Paxson's eye was one about a young prince who was sent by his father to study how to become a good ruler with a great Chinese master.

The first assignment the master gave him was to spend a year in the forest alone. When the prince returned, the master asked him to describe what he had heard, and he replied, "I could hear the cuckoos sing, the leaves rustle, the hummingbirds hum, the crickets chirp, the grass blow, the bees buzz and the wind whisper and holler."

After the prince finished, the master told him to return to the forest to listen for what more could be heard. So the prince went back and sat alone in the forest for several days and nights, wondering what the master was talking about. Then one morning, he started to hear faint sounds that he had never heard before.

Upon his return, the prince told the master, "When I listened most closely, I could hear the unheard—the sound of flowers opening, the sound of the sun warming the earth, and the sound of the grass drinking the morning dew."

The master nodded. "To hear the unheard," he said, "is a necessary discipline to be a good ruler. For only when a ruler has learned to listen closely to the people's hearts, hearing their feelings uncommunicated, pains unexpressed, and complaints not spoken of, can he hope to inspire confidence in the people, understand when something is wrong, and meet the true needs of his citizens."

Hearing the unheard. That's a skill everyone in the group needs, not just the leader. In basketball, statisticians count when players make assists, or passes that lead to scores. But I've always been more interested on having players focus on the pass that *leads to* the pass that leads to the score. That kind of awareness takes time to develop, but once you've mastered it, the invisible becomes visible and the game unfolds like a story before your eyes.

To strengthen the players' awareness, I liked to keep them guessing about what was coming next. During one practice, they looked so lackadaisical I decided to turn out the lights and have them play in the dark—not an easy task when you're trying to catch a rocket pass from Michael Jordan. Another time, after an embarrassing defeat, I had them go through a whole practice without saying a word. Other coaches thought I was nuts. What mattered to me was getting the players to wake up, if only for a moment, and see the unseen, hear the unheard.

Getting ready for the NBA playoffs is like preparing to go to the dentist. You know the visit is not going to be as bad as you think it is, but you can't stop yourself from obsessing about it. Your whole being is pointed toward that event. The anxiety often creeps up on me in the middle of the night, and I'll lie in bed thinking and rethinking our strategy for the next game. Sometimes in those wee hours, I'll turn to meditation to unlock my mind and give me some relief from the barrage of second-guessing. But the most effective way to deal with anxiety, I've discovered, is to make sure that you're as prepared as possible for whatever is coming your way. My brother Joe often talks about faith being one of the two things that can help you cope with fear. The other is love. Joe says you need to have faith that you've done all you could to make sure things turn out right—regardless of the final outcome.

There's a story I love to tell about how Napoléon Bonaparte picked his generals. After one of his great generals died, Napoléon reputedly sent one of his staff officers to search for a replacement. The officer returned several weeks later and described a man he thought would be the perfect candidate because of his knowledge of military tactics and brilliance as a manager. When the officer finished, Napoléon looked at him and said, "That's all very good, but is he lucky?"

Tex Winter called me "the luckiest coach in the world." But I don't think luck has a lot to do with it. Sure, someone might get injured or some other calamity might befall the team. But I believe that if you've taken care of all the details, the laws of cause and effect—not luck—will usually determine the result. Of course, there are plenty of things you can't control in a basketball game. That's why we focused most of our time on what we *could* control: the right footwork, the right floor spacing, the right way to handle the ball. When you play the game the right way, it makes sense to the players and winning is the likely outcome.

But there's another kind of faith that's even more important—the faith that we're all connected on some level that surpasses understanding. That's why I have players sit together in silence. Sitting silently in a group without any distractions can make people resonate with one another in profound ways. As Friedrich Nietzsche said, "Invisible threads are the strongest ties."

I've watched those ties form several times in my career. The deep feeling of connection that occurs when players pull together is a tremendous force that can wipe away the fear of losing. That was the lesson the Bulls were about to learn.

Midway through the 1990–91 season, all the pieces started falling together. As the players became more comfortable with the triangle offense, Tex started to get them to focus on a sequence of critical actions we called "automatics," which could be set in motion if the opposing team was overloading coverage in one area of the floor. The critical point was what Tex called the "moment of truth" when the player moving the ball up court encountered the defense. If the defense focused a lot of pressure on him at that point, then he could launch an automatic play to shift the action to another part of the floor and open up new scoring possibilities. One of the team's favorite automatics was what we called "the Blind Pig"—an action in which frontline players came up to relieve pressure on the point guard and the weakside forward (aka the pig) broke free, took the pass, and disrupted the defense. The Blind Pig was a critical play not only for the Bulls but also later for the Lakers, because it brought a shooter off a double screen on the weak side and put two of our best players in scoring position.

The players were enthusiastic. The Blind Pig and other automatics allowed them to adapt to what the defense was doing in a coordinated way, without having to rely on me to call plays from the sidelines. "That became our number one weapon," recalls Scottie. "We felt very good about coming down the floor and just throwing the ball into play. We all started to run to certain spots because we were comfortable there. Everyone was happy. Michael was getting his shots increasingly. We had better balance getting back on transition. We were becoming a better defensive team. And then it became second nature for us."

The automatics also taught the players how to take advantage of the defense by *moving away from pressure* rather than trying to attack it directly. This would be important when the team faced stronger, more physical teams, such as the Pistons. To beat Detroit, we needed to be resilient and not back down. But we were never going to beat them if we got into a wrestling match with them every time we came down the floor.

Just before the All-Star break, the Bulls took off on an 18-1 run, including a morale-boosting 95–93 win over the Pistons in Auburn Hills. Even though Isiah Thomas was out with a wrist injury, the game was a key turning point in how we viewed ourselves as a team. After that, the Bad Boys didn't seem so "bad" anymore.

We finished the season with a league-leading 61-21 record, which gave us home-court advantage throughout the playoffs. We swept the Knicks 3–0, then won the first two games of the series with Philadelphia easily but ran into problems in game 3. Jordan arrived with tendinitis in his knee (probably picked up playing golf between games) and the 76ers' big forwards—Armen Gilliam, Charles Barkley, and Rick Mahorn—started pushing Horace Grant around and throwing him off his game.

Horace was a six-ten power forward who had exceptional foot speed and good rebounding instincts. Johnny Bach called him "the intrepid one" because of his ability to trap quick ball handlers and make the pressure defense work. Horace, who'd grown up in rural Georgia, had bonded with Scottie early on and once told reporters that Pippen was "like my twin brother." But they'd drifted apart during the 1990–91 season, as Scottie gravitated closer to Michael. Meanwhile, Horace, who was trying hard to save his marriage, had turned to religion for solace.

The previous year Johnny had suggested that I use Horace as a "whipping boy" to motivate the team. This is a fairly common practice on pro teams. In fact, I had played that role briefly when I was with the Knicks. The point was to designate one player who would get the lion's share of criticism as a way to motivate the rest of the players to bond together. I didn't entirely buy into this type of old-school coaching, but I was willing to give it a try. I knew the players liked Horace and would rally around him if I pushed too hard. And Johnny, who had a solid relationship with Horace, assured me that he was tough enough to take the pressure.

We explained the idea to Horace and he was on board, at first. Ever since he was a kid, he'd dreamed about becoming a Marine, so strong discipline appealed to him. But as time went by, he began to bristle at the criticism. It all came to a head in the third quarter of game 3 against the 76ers.

Gilliam had been hitting Horace in the back and pushing him off position all game, and the refs had been letting him get away with it. When Horace finally retaliated out of frustration, the refs noticed and called the foul.

I was furious. I pulled Horace out of the game and started screaming at him for letting the 76ers manhandle him. Horace yelled back, "I'm tired of being your whipping boy." Then he started cursing me—unusual for him.

Needless to say, we lost the game. I admit this wasn't my finest moment. But I learned a key lesson: how important it was to relate to each player as an individual, with respect and compassion, no matter how much pressure I might be feeling. I met with Horace when the air had cleared and told him that we needed to start over. From that point on, I said, I would focus on giving him constructive criticism, and I hoped that he, in turn, would give me feedback on anything that might be troubling him.

Before the next game, I met with the team for breakfast to discuss what had happened. I said that we'd broken the tribal circle and we needed to put it back together. At the end of the meeting, I asked Horace to read the team a passage from Psalms.

Horace played like a man possessed that day. He burst out on the court, grabbed some key early rebounds, and finished with 22 points as we rolled to a 101–85 win. More important, Horace stood up to Gilliam and the other big men without getting rattled. It was a good sign. The 76ers looked tired and broken, and they folded two days later in the decisive game 5. Next stop, Detroit.

During the 1990 playoffs, I'd shown the team a video with scenes from *The Wizard of Oz*. The purpose was to illustrate how intimidated the players were by the Pistons' rough play. There was a shot of B.J. Armstrong driving to the basket and getting clobbered by the Detroit front line, followed by a clip of Dorothy saying, "This isn't Kansas anymore, Toto." Another sequence showed Joe Dumars beating out Jordan off the dribble, while the Tin Man lamented not having a heart. Yet another had Isiah Thomas waltzing by Paxson, Horace, and Cartwright as the Cowardly Lion whined about not having any courage. The players broke into laughter at first, but that died down when they realized the message I was trying to convey.

This time I didn't need to play movie scenes. Instead I put together a series of clips for the NBA's front office, showing the most egregious examples of the Pistons' cheap shots against the Bulls. I'm not sure how much impact the tape had on the officiating, but at least it showed we weren't going to roll over quietly.

It may not have mattered. The 1990–91 Pistons lineup wasn't as intimidating as before, especially since they'd lost their bruising power forward Rick Mahorn. And our team was far more confident and poised than we had been a year earlier. My advice to the players was to strike first, rather than allow the Pistons to push us around early, and to avoid getting caught up in Detroit's web of trash talk. I was pleased to see the way Scottie handled himself in game 1. When the newest Bad Boy, Mark Aguirre, threatened to mess him up, Scottie just laughed.

Jordan had an off game that day, but the second unit stepped in and built up a 9-point lead in the fourth quarter that made the difference. After the game, in a moment that surprised everyone, Jordan thanked his teammates for carrying him. I could sense that all of our efforts to shift the team's mind-set were beginning to pay off. A few days later Scottie told *Chicago Tribune* reporter Sam Smith that he had noticed a change in Michael. "You can tell M.J. has more confidence in everyone," Scottie said. "And I'd have to say it's come just in these playoffs. He's playing team ball and for the first time I can say he's not going out there looking to score. He seems to have the feeling, and we all seem to, really, that if we play together everyone can help."

In game 2 we put Scottie in charge of moving the ball up court and shifted Paxson to the wing. That move created some difficult mismatches for the Pistons, which they never could resolve. We also made a few defensive switches that worked well, putting Pippen on their center, Laimbeer, and Cartwright on their small forward, Aguirre. Our defense was so wired that nothing seemed to work for the Pistons. By game 4 they were looking at a sweep on their home court, and when they couldn't stop that, the game turned ugly. Laimbeer blindsided Paxson and Rodman knocked Scottie into the seats with a blow that could have ended his career. The worst moment, however, came at the end when the Pistons, led by Isiah Thomas, walked off the court without shaking our hands—an insult not just to the Bulls but to the game itself that bothers me to this day.

Our next opponent was L.A. The Lakers were a storied franchise that had dominated the NBA in the previous decade and were still a powerful team, led by Magic Johnson, with James Worthy, Sam Perkins, Byron Scott, and Vlade Divac. This series would be the ultimate test for Michael, who had always measured himself against Johnson. Magic not only had the rings (five) and the MVP awards (three), he also had an impressive gift for leadership. In his rookie year he had taken over a team dominated by All-Stars, including Kareem Abdul-Jabbar, and masterfully piloted it to a championship. Michael was in his seventh year with the NBA and still looking for his first ring.

We got off to a slow start and dropped game 1 in Chicago. Midway through, however, I noticed a weakness that I hadn't seen on any of the tapes. Whenever Magic left the game, his teammates weren't able to hold the lead against our second unit. Magic looked tired after the Lakers' grueling battle against Portland in the Western Conference finals, and it was clear that the Lakers were much weaker when he rested than we were when Michael was on the bench. This was something we could exploit.

Our game plan was to put Scottie on Magic.

In game 2 Michael got into foul trouble early, so moving Scottie over proved to be a good plan—the adjustment threw the Lakers' offense out of whack, and we won easily, 107–86. After the game I put a video together for Michael, showing him how Magic often left his man—Paxson—to help other players on defense. He was gambling that Michael wouldn't give up the ball. Paxson was a strong clutch shooter, and in general Michael trusted him more than others in tight situations. But in the L.A. series Michael was reverting to his old habit of trying to win games by himself. Despite our victory in game 2, this was hurting us.

The action shifted to L.A. for the next three games. In game 3 Michael tied the score with 3.4 seconds left in regulation by driving the ball to the free-throw line and nailing a quick jumper. Then we regrouped and grabbed a 104–96 win in overtime. Two days later our defense completely dominated the Lakers in game 4, holding them to their lowest point total—82—since the arrival of the shot clock, and we took a 3-1 lead in the series. Magic called it "an old-fashioned ass-kicking."

In game 5 we were ahead most of the way, but midway through the fourth quarter the Lakers fought back and took the lead. I wasn't happy with what I was seeing. Despite our discussions, Michael was still leaving Paxson in limbo. So I called a time-out and gathered the team together.

"Who's open, M.J.?" I asked, looking directly into Michael's eyes.

He didn't answer. So I asked him again, "Who's open?"

"Paxson," he replied.

"Okay, so find him."

After that exchange, the game turned. Michael and others started delivering the ball to Paxson, and he responded by hitting 4 shots in a row. The Lakers drew within 2 points with a little over a minute left. But I noticed something different as Michael moved the ball up court. I expected him to make a move toward the basket, as he usually did in this kind of situation. But instead he was luring the defense in his direction and trying to create a shot for, yes, Paxson. It was a sweet ending. John nailed the two-pointer and we went on to win, 108–101.

This was a profound moment for me. Eighteen years earlier I had won my first championship ring as a player in this stadium—the Los Angeles Forum. Now I had just won my first ring as a coach, and best of all, we had done it by playing the game the same way my Knicks team had played.

The right way.

8

A QUESTION OF CHARACTER

The way you do anything is the way you do everything.
TOM WAITS

You'd think it would get easier the second time around, but that's not how it works. As soon as the cheering stops, the dance of the wounded egos begins. Former UCLA head coach John Wooden used to say that "winning takes talent, to repeat takes character." I didn't really understand what he meant until we started our second run for the ring. All of a sudden the media spotlight turned in our direction, and everyone connected to the Bulls whose name wasn't Jordan began to vie for more attention. As Michael put it, "Success turns we's back into me's."

The first glimmer I got of this came when Horace unloaded on Michael in the media for skipping out on the championship celebration at the White House. Attendance was optional, and before the event, Michael had informed Horace that he wasn't planning to attend. Horace didn't seem to have a problem with it at the time, but when we returned from Washington, he told reporters he was upset that Jordan hadn't shown up. Michael felt betrayed by Horace but chose not to respond to his comments. I presumed that Horace had been hoodwinked by reporters into saying something he didn't believe, so I didn't fine him. But I warned him to be careful in the future about saying things to the press that might be divisive to the team.

Horace wasn't the only player who was envious of Michael's fame, but he was the most outspoken. He had a hard time understanding that I had no control over Michael's celebrity. It transcended the Bulls and the sport itself.

As soon as the White House kerfuffle ended, another controversy arose that had a much longer-lasting impact on the team. It surrounded the publication of Sam Smith's best-selling book *The Jordan Rules,* an account of the 1990–91 championship season that tried to demythologize Michael and provide an inside look at the secret world of the Chicago Bulls. Smith, a smart, hardworking reporter whom I liked, based the book on his coverage of the Bulls for the *Chicago Tribune.* Some of the anecdotes portrayed Michael and Jerry Krause in a less-than-flattering light.

Michael wasn't happy with the book, but he shrugged it off, presuming, no doubt, that it wasn't going to have a serious impact on his public image. However, Krause was far less detached. One night shortly after the book came out, he called me into his hotel room during a road trip and started ranting about Smith. He said he had uncovered "176 lies" in the book and pulled out his heavily marked-up copy to prove it. As soon as he started pointing out each alleged lie page by page, I cut him off, saying, "You've really got to let this thing go, Jerry."

But he couldn't. Jerry had been suspicious of reporters ever since he got caught in a media flare-up in 1976 that caused him to lose his position as executive of the Bulls after just three months on the job. He was in the middle of hiring a new head coach for the team when the papers reported that he'd offered the position to DePaul coach Ray Meyer. Jerry denied it, but the story wouldn't die. Disappointed by Jerry's handling of the situation, Bulls chairman Arthur Wirtz let him go.

As the weeks went by, Jerry became obsessed with trying to suss out who had been Sam's primary source for the book. There were dozens of sources, of course. Sam talked regularly with almost everybody connected with the team, including owner Jerry Reinsdorf. I arranged for Krause to meet with Sam and try to work things out, but that conversation went nowhere. Finally Jerry concluded that assistant coach Johnny Bach was the main culprit. I thought that was absurd, but the suspicion lingered and figured in Johnny's dismissal years later.

This was the first chink in my relationship with Jerry, which until then had been extremely productive. I was grateful to Jerry for believing in me and giving me the opportunity to coach the Bulls. I also admired the way he'd constructed the team, recruiting the right talent to complement Jordan, even though he often took a lot of heat from Michael and others for the moves he made. I enjoyed working with Jerry on creating the first incarnation of the Bulls' championship team, then rebuilding it later after Michael returned from his baseball sojourn. One thing I liked about Jerry was that he always sought a wide range of perspectives from coaches, players, and the scouting staff before making key decisions. He also placed great importance on finding players with a high degree of character and was relentless about digging into a potential recruit's background to find out what he was made of.

Early in my tenure as head coach, Jerry would greet the players on the first day of training camp and tell the same story, which summed up how he envisioned our relationship. Jerry was an only child, and when he was young, he said, he tried to play his parents against each other, going back and forth between them until he got the response he wanted. One day his father figured this out and said, "Look, Jerry, don't ever come between your mother and me. We have to sleep together." I'd roll my eyes when he told this story and say something like, "Sorry, Jerry. No can do"—and it would get a good laugh.

Obviously I had a different vision of how we should work together. I wanted to be supportive of Jerry, and I spent a lot of time mediating between him and the players. But I didn't want to do anything that would jeopardize the bond of trust I'd developed with the team.

Most of the players resented Jerry for one reason or another. It started with Michael. During his second year with the Bulls, Michael broke his left foot and had to sit out most of the season recovering from the injury. At a certain point, Michael insisted that his foot was fully healed, but Jerry refused to let him play until the doctors gave him the final okay. When Michael pushed back, Jerry told him that management had made the decision because he was *their* property, an unfortunate gaffe that alienated Michael and tainted his relationship with Krause from that day forward.

Other players had issues with Jerry too. They didn't like the way he stretched the truth about his past achievements as a scout to make himself look good. They were also annoyed when he became obsessed with recruiting Toni Kukoc, a promising forward from Croatia who Jerry predicted would be the next Magic Johnson, even though Toni had never played a game in the NBA. Scottie and Michael felt that Jerry's flirtation with Toni, who later signed with the Bulls, was an insult to his own players, and they went out of their way to crush Kukoc and the Croatian national team during the 1992 Olympics.

Most of all, the players were put off by Jerry's constant attempts to hang out with them and be one of the guys. His short, roly-poly physique didn't help his case, either. Michael nicknamed him "Crumbs" because of his less-than-perfect table manners and often poked fun at his weight and other idiosyncrasies when he rode on the team bus.

This kind of tension on a team always makes me feel uneasy.

When I was a kid, I hated discord of any kind. My older brothers, who were less than two years apart, fought constantly, and I was the peacemaker. My father used to discipline my brothers with his belt, and I remember sitting at the top of the cellar stairs bursting into tears listening to them get their whippings.

The way I handled Jerry was to keep things light. I knew that his overreaction to *The Jordan Rules* stemmed from his feeling that he wasn't getting the credit he deserved for building this great team. I understood. But I couldn't fix it, so I tried to shift his mind with a touch of humor and compassion. I also tried to keep our relationship as professional as possible. As the team's fame grew, the rift between Jerry and me widened. But professionalism sustained us. Despite the turmoil, Jerry and I were able to stay focused and get the job done.

With the players it was a different matter. I told them they needed to tune out the distractions—whether they came from the media, Krause, or another source—and focus their attention on winning a second championship. To that end, I redoubled my efforts to turn practice into a sanctuary from the messiness of the outside world. "We were a very popular team," says Scottie. "So we had to secure and protect each other. We couldn't have people bringing their friends to practice and bugging guys for autographs. Because if you can't have freedom of life with your teammates, where are you going to get it?"

As the team turned its attention inward, the bond among the players began to re-form. The "me's," to use Michael's phrase, slowly transformed into a powerful We—and one of the strongest all-around teams I've ever coached. The system was clicking, and our defense was unstoppable. We got off to a 15-2 start and finished the season with 67 wins, 10 more than anyone else in the league. Our biggest losing streak was two games. At one point, Reinsdorf called and said, "I hope you're not pushing the team to break the record." No, I told him, it was just happening spontaneously. B. J. Armstrong said he felt the Bulls were "in tune with nature" that season and that everything was fitting together "like fall and winter and spring and summer."

Then came the playoffs. After beating Miami in three games, we faced a tough New York Knicks team, coached by Pat Riley, who had done a good job of turning the Knicks into a new version of the old Detroit Pistons. In fact, Riley had hired a former Pistons defensive coach, Dick Harter, to bring that kind of toughness to the Knicks. The NBA had put up with the Bad Boys of Detroit for the past five years, and after we'd dispatched them the previous year, there had been a collective sigh around the league. Muscle ball was out and finesse basketball was slowly coming back in vogue. Still, the Knicks had a powerful front line—made up of Patrick Ewing, Charles Oakley, and Xavier McDaniel, with Anthony Mason as the backup. Their strategy was to use their muscle to dominate the boards, slow down the tempo of the game, and take away the fast break. Their most effective weapon, however, was Riley's ability to spin the media. He had learned a lot in L.A. about using the press to play the refs, and he fired his first salvo before the first playoff game. His point? If the refs didn't get enamored with M.J., he said, and called a fair game, the Knicks would have a chance to win. I fired back, saying that Ewing was getting away with murder, taking extra steps every time he drove to the basket. The battle was on.

I've always felt comfortable talking with reporters because I spent so much time hanging out with them during my playing days with the Knicks. I also learned from some of the stupid mistakes I made. In my first year as a starter—1974–75—the Knicks took off on a roll, but we didn't have much depth and finished the season with a disappointing 40–42 record. So I told reporters that we might have made the playoffs, but we were "still losers." That was the big headline the next day: "Jackson Calls Knicks Losers."

My other gaffe was even worse. During a fight between the Lakers and the Rockets in 1977, L.A.'s Kermit Washington threw a punch at Houston's Rudy Tomjanovich that smashed his face and nearly killed him. I told reporters that I thought it was an unfortunate situation but that I'd narrowly ducked a similar blow from 76er George McGinnis a week earlier and nobody had even noticed. "It seemed you had to be a star to get the league to notice," I complained. I still wish I could take back those words.

The Knicks outmuscled us and got an easy ride from the refs en route to a surprising win in game 1. Early on Scottie Pippen severely sprained his ankle and the game slowed down to the Knicks' pace. We bounced back in game 2, lifted by several key shots by B.J. Armstrong. And Michael broke loose from the Knicks' crowbar defense to allow us to take back home-court advantage in game 3.

Horace compared game 4 to a World Wrestling Federation match, and Michael said the officiating was so bad he thought it would be impossible for us to win. I blamed the refs and got thrown out in the second half, as the Knicks took over and won, 93–86.

My bad-boy side came out in the postgame interviews. I said, "I think they're probably licking their chops on Fifth Avenue where the NBA offices are. I think they kind of like that it's a 2-2 series. I don't like 'orchestration.'. . . But they control who they send as referees. And if it goes seven, everybody will be really happy."

Riley loved it. I had just handed him the perfect opening. The next day he told reporters that I was insulting his team. "I was part of six championship teams and I've been to the finals 13 times. I know what championship demeanor is about. The fact that he's whining and whimpering about the officiating is an insult to how hard our guys are playing and how much our guys want to win. . . . That's what championship teams are about. They've got to take on all comers. They can't whine about it."

The New York press bought it wholesale. The next day the papers were filled with Phil the Whiner stories. Before then New York fans had treated me like one of the family, even though I now worked for the enemy. But after Riley's holier-than-thou speech, they started hurling catcalls at me in the street. It was strange, but I realized there was nothing I could say to undo what had been done. Winning was the best revenge.

It took us seven games. My Lakota friends told me that I should "count coup" on Riley before game 7, so I did. As I walked by the Knicks bench, I stopped and reached out my hand to Pat and said: "Let's give them a good show." He nodded, a little nonplussed that I was talking to him. As it turned out, the game was a good Michael Jordan show. Early on Xavier McDaniel was pushing around Scottie, who was recovering from his sprained ankle, so Michael stepped in and confronted the bigger, stronger power forward until he backed down. (I was so impressed by the way Michael defended his teammate, I later hung a picture of the stare-down over my office desk.) In the third quarter Jordan stymied McDaniel with one of the best turn-around plays I've ever seen. It started when Michael hit a jumper, then stole the Knicks' inbound pass and started driving to the basket for another quick 2 points. But Xavier knocked the ball out of his hands and charged downcourt for what looked like an easy layup. Except that Jordan was on his heels and knocked the ball away from behind just as McDaniel went up for the shot. That play destroyed the Knicks' spirit, and they never got close again. Afterward Riley graciously summarized what the Bulls had done. "They played like they are," he said.

Still, nothing came easy. After winning another hard-fought series against Cleveland, we faced the playoffs-hardened Portland Trail Blazers in the championship finals. They were a fast, dynamic team led by Clyde Drexler, whom some observers not based in Chicago considered on par with Jordan. Our plan was to play strong transition defense and force them to beat us with their outside shooting. M.J.'s plan was to show the world that Drexler was no Michael Jordan. Michael was so determined Drexler's teammate Danny Ainge later told author David Halberstam it was like watching "an assassin who comes to kill you and then cut your heart out."

We came out strong and won the opener in Chicago, then let the next game slip away in overtime. Rather than take a late-night flight to Portland, as the Blazers did, I decided to fly the team out the next day and give them time off rather than make them slog through practice. The next day we burst out and took back the series lead, 2–1. After splitting the next two games, we returned to Chicago with a chance to put the series away on our home court.

The Blazers were on a roll in game 6, running up a 17-point lead in the third quarter. Tex insisted that I take Jordan out because he had gone rogue and wasn't playing within the system. I usually pulled Michael out two minutes before the end of the third period, but this time I took him out early and left the reserves in longer because they'd gone on a 14–2 run, helped by M.J.'s backup, Bobby Hansen, who threw down a key three-pointer. Michael was not happy when I didn't put him back in at the start of the fourth quarter. But I liked the backup players' energy and enthusiasm, and the Blazers seemed baffled about how to defend them. By the time Michael and the other starters returned to the game, the lead had shrunk to 5 points and the

Blazers were reeling. Michael scored 12 of his 33 points and Scottie made some key shots to finish them off 97–93.

Bring on the champagne. This was the first time we'd won a championship at home, and the fans went wild. After the traditional craziness in the locker room, I led the players back to the floor to join in the celebration. Scottie, Horace, and Hansen jumped on the scorers' table and started to dance, and Michael followed, waving the championship trophy. It was a joyous celebration.

After a while I returned to my office to reflect on what had just transpired. Later, when I met with the players privately, I told them that winning back-to-back championships was the mark of a great team. But what pleased me even more was that we'd had to navigate so many unexpected twists and turns to get there. Paxson called the season "a long, strange trip," referring to the famous Grateful Dead song. He was right. Our first championship run had been a honeymoon. This was an odyssey.

9

BITTERSWEET VICTORY

*Human beings are not born once and for all on the day
their mothers give birth to them, but . . . life obliges
them over and over again to give birth to themselves.*

GABRIEL GARCÍA MÁRQUEZ

That summer Michael and Scottie headed to Barcelona to play for the Dream Team. Jerry Krause was not pleased. He argued that they should skip the Olympics and rest up for the coming season. But they ignored his request, and I'm glad they did. An important shift took place in Barcelona that would have an enormous impact on the future of the Bulls.

Michael returned from the games raving about Scottie's performance. Before the summer, Michael had regarded Pippen as the most talented member of his supporting cast. But after watching him outplay Magic Johnson, John Stockton, Clyde Drexler, and other future Hall of Famers in Barcelona, Michael realized that Scottie was the best all-around player on what many consider the best basketball team ever assembled. Scottie, Michael had to admit, had even outshone him in several of the games.

Scottie came back with renewed confidence and took on an even bigger role with the Bulls. NBA rules prevented us from adding a third cocaptain to the roster (in addition to Michael and Bill Cartwright), but we gave Scottie that role ex officio. We also made B.J. Armstrong a starter, since John Paxson was recovering from knee surgery and his playing time was limited.

In *The Tao of Leadership*, John Heider stresses the importance of interfering as little as possible. "Rules reduce freedom and responsibility," he writes. "Enforcement of rules is coercive and manipulative, which diminishes spontaneity and absorbs group energy. The more coercive you are, the more resistant the group will become."

Heider, whose book is based on Lao-tzu's *Tao Te Ching*, suggests that leaders practice becoming more open. "The wise leader is of service: receptive, yielding, following. The group member's vibration dominates and leads, while the leader follows. But soon it is the member's consciousness which is transformed, the member's vibration which is resolved."

This is what I was trying to do with the Bulls. My goal was to act as instinctively as possible to allow the players to lead the team from within. I wanted them to be able to flow with the action, the way a tree bends in the wind. That's why I put so much emphasis on having tightly structured practices. I would assert myself forcefully in practice to imbue the players with a strong vision of where we needed to go and what we had to do to get there. But once the game began, I would slip into the background and let the players orchestrate the attack. Occasionally I would step in to make defensive adjustments or shift players around if we needed a burst of energy. For the most part, though, I let the players take the lead.

To make this strategy work, I needed to develop a strong circle of team leaders who could transform that vision into reality. Structure is critical. On every successful team I've coached, most of the players had a clear idea of the role they were expected to play.

When the pecking order is clear, it reduces the players' anxiety and stress. But if it's unclear and the top players are constantly vying for position, the center will not hold, no matter how talented the roster.

With the Bulls, we didn't have to worry about who the top dog was, as long as Michael was around. Once I forged a strong bond with Michael, the rest fell into place. Michael related strongly to the "social bull's-eye" I described earlier because he envisioned the leadership structure as a series of concentric circles. "Phil was the centerpiece of the team, and I was an extension of that centerpiece," he says. "He relied on me to connect with all the different personalities on the team to make the team bond stronger. He and I had a great bond, so everything I did, Scottie did, and then it fell down the line. And that made the whole bond stronger so that nothing could break it. Nothing could get inside that circle."

Scottie was a different kind of leader. He was more easygoing than Michael. He'd listen patiently to his teammates vent, then try to do something about whatever was troubling them. "I think guys gravitated toward Scottie because he was more like us," says Steve Kerr. "Michael was such a dominant presence that, at times, he didn't appear human. Nothing could get to Michael. Scottie was more human, more vulnerable like us."

The 1992–93 season was a long winter of discontent. Cartwright and Paxson were recovering from off-season knee surgeries, and Scottie and Michael were bothered by overuse injuries. I'd promised the players the year before that if we won a second championship we wouldn't have grueling two-a-day practices during training camp. Instead we held one long practice each day, interrupted by breaks to watch game videos. But that schedule didn't work out very well because the players stiffened up during the breaks.

Some coaches like to run long practices, particularly after they've suffered a hard loss. My college coach, Bill Fitch, was a classic example. Once he got so exasperated with our lackadaisical performance at a game in Iowa, he made us practice when we got back to the UND campus, even though the plane didn't arrive until after 10:00 P.M. I don't believe in using practice to punish players. I like to make practices stimulating, fun, and, most of all, efficient. Coach Al McGuire once told me that his secret was not wasting anybody's time. "If you can't it get done in eight hours a day," he said, "it's not worth doing." That's been my philosophy ever since.

Much of my thinking on this subject was influenced by the work of Abraham Maslow, one of the founders of humanistic psychology who is best known for his theory of the *hierarchy of needs*. Maslow believed that the highest human need is to achieve "self-actualization," which he defined as "the full use and exploitation of one's talents, capacities and potentialities." The basic characteristics of self-actualizers, he discovered in his research, are spontaneity and naturalness, a greater acceptance of themselves and others, high levels of creativity, and a strong focus on problem solving rather than ego gratification.

To achieve self-actualization, he concluded, you first need to satisfy a series of more basic needs, each building upon the other to form what is commonly referred to as Maslow's pyramid. The bottom layer is made up of physiological urges (hunger, sleep, sex); followed by safety concerns (stability, order); love (belonging); self-esteem (self-respect, recognition); and finally self-actualization. Maslow concluded that most people fail to reach self-actualization because they get stuck somewhere lower on the pyramid.

In his book *The Farther Reaches of Human Nature*, Maslow describes the key steps to attaining self-actualization:

1. experiencing life "vividly, selflessly, with full concentration and total absorption";
2. making choices from moment to moment that foster growth rather than fear;
3. becoming more attuned to your inner nature and acting in concert with who you are;
4. being honest with yourself and taking responsibility for what you say and do instead of playing games or posing;
5. identifying your ego defenses and finding the courage to give them up;
6. developing the ability to determine your own destiny and daring to be different and non-conformist;
7. creating an ongoing process for reaching your potential and doing the work needed to realize your vision.
8. fostering the conditions for having peak experiences, or what Maslow calls "moments of ecstasy" in which we think, act, and feel more clearly and are more loving and accepting of others.

When I first encountered Maslow's ideas in grad school, I found them extremely liberating. As an athlete I was familiar with peak experiences, but I'd never fully understood the complex psychology behind them. Maslow's work opened a door for me to think more expansively about life. I was particularly drawn to his insights about how to get out of your own way and let your true nature express itself. Later when I became a coach, I found that Maslow's approach of balancing physical, psychological, and spiritual needs provided me with a foundation for developing a new way of motivating young men.

Our biggest enemy during the 1992–93 season was boredom. Life in the NBA can be a stultifying, mind-numbing experience, particularly when you're on a long road trip and every minute of every day is scheduled. My goal was to get the players to break free from their confining basketball cocoon and explore the deeper, more spiritual aspects of life. By "spiritual" I don't mean "religious." I mean the act of self-discovery that happens when you step beyond your routine way of seeing the world. As Maslow puts it, "The great lesson from the true mystics . . . [is] that the sacred is in the ordinary, that it is to be found in one's daily life, in one's neighbors, friends, and family, in one's backyard."

To make your work meaningful, you need to align it with your true nature. "Work is holy, sacred, and uplifting when it springs from who we are, when it bears a relationship to our unfolding journey," writes activist, teacher, and lay monk Wayne Teasdale in *A Monk in the World*. "For work to be sacred, it must be connected to our spiritual realization. Our work has to represent our passion, our desire to contribute to our culture, especially to the development of others. By passion I mean the talents we have to share with others, the talents that shape our destiny and allow us to be of real service to others in our community."

To tap into the sacred in work as well as in life, it's essential to create order out of chaos. Teasdale quotes Native American songwriter James Yellowbank, who says, "The task of life is to keep your world in order." And that takes discipline, a healthy balance between work and play, and nourishment of mind, body, and spirit within the context of community—values deeply rooted in my own being, as well as my objectives for the teams I've coached.

Getting the players to turn inward wasn't always easy. Not everyone on the Bulls was interested in "spiritual" realization. But I didn't hit them over the head with it. My approach was subtle. Every year the team went on a long West Coast road trip in November when the circus took over the stadium for a few weeks. Before the trip I would select a book for each of the players to read, based on what I knew about them. Here's a typical list: *Song of Solomon* (for Michael Jordan), *Things Fall Apart* (Bill Cartwright), *Zen and the Art of Motorcycle Maintenance* (John Paxson), *The Ways of White Folks* (Scottie Pippen), *Joshua: A Parable for Today* (Horace Grant), *Zen Mind, Beginner's Mind* (B.J. Armstrong), *Way of the Peaceful Warrior* (Craig Hodges), *On the Road* (Will Perdue), and *Beavis & Butt-Head: This Book Sucks* (Stacey King).

Some players read every book I gave them; others dumped them in the trash. But I never expected everyone's 100 percent engagement. The message I wanted to convey was that I cared enough about them as individuals to spend time searching for a book that might have special meaning for them. Or at least make them laugh.

Another way I pushed the envelope was to have experts come in and teach the players yoga, tai chi, and other mind-body techniques. I also invited guest speakers—including a nutritionist, an undercover detective, and a prison warden—to show them new ways of thinking about difficult problems. Sometimes when we were traveling short distances—between Houston and San Antonio, for instance—we'd load everybody onto a bus to give them a chance to see what the world looked like beyond airport waiting rooms. Once, after a hard loss in a playoff series with the Knicks, I surprised everyone by taking the team on a ferry ride to Staten Island, rather than making them go through another round of enervating interviews with the New York media. On another occasion I arranged to have the team visit my former teammate, Senator Bill Bradley, in his Washington, D.C., office, where he gave us a talk about basketball, politics, and race. He'd just delivered a resounding speech on the Senate floor (shortly after Rodney King had been beaten by L.A. police officers) in which he banged a pencil against the mic fifty-six times for the number of hits that King had taken. On one wall in Bradley's office hung a photo of the jump shot he missed in game 7 of the 1971 Eastern Conference finals that effectively ended the Knicks' hope of repeating as champions that year. Bill kept it there as a reminder of his own fallibility.

All these activities made us stronger not just as individuals but also as a team. "One of the best things about our practices," says Steve Kerr, who joined the Bulls in 1993, "was that they delivered us from the mundane. In the NBA if you have a coach that says the same thing every day and the practices are the same too, it gets old fast. But our communal gatherings were really important. Our team bonded in ways that the other teams I've played for never did."

For Paxson, our adventures outside of basketball routines were transcendent. "It felt as if we were part of something really important," he says. "We felt like the good guys because we were trying to play the game the right way. It was as if we were part of something bigger than the game. And it was reinforced after we started to win, because the fans would let you know how important it was to them. I still have people come up and talk to me about where they were when we won our first championship and why it was such a priceless moment for them. We were playing the game the right way, and that's what people long for."

"Transcendent" isn't exactly the word I would use to describe the Bulls as the playoffs began in late April. We had struggled all season,

limping along without Cartwright and other players who were nurs-
ing injuries. Although we ended up winning the division, we finished
with 57 wins, 10 fewer than the year before. What's more, we couldn't
count on home-court advantage throughout the playoffs, as we had
in the previous season.

As soon as the playoffs began, however, the players shifted to another level. At least, that's how it seemed as we swept both Atlanta
and Cleveland in the first rounds. But then we ran into the Knicks in
New York and lost two games straight. This time the aspiring king
slayer was John Starks, a quick, hard-driving guard with a deadly
three-point shot who was giving Jordan endless grief on defense. With
forty-seven seconds left in game 2, Starks went airborne over Michael
and Horace for an in-your-face dunk that put the Knicks up by five.
Pat Riley called Starks's move "the exclamation mark."

When we returned to Chicago, I showed the players a video of the
dunk and told Michael we needed to stop Starks from penetrating
our defense and cut off his post passes to Ewing. That got Michael's
attention.

But Michael's challenges weren't restricted to the basketball court.
That week *New York Times* columnist Dave Anderson revealed that
Michael had been spotted gambling in Atlantic City on the day of
game 2, and Anderson questioned whether his late-night field trip
had hampered his performance. All of a sudden an army of reporters
descended on our training facility, asking detailed questions about
Michael's gambling habits, which he found offensive. He stopped
talking to the media, and so did his teammates. I thought the story
was ludicrous. "We don't need a curfew," I told reporters. "These are
adults. You have to have other things in your life or the pressure becomes too great."

Unfortunately, the story wouldn't die. Soon afterward a book was
published by businessman Richard Esquinas claiming that Michael

owed him $1.25 million for gambling losses on golf. Michael denied that the losses were that big, and it was later reported that he'd agreed to pay Esquinas a $300,000 settlement. Other stories began to surface about Michael getting fleeced for large sums of money by shady golf hustlers. As the coverage escalated, Michael's father, James Jordan, came to his son's defense. "Michael doesn't have a gambling problem," he said. "He has a competitiveness problem."

Fortunately, none of these distractions affected the team's play. If anything, they helped to focus everyone's energy on the task at hand. Michael roared out in game 3, shutting down Starks and leading the Bulls to a decisive four-game sweep. "The big thing about this team is everyone in here has a burning desire to win," said Cartwright. "Everyone in here really hates to lose. That's the attitude we take onto the court. We just hate to lose, and when you have guys like that, they'll do anything to win."

The next series—the championship finals against Phoenix—was billed as a showdown between Michael and Charles Barkley, who had emerged as a superstar that year after winning the MVP award and piloting the Suns to a league-leading 62-20 record. I wasn't that concerned about Barkley because our players knew most of his moves from his days on the 76ers. A bigger threat, I thought, was point guard Kevin Johnson, who spearheaded their lightning-quick fast break, the key to their high-scoring offense. I was also concerned about guard-forward Dan Majerle and his maddening three-pointers.

Johnny Bach encouraged me to stay with our full-court defensive pressure to contain Johnson—using B.J., Pax, and Horace to trap him in the backcourt—and it helped us steal the first two games in Phoenix. But when we returned to Chicago, the Suns came back to life and won two of the next three games, including a triple-overtime marathon in game 3. But Michael was unflappable. As we boarded the plane for game 6, he showed up smoking a footlong cigar. "Hello, world champs," he said. "Let's go to Phoenix and kick some ass."

The game was an all-out battle. Afterward I thought the best slogan for this series would be "Three the Hard Way," because the Suns defense held us to only 12 points in the fourth quarter. But *our* defense was even more effective, restricting the Suns to a paltry 24 percent shooting average in the final period.

It all came down to a play that put a smile on Tex Winter's face. Jordan came into the game with eight minutes left and took over, scoring our first 9 points in the period, including a breakaway jam that put us within 2 points at the thirty-eight-second mark. At the break, I called the players together and said with a straight face, "Let's go away from M.J." Some of the players looked at me as if I were mad. Then they realized I wasn't serious and the tension broke.

As it turned out, it wouldn't be Michael who took the final shot. He dribbled up court and hit Pippen, who passed it back to M.J. But when the Suns' defense collapsed on him, he passed the ball back to Scottie, who started driving toward the basket. At the last moment Scottie dished off to Horace on the baseline. Then Horace, who saw Danny Ainge closing in to foul him, tossed the ball to Paxson, who was wide open at the top of the key. And John nailed the three-pointer.

Talk about a peak experience. Years later, in an interview with author Roland Lazenby, Paxson described what was going through his mind. "It was a dream come true," he said. "You're a kid out in your driveway shooting shots to win championships. When you get down to it, it's still just a shot in a basketball game. But I think it allowed a lot of people to relate to that experience, because there are a lot of kids and adults who lived out their own fantasies in their backyards. It made the third of the three championships special. It's a real nice way of defining a three-peat, by making a three-point shot."

It wasn't the shot that captivated me, however. It was the pass from Michael that led to the pass from Scottie that led to the pass from Horace that led to the shot. That sequence of passes would never have happened if we hadn't spent all those months and years not only mastering all of Tex's drills but also developing the kind of group intelligence needed for a team to perform as one. That night the triangle was a thing of beauty.

After the game, the sports pundits began comparing the Bulls with the giants of the past. With this victory, we became only the third team in history—along with the Minneapolis Lakers and the Boston Celtics—to win three NBA championships in a row. It was flattering to be included in the same sentence with those hallowed teams. But what they missed was the real story: the inner journey the players had gone through to transform the Bulls from a stage 3 ("I'm great, you're not") team into a stage 4 ("We're great, they're not") team.

I've always been against packing suitcases before a big game, just in case the basketball gods favor our opponent and we have to stay around to play another day. So after the win, we returned to our hotel, packed our luggage, and celebrated on the plane back to Chicago, where a huge, ecstatic crowd of fans was waiting to greet us.

This season had been a hard ride. The pressure kept building and building until it felt like it might never stop. But the players turned to one another for strength, and then ended it all with a moment of pure basketball poetry that made all the pain and ugliness melt away. That night I awoke suddenly after a few hours of sleep, overwhelmed by a feeling of deep satisfaction. Then I drifted back and was out for hours.

Soon the feelings of joy turned to sorrow. In August Michael Jordan's father was murdered on his way home from a funeral in Wilmington,

North Carolina. Michael was shattered. He was very close to his father, who had retired and spent a good deal of time in Chicago as Michael's chief supporter. The media hordes shadowed Michael everywhere after his dad's death, and it pained him that his fame made it difficult for his family to mourn in private. There was a time when all Michael had to deal with was a handful of sportswriters, many of whom he knew personally. Now he was being stalked by a large, faceless crowd of celebrity journalists who had no qualms about invading corners of his personal life that had once been off limits.

For a long time I suspected Michael might want to step away from the game—and all the pressures it entailed—and do something else with his life. He'd been dropping hints for months that he might be interested in switching to professional baseball, and he'd even gone as far as having his trainer, Tim Grover, design a baseball-oriented workout program. So it didn't surprise me when Michael met with Jerry Reinsdorf over the summer and told him he wanted to leave the Bulls to play for Jerry's other club: the White Sox. Jerry told Michael that before he could give him an answer, he needed to talk it over with me.

I wasn't interested in trying to talk Michael out of following his dream, but I wanted to make sure he'd examined the move from every possible angle. I talked to him more as his friend than as his coach, never raising my own personal interest in the matter. For starters, I appealed to his sense of a higher calling. I said that God had given him a remarkable talent that made millions of people happy, and I didn't think it was right for him to walk away. But he had an answer for that. "For some reason, God is telling me to move on, and I must move on," he said. "People have to learn that nothing lasts forever."

Then we tried to figure out a way that he could compete in the playoffs without playing the whole regular season. But he'd already considered everything I suggested and rejected the idea. Finally I realized he had made his mind up and was serious about leaving the game he had dominated for so long. It was very moving.

"We sat in that room getting all emotional and talking about the steps I needed to take," Michael recalls. "And I walked away with the understanding that Phil was a great friend. He made me think about a lot of different things, and didn't let me rush into the decision. But at the end of the day he totally understood that I needed a break. That I had gotten to a point when I was battling a lot of demons rather than focusing on basketball. And walking away was what I needed to do at that particular time."

But as Michael walked out the door, somehow I sensed that this wasn't going to be the end of the story.

10

WORLD IN FLUX

If you live in the river you should make
friends with the crocodile.

INDIAN PROVERB (PUNJABI)

t was supposed to be a night of celebration. Michael Jordan was there with his family for the 1993 ring ceremony and home opener at Chicago Stadium. This was his first public appearance since he'd announced his retirement on October 6, and the fans were eager to express their gratitude. "Deep down in my heart," Michael said to the crowd after receiving his third ring, "I will always be a Chicago Bulls fan and I'll support my teammates to the fullest."

What we needed that night, however, wasn't just another fan. I'm not sure if it was Michael's presence in the front row or the fact that we were playing the Miami Heat, an oft-beaten rival that was looking for vengeance, but we went on to play one of the worst games in franchise history. How bad was it? We set team records for fewest points scored in a period (6), in a half (25), and in our beloved stadium (71). It was so bad the Miami bench trash-talked us shamelessly all night without any consequences and the fans started streaming out midway through the third period.

After the 95–71 blowout, Miami's center, Rony Seikaly, said he was worried that Michael was going to "take his suit coat off and be

Superman against us again." Actually, I'm glad he didn't. What better way for the players to learn that they no longer could count on Michael to bail them out than to lose by such historic proportions with the man himself sitting in the front row?

The sports pundits thought we were on life support now that Michael had retired. If we were lucky, they said, we might win thirty games. And the odds in Vegas were twenty-five to one against our winning a fourth championship. But I was guardedly optimistic. The core of our championship team sans Michael was still intact, and I believed the team spirit we'd built over the years could carry us into the playoffs. I wrote down what I thought would be a reasonable goal for the season: forty-nine wins. But I didn't feel confident enough yet to share it with anyone.

My biggest concern was figuring out how to replace the 30-plus points Michael averaged every game. Because Jordan's retirement happened so late in the year, Jerry Krause didn't have many options left. So he signed Pete Myers, a reliable free-agent guard (and former Bull) who was a solid defender, an exceptional passer, and a quick study on the triangle offense. But in his seven years in the NBA he had averaged only about 3.8 points per game—not exactly Jordanesque numbers. A stronger possibility was Toni Kukoc, whom Jerry had finally persuaded to join the Bulls after a long courtship. Kukoc, a six-eleven forward billed as "the best player in the world outside of the NBA," was a gifted shooter who had averaged 19 points per game in the Italian pro league and had led Croatia's national team to a silver medal in the 1992 Olympics. But Toni had yet to be tested in the NBA, and I questioned whether he was tough enough to withstand the punishment. Two other additions were guard Steve Kerr and center Bill Wennington, both of whom showed promise but had yet to post big numbers. Clearly, it was going to take a village to fill the Jordan gap.

In the preseason I'd invited George Mumford, a sports psychologist and meditation teacher, to join us at training camp to give the players a mini workshop on coping with the stress of success. But a few days before George arrived, Michael announced his retirement, and the team was going through an identity crisis. So George talked about the two aspects of every crisis: danger and opportunity. If you have the right mind-set, he said, you can make the crisis work for you. You have the chance to create a new identity for the team that will be even stronger than before. Suddenly, the players perked up.

George had an interesting background. He'd played basketball at UMass and roomed with NBA great Julius Erving and Boston College coach Al Skinner. But he had a serious injury that forced him off the team. During recovery he grew interested in meditation, and he spent several years studying at the Cambridge Insight Meditation Center. He later started exploring new ways to integrate meditation, psychology, and organizational development. When I met him, he was working with Jon Kabat-Zinn, founder of the Stress Reduction Clinic at the University of Massachusetts Medical School and a pioneer in research on the effects of mindfulness on pain management and overall health.

George had a gift for demystifying meditation and was able to explain it in language that made sense to the players. He also had an intuitive feel for the issues they were grappling with because of his friendship with Dr. J and other elite athletes. I'd already introduced mindfulness meditation to most of the players, and they knew how much it could help them improve their ability to read what was happening on the floor and react more effectively. But George wanted to move them to the next level. He believed that mindfulness training would help them become both more focused as individuals and more selfless as a team.

The word "mindfulness" has become so diluted in recent years that it's lost much of its original meaning. It comes from the Sanskrit word *smriti*, which means "remember." "Mindfulness is remembering to come back to the present moment," writes Zen teacher Thich Nhat Hanh. This is an ongoing process that is not limited to the act of meditation itself. "Sitting and watching our breath is a wonderful practice, but it is not enough," he adds. "For transformation to take place, we have to practice mindfulness all day long, not just on our meditation cushion." Why is this important? Because most of us—basketball players included—spend so much time bouncing back and forth between thoughts of the past and the future that we lose touch with what's happening right here, right now. And that prevents us from appreciating the deep mystery of being alive. As Kabat-Zinn writes in *Wherever You Go, There You Are*, "The habit of ignoring our present moments in favor of others yet to come leads directly to a pervasive lack of awareness of the web of life in which we are embedded."

George taught mindfulness as a way of life, what he called "meditation off the cushion." That meant being fully present not just on the basketball floor but throughout the rest of the day as well. The key, he said, was not just to sit and calm your mind but to learn to read and react effectively in any situation based on what's happening at that very moment.

One of the first things he noticed about the players, particularly the younger ones, was that they were trapped in a restrictive mind-set that made it difficult for them to adapt to their new reality. "Many of these guys were the main dude on their college teams," he says. "But now they were in the NBA and there were a lot of players who were faster, quicker and stronger. So they had to figure out a new way to compete and be successful. The thing that got them here was not going to get them to the next level."

The example George gives is Jared Dudley, a forward for the Phoenix Suns whom he has worked with. At Boston College, Dudley was a high-scoring post-up player with an aggressive style that won him the nickname "Junkyard Dog." But when he got to the pros, he realized he had to take on a different role. Working with George, he discovered how to adapt to the situation and grow as a player. George remembers: "Jared looked around and said, okay, they need somebody to play defense—I'll do that. They need somebody to hit three's—I'll do that. He was always thinking: How do I want to play and how do I need to change?" The result: Jared flourished in his new role, and averaged 12-plus points per game in 2011–12.

Our goal was to help the players make a similar shift. They each needed to find a role for themselves that played to their strengths. At first George focused on getting them simply to pay attention and adjust their behavior to the team's goals. But after working with the players for a while, he realized that the first step was to help them understand that what they were learning to do on the court would also enhance their own individual growth. As George says, they needed to see how "in the process of becoming a *we*, they could also be their best *me*."

None of this was accomplished overnight. For most people, the process of waking up to the connectedness between oneself and others, as well as to the wisdom of the present moment, takes years. But the members of the 1993–94 team were especially receptive. They wanted to prove to the world that they could be more than Michael's supporting cast and win a championship on their own. They weren't as talented as some of the other teams I've coached, but they knew intuitively that their best hope was to bond together as seamlessly possible.

At first it looked as if the home opener might be prophetic. Several players were sidelined with injuries—including Scottie, John Paxson, Scott Williams, and Bill Cartwright—and by the end of November our record was 6-7. But I was beginning to see signs that the team was gelling—including last-minute wins against the Lakers and the Bucks. And when Scottie returned, the team erupted, winning thirteen of the next fourteen games. At the All-Star break, we were 34-13 and on track to win sixty games.

Scottie was the ideal leader for this team. At the start of the season he took over Michael's extralarge locker to make a statement, but to his credit he didn't try to turn himself into a clone of M.J. "Scottie hasn't tried to be something he's not," Paxson said at the time. "He hasn't tried to score 30 a game. He just plays the way Scottie Pippen plays, and that's to distribute the ball. It's the old standard: Great players make other players better. And Scottie has definitely done that." To wit: Horace and B.J. made the All-Star team for the first time. Toni blossomed into a strong clutch shooter. And Kerr and Wennington turned into reliable go-to scorers.

Coaching Toni was a challenge for me. He was used to playing a more freewheeling style of basketball in Europe and was frustrated by the constraints of the triangle offense. He couldn't understand why I gave Scottie so much freedom and slapped his wrist whenever he made the same move. I explained that Scottie might look like he's freelancing, but every move he made was geared toward making the system work more effectively. When Toni went rogue, there was no telling what was going to happen next.

Toni was especially unpredictable on defense, which drove Scottie and other players crazy. To increase his level of mindfulness, I developed a special form of sign language to help us communicate with each other during games. If he strayed from the system, I'd give him a look, and I expected him to give me a sign of acknowledgment. This is the essence of coaching: pointing out mistakes to players and having them signify to you that they know they've done something wrong. If they don't acknowledge the mistake, the game is lost.

The Bulls fell into a slump after the All-Star break, and we didn't push out of it until March. But we finished the season with a 17-5 run and a convincing 55-27 record. The surge continued through the first round of the playoffs with Cleveland, which we swept 3–0. Then we ran into a roadblock in New York, losing the first two games of the series.

Game 3 had the most bizarre finish of any game I've coached. But it also was a key turning point for the team.

Patrick Ewing drove across the lane and lofted a hook shot that tied the score, 102–102. I called a time-out and designed a play that had Scottie inbounding a pass to Kukoc for the final shot. Scottie wasn't happy with the play, and when the huddle broke up, he retreated to the far end of the bench, sulking.

"Are you in or out?" I asked him.

"I'm out," he replied.

I was surprised by his answer, but the clock was ticking, so I had Pete Myers toss in the pass to Kukoc, who put in a jumper for the win.

As I walked off court into the locker room, I was puzzled about what to do. This was unusual behavior for Scottie. He had never challenged one of my decisions before. In fact, I considered him the ultimate team player. I presumed that the pressure of not being able to put the game away on the previous possession had made him crack. If I came down too heavily on him at that moment, I feared, Scottie might sink into a funk that could last for days.

As I was taking out my contact lenses in the bathroom, I heard Bill Cartwright groaning in the shower, gasping for air. "Bill, are you okay?" I asked.

"I can't believe what Scottie did," he said.

A few minutes later I gathered the players in the dressing room and gave Bill the floor. "Look, Scottie, that was bullshit," he said, staring at his fellow cocaptain. "After all we've been through on this team. This is our chance to do it on our own, without Michael, and you blow it with your selfishness. I've never been so disappointed in my whole life."

He stood there with tears in his eyes and everyone sat in stunned silence.

After Bill finished talking, I led the team in the Lord's Prayer and left for the press conference. The players stayed behind and talked over the situation. Scottie apologized to them for letting the team down, saying he was frustrated by the way the game ended. Then others chimed in about how they felt. "I really think it cleansed us as a team," said Kerr later. "We got some things out of our system and realized what our goals are again. The crazy thing is, it helped us."

It's amusing to look back on how the media handled the story. They went into high moralizing mode, arguing that I should do everything short of incarcerating Scottie. Most coaches would probably have suspended him or worse, but I didn't think being punitive was the best way to handle the situation. The next day Scottie assured me that he had put the incident behind him, and that was that. And I could tell by the way he moved during practice that this wasn't going to be a big issue for him.

Some people applauded my clever management strategy. But I wasn't trying to be clever. In the heat of the game, I simply tried to stay in the moment and make decisions based on what was actually happening. Rather than asserting my ego and inflaming the situation fur-

ther, I did what needed to be done: find someone to throw in the ball
and go for the win. Afterward, rather than trying to fix things myself,
I let the players solve the problem. I acted intuitively, and it worked.

The team came alive in the next game, led by Scottie, who amassed
25 points, 8 rebounds, and 6 assists, en route to a 95–83 victory that
tied the series 2–2. "All of a sudden there was a lovefest going on,"
said Johnny Bach after the game. "It was in Chicago instead of
Woodstock."

I wish there were a fairy-tale ending to this story, but the plot took
another bizarre turn. We were leading by one point in the final seconds of game 5 when referee Hue Hollins decided to step through the
looking glass. Most refs try to avoid making calls that decide big
games as the clock is running down. But this was Madison Square
Garden, and the age-old rules of basketball didn't seem to apply.

With 7.6 seconds left, John Starks got trapped along the sideline
and tossed a desperation pass to Hubie Davis at the top of the key.
Scottie stormed out to cover Davis, and Hubie got off a rushed, off-
kilter jumper that didn't come close to the basket. Or at least that's
how it looked on the replay. But that's not what happened in Hollins's
parallel universe. He called a foul on Scottie, saying he had made
contact with Hubie and disrupted the shot. (Davis had kicked out
his legs and Scottie collided with them, a move the NBA has since
deemed an offensive foul.) Needless to say, Hubie hit the two free
throws, and the Knicks went ahead in the series, 3–2.

We beat the Knicks decisively in game 6, but the fairy tale ended
in game 7. After the 87–77 loss, I gathered the players together to pay
homage to our achievement. This was the first time in years that we'd
ended a season without being surrounded by TV cameras. We should
absorb this moment, I told the team, because losing is as much a part
of the game as winning—and I really meant it. "Today they beat us,"
I said. "We were not defeated."

It was a difficult summer. Suddenly, the team started to come apart. Paxson retired and became a radio announcer for the team. Cartwright announced his retirement but changed his mind after being offered a lucrative deal by the Seattle SuperSonics. Scott Williams grabbed a big contract with Philadelphia. And Horace Grant, who was eligible for free agency, initially accepted an offer from Jerry Reinsdorf to stay with the Bulls but shifted and went to Orlando instead.

I also had to let go of Johnny Bach. Tensions between Jerry Krause and Johnny had hit the boiling point and were making it difficult for us to work together as a group. Jerry, whose nickname in the media was "the Sleuth" because of his reputation for surreptitiousness, was already suspicious of Johnny because of his supposed leaks to Sam Smith for *The Jordan Rules*. Now Jerry was claiming that Johnny was responsible for leaking confidential information about our interest in seven-seven Romanian center Gheorghe Muresan. This was an outrageous accusation. Even though we'd been following Muresan closely in Europe and had even brought him in for a secret tryout, there were several other teams that had been scouting him, including Washington, which ended up drafting him.

Nevertheless, I thought it would be best for everyone concerned, including Johnny, to have him move on, and he landed a spot as an assistant coach for the Charlotte Hornets. Johnny's departure had a dispiriting effect on my staff and the players, and it created a crack in my relationship with Krause.

Another troubling development in the 1993–94 off-season was the conflict between Pippen and Krause over the possible trade of Scottie to the Seattle SuperSonics for forward Shawn Kemp and swingman Ricky Pierce. Scottie was stunned when he heard about the deal from reporters and didn't believe Krause when he told him that he was just listening to trade offers, as he would with any player. Seattle's owner eventually pulled the plug on the deal under pressure from the Sonics' fans. But the damage had been done. Scottie felt insulted by the way he'd been treated, and it tainted his perception of Jerry from that point on.

Team morale began to improve in late September when we signed free-agent shooting guard Ron Harper and formally announced that we didn't have any plans to trade Pippen. I warned Scottie against getting caught in a media war with Krause. "I know you've got this feud going on," I said, "but it's not helping you and it's not helping the team. Frankly, it's making you look bad. Things are going to work out for you, Scottie. You had an MVP-like season last year. Why don't you just let it go?"

"Yes, I know," he said, with a shrug. "It is what it is." Nevertheless, the flare-ups between Pippen and Krause continued for some time, and as late as January 1995 Scottie was asking to be traded.

Still, the acquisition of Harper was promising. He was six feet six, with a strong drive and a nice shooting touch and had averaged close to 20 points a game during his nine years with the Cavaliers and the Clippers. Ron had had a devastating ACL injury in 1990 and had recovered, but he wasn't the same threat we'd faced in the '89 play-offs against Cleveland. Yet we were optimistic that he could fill at least part of the Jordan scoring gap. As for the rest of the lineup, I was less certain. Our biggest weakness was our two untested newcomers at power forward—Corie Blount and Dickey Simpkins.

As the season got under way, I was troubled by the team's lack of competitive spirit. This was a new problem for us. Michael had such an overpowering drive to win that it rubbed off on everybody else. But now that all the players on the core championship teams had left, except for Scottie, B.J. Armstrong, and Will Perdue, that drive was

only a faint memory. Typically, we'd build up leads in the first half
then succumb to pressure in the fourth quarter when the games
got more physical. By the All-Star break we were struggling to stay
above .500 and losing games on the road that in years past would
have been victories for us.

Then one morning in early March, Michael Jordan showed up at
my office in the Berto Center. He'd just left spring training and returned home, after refusing the White Sox's offer to be a replacement
player during Major League Baseball's upcoming lockout season. Michael said he was considering a return to basketball and wondered if
he could come to practice the next day and work out with the team.
"Well, I think we've got a uniform here that might fit you," I replied.

What followed was the weirdest media circus I've ever witnessed. I
did everything I could to protect Michael's privacy, but word soon
got out that Superman was in the house. Within days an army of reporters were gathered outside our training facility, waiting to hear
when Michael was going to suit up again. After more than a year
of being fixated on the O.J. Simpson murder case, America was
yearning for good news about a sports superhero. And the mystery
surrounding Michael's comeback gave the story an additional allure.
When Michael finally decided to return, his agent sent out what may
be the pithiest press release in history. All it said was, "I'm back."

Michael's first game—on March 19, against the Pacers in
Indianapolis—was a worldwide media event that attracted the largest
television audience ever for a regular-season game. "The Beatles and
Elvis are back," quipped Indiana's coach, Larry Brown, as a phalanx
of TV cameras crowded into the locker rooms before the game. And
during warm-ups, Corie Blount saw a TV crew taking a shot of Michael's Nikes and said, "Now they're interviewing his shoes."

Michael's arrival had an enormous impact on the team. Most of the new players were in awe of his basketball skills and competed intensely during practice to show him what they could do. Still, there was a vast gulf between Michael and his teammates that was difficult for him to bridge. To build the deep level of trust that a championship team requires usually takes years of hard work. But this team didn't have that luxury. Michael didn't know many of the players very well, and there wasn't enough time left in the season to change that.

At first it didn't seem to matter. Though Michael had trouble finding his shooting rhythm in that first game in Indiana, he erupted in the next game against Boston and the team began a 13-3 run. If anyone had doubts about Michael's ability the second time around, he erased them six days later when he scored 55 points against the Knicks in Madison Square Garden—the highest total for any player that year.

After the game, however, Michael came to my office and voiced some reservations. "You've got to tell the players they can't expect me to do what I did in New York every night," he said. "In our next game, I want them to get up and get going—to play as a team."

This was a new Michael. In the past he would have reveled in his triumph over the Knicks—and most likely attempted a repeat performance the following day. But he'd returned from his baseball sabbatical with a different perspective on the game. He wasn't interested in going solo anymore; he longed for the team harmony that had made the Bulls champions.

He would have to wait. After we pushed past the Charlotte Hornets, 3–1, in the first round of the playoffs, we faced Orlando, a young, talented team designed to exploit our weaknesses. The Magic had Shaquille O'Neal, one of the most dominant centers in the league, and Horace Grant, who matched up well against us at power forward. It also featured a deadly trio of three-point shooters—Anfernee Hardaway, Nick Anderson, and Dennis Scott. Our strategy was to double-team Shaq and force him to beat us at the foul line. We also decided to put Michael on Hardaway and have the defenders covering Horace slide off him, when necessary, to collapse on Shaq or chase down three-point shooters. This approach might have worked if our offense had been more in sync throughout the series.

One of the most startling moments came in game 1 when Michael, who was having an off night, got stripped by Anderson with ten seconds left and the Bulls up by one. Then after the Magic went ahead, he threw the ball away, ending our chance of winning. After the game I put my arm around Michael and tried to console him. I told him we'd turn the experience around and use it in a positive way to help guide us going forward. "You're our guy, and don't ever forget that," I said.

Michael bounced back in game 2, leading us to victory with a 38-point surge. We split the next two games in Chicago, but Horace made us pay for leaving him open too often in game 5. He hit 10 of 13 from the field on the way to 24 points, to pilot the Magic to a 103–95 win.

Horace's performance was a minor blip, though, compared to our embarrassing collapse at the end of game 6. It looked like we were in pretty good shape when B.J. put us ahead 102–94 with 3:24 left. Then the whole team imploded and we went scoreless from that point on. We missed 6 shots in a row and turned the ball over twice, while the Magic went on a maddening 14–0 romp, including a breakaway dunk by Shaq to end the game. The season was over.

Michael was remarkably calm afterward. He spent half an hour talking to reporters about how challenging it was for him to gel with his new teammates. "I came back with the dream of winning," he said. "I thought it was realistic. Now looking back, maybe it wasn't, because we lost."

This was the kind of game that can haunt you for years, if you let it. "Just swallow this loss and digest it," I advised the players. "Then get on with your lives." Still, I knew it wasn't going to be easy to let this one go.

A few days later, however, while I was still struggling to get a handle on what had gone wrong, I suddenly came up with a vision of how to turn the Chicago Bulls into a champion team again.

I couldn't wait to get started.

11

BASKETBALL POETRY

It's more fun to be a pirate than to join the Navy.

STEVE JOBS

'm often asked to reveal the secret of the 1995–96 Bulls, which some consider the greatest basketball team ever assembled. How could a team that was going nowhere in May transform a few months later into a team that couldn't be beaten?

The simple answer would be that it was all about the superstars: Michael Jordan, Scottie Pippen, and Dennis Rodman. But talent can only get you so far in this game. Other teams have been far more loaded than the Bulls but couldn't achieve anything close to this team's success. Another explanation might be the magic of the triangle offense. But even Tex Winter would admit that the triangle was only part of the answer.

In truth, it was a confluence of forces that came together in the fall of 1995 to transform the Bulls into a new breed of championship team. From a tribal-leadership perspective, the Bulls were moving from being a stage 4 team to a stage 5. The first series of championships transformed the Bulls from an "I'm great, you're not" team to a "We're great, they're not" team. But for the second series, the team adopted a broader "Life is great" point of view. By midseason it became clear to me that it wasn't competition per se that was driving the team; it was simply the joy of the game itself. This dance was ours, and the only team that could compete against us was ourselves.

The first breakthrough was a shift in vision. Right after our loss to Orlando in the '95 playoffs, it struck me that we needed to reimagine the way we used our backcourt. In the midnineties most teams had small guards. It was dogma in the NBA that unless you could find another Magic Johnson, the smart strategy was to go small in the backcourt to keep pace with the quick, undersized point guards who dominated the league at the time. But I'd learned from watching Scottie Pippen play point guard that having a six-seven player with an extralong wingspan in that position created all kinds of fascinating possibilities.

What would happen, I wondered, if we had three tall, long-armed guards on the court at the same time? Not only would it create confusing mismatches for other teams, but it would also improve defense immeasurably because big guards could switch off and defend post players without resorting to double-teaming. It would also allow us to move away from using full-court pressure all the time, which was taking its toll on some of our older players. With big guards, we could apply pressure more effectively inside the three-point line.

In the off-season we had to figure out which players we were going to leave unprotected for the expansion draft. It came down to a decision between B.J. Armstrong, our current point guard, and Ron Harper, our former starting shooting guard who had been displaced when Michael returned to the lineup. I hated to give up B.J. He was a solid point guard with a good three-point shot, and he played dependable defense. But at six feet two, 175 pounds, he wasn't big enough to switch and defend larger players or trap big centers like Shaquille O'Neal. Although Ron had not lived up to expectations as a scorer, he was adapting well to the triangle and was a great team defender. Ron was also big for a guard—six feet six, 185 pounds, with the strength and athleticism to play almost any position. So Jerry Krause and I decided to stick with Ron instead of B.J. During our end-of-the-year meeting I told Ron that I had big plans for him in 1995–96, but he needed to get in better condition and reinvent himself as more of a defensive player than a scoring threat. Moving to a big-guard strategy represented a significant philosophical shift for the team. But if it worked, it would make us more flexible, more explosive, and impossible to contain.

The second breakthrough was acquiring Dennis Rodman as our new power forward. During the off-season we drew up a list of possible candidates for the job, and Rodman's name was at the bottom. We'd discussed Dennis before, but Krause was always cool to the idea, saying Rodman wasn't "our kind of person." After being traded by Detroit to San Antonio in 1993, Dennis had had a difficult time adjusting to the Spurs culture, even though he excelled as the league's leading rebounder. He flouted the rules, showing up late for practices, acting out on court, and wearing gaudy clothing and jewelry. In fact, San Antonio's management got so fed up with his rebellious antics, it fined him thousands of dollars multiple times and benched him during the crucial game 5 of the 1995 Western Conference finals, which the Spurs ended up losing to the Houston Rockets.

Although I shared some of Jerry's concerns, I was less troubled by Dennis's eccentricities than I was by his selfish style of play. I'd heard from coaches who'd worked with him that he was so fixated on rebounding that he was reluctant to help teammates on defense. I also questioned whether he could work with Michael and Scottie, who resented him for the brutal way he had manhandled the Bulls when he was with the Pistons. But scout Jim Stack thought we might lose Rodman if we didn't act quickly, so Jerry decided to give him a serious look.

Two weeks later Jerry invited me to his house to meet Rodman and his agent, Dwight Manley. When I arrived, Dennis was lounging on the couch in sunglasses and a "poor boy" hat. He remained mute during the whole conversation, so I asked to speak to him privately on the patio. But all he wanted to talk about was how much he was going to get paid. I told him that the Bulls paid for production, not promise, and if he played up to his potential we would take care of him.

The next day I met with Dennis again, in the tribal room at the Berto Center. This time Dennis was more open. I asked him what had gone wrong in San Antonio. He said it had started when he invited Madonna, whom he was dating at the time, to visit the locker room after a game. The media feeding frenzy that ensued had ticked off the guys in the front office.

I expressed my concern over his reputation for selfishness. He said that his real problem in San Antonio was that he was sick of helping out center David Robinson, who, he said, was intimidated by Houston's Hakeem Olajuwon. "Half the Spurs players had their balls locked up in the freezer every time they left the house," he added sarcastically.

I laughed. "So do you think you can master the triangle?" I asked.

"Oh yeah, that's no problem for me," he said. "The triangle's about finding Michael Jordan and getting him the ball."

"That's a good start," I replied. Then we got serious. "If you think you're up for this job," I said, "I'm going to sign off on this deal. But we can't screw it up. We're in position to win a championship, and we really want to get back there."

"Okay."

After that, Dennis took a look at the Native American artifacts in the room and showed me the necklace he'd been given by a Ponca from Oklahoma. Then we sat silently together for quite a while. Dennis was a man of few words, but sitting with him, I felt reassured that he would come through for us. We connected on a nonverbal level that afternoon. A bond of the heart.

The next day Jerry and I had a follow-up meeting with Dennis to go over the team's rules about attendance, punctuality, and other issues. It was a short list. After I finished reading it, Dennis said, "You won't have any problem with me, and you'll be getting an NBA championship."

I checked with Michael and Scottie later that day to see if they had any reservations about playing with Rodman, and they said no. So Jerry went ahead and sealed the deal, trading Will Perdue to the Spurs for Rodman. And I braced myself for the ride of my life.

Before Dennis arrived at training camp, I had a long discussion with the players. I warned them that he was probably going to ignore some of the rules because it was hard for him to abide by certain guidelines. I would probably have to make some exceptions for him at times, I said. "You're going to have to be grown up about this," I added. And they were.

Most of the players developed a fondness for Dennis right away. They soon realized that all his wild offstage theatrics—the nose rings, the tattoos, the late-night parties in gay bars—were all part of an act he'd created, with the help of Madonna, to get attention. Underneath, he was just a quiet boy from Dallas with a generous heart who worked hard, played hard, and would do anything to win.

Somewhere in the middle of training camp, I realized that Dennis was going to bring a new dimension to our team that I hadn't anticipated. Not only was he a magician on the boards, but he was also a smart, mesmerizing defender who could guard anyone, even Shaq, who had six inches and close to a hundred pounds on him. With Dennis in the lineup, we could run fast breaks and also settle back and play a tough half-court game. Most of all, I just liked watching him play. He was so uninhibited and joyful when he stepped on the floor, like a boy discovering how to fly. On some level, I told the other coaches, he reminded me of me.

The shadow side of Dennis was more of a challenge. Sometimes he was like a pressure cooker about to explode. He went through periods of high anxiety that lasted forty-eight hours or more, and the pressure would build inside of him until he had to release it. During those times, his agent would often ask me to give Dennis the weekend off, if we didn't have any games, and they would go to Vegas and party for a couple days. Dennis would be a wreck by the end of it, but then he'd come back and work out until he got his life back together.

That year I stopped pacing along the sidelines during games because I noticed that whenever I got agitated, Dennis would become hyperactive. And if I argued with a ref, it would only give him license to do the same. So I decided to become as quiet and restrained as possible. I didn't want to set Dennis off, because once he got agitated, there was no telling what he might do.

The third breakthrough was Michael's new approach to leadership. During the first run of championships, Michael had led primarily by example, but after the loss to Orlando he realized he needed to do something dramatically different to motivate this team. Simply glaring at his teammates and expecting them to be just like him wasn't going to cut it anymore.

Michael was at a tipping point. He had been stung by press commentary during the Orlando series contending that he had lost his edge and wasn't the same Michael Jordan anymore. So he returned to the gym that summer determined to get his body back in basketball shape. He even had a basketball court set up in the studio in L.A. where he was filming *Space Jam* so he could practice between takes and work on a new fadeaway jumper that would eventually become his trademark shot. By the time he arrived at training camp in October, he had the hard look of vengeance in his eyes.

A week into camp I was scheduled to do a phone conference with the media at a time that conflicted with our morning practice. When my assistant came down to the court to tell me it was time to get on the phone, I instructed the other coaches to postpone the scrimmage and give the players some shooting drills until I returned. The call was only fifteen minutes long, but before I was off the phone our equipment manager, Johnny Ligmanowski, was at my door saying, "You'd better come. M.J. just punched Steve and he's in the locker room getting ready to leave practice." Apparently, Kerr and Jordan had gotten into a bit of a scuffle that escalated back and forth until Michael popped Steve in the face and gave him a black eye.

When I got to the locker room, M.J. was about to step into the shower. He said, "I've got to go." And I told him, "You'd better call Steve and get it straight before tomorrow."

This was a major wake-up call for Michael. He had just gotten into a fight with the smallest guy on the team over nothing. What was going on? "It made me look at myself, and say, 'you know what? You're really being an idiot about this whole process,'" Jordan recalls. "I knew I had to be more respectful of my teammates. And I had to be more respectful of what was happening to me in terms of trying to get back into the game. I had to get more internal."

I encouraged Michael to start working more closely with George Mumford. George understood what Michael was going through because he had seen his friend Julius Erving experience similar pressures after he turned into a superstar. It was difficult for Michael to develop close relationships with his teammates because, as George puts it, he was "a prisoner in his own room." He couldn't go out with them in public and just hang out, as Scottie often did. Many of the new players were still in awe of him, and that too created a distance that was hard to bridge.

Michael was impressed with the mindfulness training George had been doing with the team because it helped bring the players closer to his level of mental awareness. In George's view, Michael needed to shift his perspective on leadership. "It's all about being present and taking responsibility for how you relate to yourself and others," says George. "And that means being willing to adjust so that you can meet people where they are. Instead of expecting them to be somewhere else and getting angry and trying to will them to that place, you try to meet them where they are and lead them where you want them to go."

While Michael had been away playing baseball, George and I had made changes in the team's learning environment to enhance the players' ability to grow mentally, emotionally, and spiritually. If Michael was going to gel with this team and be its floor leader, he would have to get to know his teammates more intimately and relate to them more compassionately. He would need to understand that each player was different and had something important to offer the team. It was his job, as leader, to figure out how to get the best out of each one of them. As George puts it, Michael had to "take his ability to see things on the basketball court and use that to improve the way he related to others."

Michael was open to the challenge, because he too had changed during his time away. He was still a fierce competitor, but he had also mellowed in certain ways. He was less judgmental of others and more conscious of his own limitations. Playing minor-league baseball, where he spent long hours passing the time with his teammates, Michael had rediscovered the joy of bonding with other men, and more than anything he wanted to have that experience again with the Bulls.

Working with Mumford, Michael adopted a new way of leading based on what worked best with each player. With some players, he decided, he would get *physical*, either by demonstrating what needed to be done with his body or, in Scottie's case, simply by being present. "Scottie was one of those guys for whom I had to be there every single day," says Michael. "If I took a day off, he would take a day off. But if I was there every single day, he would follow." With other players—Dennis in particular—Michael would go *emotional*. "You couldn't yell at Dennis," he says. "You had to find a way to get into his world for a few quick seconds so that he could understand what you were saying." With still others Michael would communicate primarily on a *verbal* level. Example: Scott Burrell, a forward on the 1997–98 Bulls. "I could yell at him and he would get it," says Michael, "but it didn't hurt his confidence at all."

One person he didn't have to worry about was Kerr. The fight had forged a strong bond between the two players. "From that day forward Michael looked at me differently," Steve says. "He never picked on me again. He didn't trash talk with me anymore. And he started trusting me on the court too." Adds Michael, "I have the most respect for Steve because, one, he was thrown into a situation where he really had no chance of winning. And, two, he stood up. When I started fouling him, he came back at me. Which got me angry. But that's where the mutual respect comes from."

From Michael's perspective, the second run of championships was harder than the first because of the personalities involved. Most of the players on the first championship teams had been together for several years and, together, had fought many battles. As M.J. says, "We'd go up the hill and get knocked down, knocked down, and knocked down, until we climbed over it as a group." But during the second run, most of the players didn't know one another very well, yet everybody expected the team to win right out of the gate. "I think we needed Phil more for the second run than the first," says Michael now. "In the first run, the egos hadn't set in yet. But in the second run, we had a lot of different personalities to mesh together and the egos were really strong. And Phil had to bring us together as a brotherhood."

All the pieces fell together beautifully. We didn't have a dominant big man like the sixties Celtics and other great teams from the past, but these Bulls had a remarkable sense of unity, on both offense and defense, and a powerful collective spirit.

Everything we did was designed to reinforce that unity. I had always insisted on structured practices with a clear agenda that the players would receive ahead of time. But we also started organizing other aspects of the team process to create a sense of order. In general, I used discipline not as a weapon but as a way to instill harmony into the players' lives. This was something I'd learned from years of mindfulness practice.

That season we asked the players to arrive at the training facility at ten every morning to do forty-five minutes of strength training and warm-ups. Michael preferred to work out earlier at home with his private trainer, Tim Grover, and that year he invited Scottie and Harper to take part in the program, which they dubbed "the Breakfast Club." By ten they, too, would show up to warm up for practice, which started at eleven. We'd focus on refining our triangle skills, as well as our defensive goals for the upcoming game or week. Then we'd move into an offensive segment, including a full-court scrimmage. I'd often put Pip or M.J. with the second unit and see what influence their presence would bring to the practice. Afterward, the guys would hang around and work on their shots, and our trainer, Chip Schaefer, would get them recharged with fresh blended fruit drinks. If we were headed for a road trip, we might go upstairs to our team room and have a short video session.

At first Dennis tried to skirt the rules, as if he were playing a game. One rule was that players had to show up for practice on time with their shoelaces tied and all their jewelry put away. Dennis would often appear with one shoe untied or a piece of jewelry hidden somewhere. Sometimes I'd give him a silly fine or make a joke about his appearance, and other times we'd just ignore him. I told him that it wasn't me he had to worry about if he came late to practice; it was his teammates. Once he realized that none of us were really interested in his little rebellions, the problem went away.

One thing I loved about this team was that everyone had a clear idea about their roles and performed them well. Nobody groused about not getting enough playing time or enough shots or enough notoriety.

Jordan focused on being consistent and stepping up, when needed, to deliver a decisive blow. In early December, after scoring 37 points against the Clippers, he announced to reporters that he felt "pretty much all the way back now as a player." He joked about being compared to his former self all the time. "According to some people," he said, "I'm even failing to live up to Michael Jordan. But I have the best chance of being him because I am him."

Scottie felt liberated not having to live up to the Jordan legacy anymore and gave an MVP-level performance in his new role as chief orchestrator of the action, which felt much more natural to him. Harper also adapted extremely well to his job as multipurpose guard and defensive bulldog. Meanwhile, Dennis exceeded all expectations. Not only did he master the system in a short period of time, but he also blended perfectly with Michael, Scottie, and Harper on defense. "We basically had four attack dogs in the starting lineup," says Kerr, "and they could all guard four or five positions on the floor. It was incredible."

Dennis played the game with such wild enthusiasm that he soon became a fan favorite. People loved to watch him hustle for loose balls and pull down rebounds to ignite fast breaks. Early in the season Dennis started dyeing his hair different colors and tearing off his jersey after games and tossing it to the crowd. The fans loved it. "All of a sudden," he said, "I'm like the biggest thing since Michael Jordan."

The fifth starter was Luc Longley, a seven-two, 265-pound center from Australia who wasn't as mobile and explosive as Shaq but was big enough to plug up the middle and force other centers off their games. His backup was Bill Wennington, who had a good short-range jumper that he often used to lure his man away from the basket. Later in the season, we also added two other big men to the lineup, James Edwards and John Salley, both of whom, like Dennis, were former Detroit Bad Boys.

At first Toni Kukoc balked when I made him the team's sixth man, but I persuaded him that it was the most effective role for him. As a starter he often had trouble playing forty minutes without getting worn down. But as sixth man he could come in and give the team a scoring boost, which he did in several key games. He could also use his exceptional passing skills to reenergize the team when Scottie wasn't on the floor. Meanwhile Steve Kerr played a key role as a long-range scoring threat; guard Randy Brown was a high-energy defensive specialist; and Jud Buechler was a talented swingman. In addition, we had two backup power forwards, Dickey Simpkins and rookie Jason Caffey.

We had absolutely everything in place that we needed to fulfill our destiny—talent, leadership, attitude, and unity of purpose.

When I look back on the 1995–96 season, I'm reminded of another parable that John Paxson discovered about the emperor Liu Bang, the first leader to consolidate China into a unified empire. In W. Chan Kim and Renée A. Mauborgne's version of the story, Liu Bang held a lavish banquet to celebrate his great victory and invited master Chen Cen, who had advised him during the campaign. Chen Cen brought as guests three of his disciples, who were perplexed by an enigma at the heart of the celebration.

When the master asked them to elaborate, they said that the emperor was sitting at the central table with his three heads of staff: Xiao He, who masterfully administered logistics; Han Xin, who led a brilliant military operation, winning every battle he fought; and Chang Yang, who was so gifted at diplomacy that he could get heads of state to surrender before the fighting began. What the disciples had a hard time understanding was the man at the head of the table, the emperor himself. "Liu Bang cannot claim noble birth," they said, "and his knowledge of logistics, fighting, and diplomacy does not equal that of his heads of staff. How is it then that he is emperor?"

The master smiled and asked them "What determines the strength of a chariot's wheel?"

"Is it not the sturdiness of the spokes?" they replied.

"Then why is it that two wheels made of identical spokes differ in strength?" asked the master. "See beyond what is seen. Never forget that a wheel is made not only of spokes, but also of the space between the spokes. Sturdy spokes poorly placed make a weak wheel. Whether their full potential is realized depends on the harmony between them. The essence of wheel-making lies in the craftman's ability to conceive and create the space that holds and balances the spokes within the wheel. Think now, who is the craftsman here?"

After a long silence, one of the disciples asked, "But master, how does a craftsman secure the harmony among the spokes?"

"Think of sunlight," replied the master. "The sun nurtures and vitalizes the trees and flowers. It does so by giving away its light. But in the end, in which direction do they grow? So it is with a master craftsman like Liu Bang. After placing individuals in positions that fully realize their potential, he secures harmony among them by giving them all credit for their distinctive achievements. And in the end, as the trees and flowers grow toward the sun, individuals grow toward Liu Bang with devotion."

Liu Bang would have made a good basketball coach. The way he organized his campaign was not unlike the way we brought the Bulls into harmony for the next three seasons.

The start of the 1995–96 season reminded me of Joshua fighting the battle of Jericho. The walls just kept tumbling down. Every time we moved to a new city, it seemed, something would go wrong with the other team. A star player would be injured or a key defender would foul out at just the right moment or the ball would bounce in the right way at just the right time. But it wasn't all luck. Many of our opponents didn't know how to deal with our three big guards, and our defense was remarkably skilled at breaking down offenses in the second and third periods. By the end of January, we were 39-3, and the players started to talk about breaking the record of sixty-nine wins held by the 1971–72 Lakers.

I was worried that they might get drunk on winning and run out of steam before we reached the playoffs. I considered slowing down the pace, but nothing seemed to stop this juggernaut. Not even injuries. Rodman injured his calf early in the season and was out for twelve games. During that time we were 10-2. Then in March Scottie missed five games with an injury, while Dennis reverted to his old ways and got suspended for six games for head-butting a ref and defaming the commissioner and head of officials. Still, we lost only one game during that period.

As we approached the seventy-game mark, the media hype was out of control. ABC News reporter Chris Wallace dubbed the team "the Beatles of basketball" and designated Michael, Scottie, Dennis, and me as the new Fab Four. The day of the big game—against the Bucks—TV helicopters shadowed our team bus all the way to Milwaukee, with crowds massed at the overpasses on the interstate holding up signs of support. When we arrived at the Bucks' stadium, a crush of fans was gathered outside hoping to get a peek at Rodman's hair.

Naturally, we had to make the game dramatic. We were so wound up by the time the game started that we fell apart in the second quarter, hitting only 5 of 21 from the field for 12 points. But then we slowly clawed our way back in the second half and won in the final seconds, 86–80.

The main emotion we felt was relief. "It was a very ugly game, but sometimes ugly is beautiful," said Michael. But his mind was already on the future. "We didn't start out the season to win 70 games,'" he added. "We started out the season to win the championship and that's still our motivation."

We finished the season with two more wins, and Harper came up with a new Gershwinesque team slogan, "72 and 10 don't mean a thing without the ring." To inspire the players, I adapted a quote from Walt Whitman and taped it on their lockers before the first game of the playoffs, against the Miami Heat. "Henceforth we seek not good fortune, we are ourselves good fortune." Everyone expected us to dance our way to the championship, and those are always the hardest kinds of games to win. I wanted the players to know that despite our remarkable season, the rest of the way wasn't going to be easy. They would have to make their own luck.

And they did. We swept Miami and rolled over New York in five games. Next up was Orlando. To prep the players for the series, I spliced a few clips from *Pulp Fiction* into the game tapes. The players' favorite scene showed a seasoned criminal, played by Harvey Keitel, instructing two hit men (Samuel L. Jackson and John Travolta) on how to clean up a particularly gruesome murder scene. Midway through the proceedings he quips, "Let's not start sucking each other's dicks quite yet."

Ever since we were humiliated by the Magic in the 1995 playoffs, we had set our sights on a rematch. In fact, we had rebuilt the team primarily with Orlando in mind. But the first game was anticlimactic. Our defense was just too overpowering. Dennis held Horace Grant to no points and 1 rebound in the first part of the game. Then Horace hyperextended his elbow in a collision with Shaq and was out for the rest of the series. We also shut down two other players who had hurt us badly the year before: Dennis Scott (0 points) and Nick Anderson (2). We ended up winning 121–83.

The Magic rebounded in game 2, but we broke their spirit when we erased an 18-point deficit in the third period and went on to win. They were also crippled by injuries to Anderson (wrist), Brian Shaw (neck), and Jon Koncak (knee). The only Magic players who posed any kind of scoring threat were Shaquille O'Neal and Penny Hardaway, but that wasn't enough. The series ended, appropriately, with a 45-point scoring blitz by Michael in game 4 on the way to four-game sweep.

The odds against our next rival, the Seattle SuperSonics, winning the championship finals were nine to one. But they were a young, talented team that had won sixty-four games that season and could give us trouble with their out-of-the-box pressure defense. The key was to stop their stars, point guard Gary Payton and power forward Shawn Kemp, from building up momentum and outrunning us. I decided to put Longley on Kemp to capitalize on Luc's size and strength, and I gave Harper the assignment of covering Payton.

At first it looked as if the series might be over early. We won the first two games in Chicago, buoyed by our defense and Rodman's 20 rebounds in game 2, during which he also tied an NBA finals record with 11 offensive boards. But Harper reinjured his knee that night and had to sit out most of the next three games. Luckily, the Sonics made a tactical error after game 2, flying back to Seattle Friday night after the game rather than waiting, as we did, until Saturday morning to take a more leisurely flight. The Sonics still looked bleary-eyed on Sunday afternoon, and we were able to put them away 108–86.

At that point the debate over whether the Bulls were the greatest team ever became pretty intense. I ignored most of the chatter, but I was pleased when former Portland Trail Blazers coach Jack Ramsay said the Bulls had the kind of defense that "defies a period of time." In my view, the team the Bulls most closely resembled was the 1972–73 New York Knicks. Like the Bulls, that Knicks team was made up largely of newcomers. The players were very professional and liked playing together, but they didn't spend a lot of time together off the court. I told the Bulls early in the year that as long as they kept their professional lives together, it didn't matter to me what they did with the rest of their time. These players weren't that close, but they weren't that distant either. Most important, they had a deep respect for one another.

Unfortunately the basketball gods weren't cooperating. With Harper injured, it was harder for us to contain the Sonics' attack, and we lost the next two games. Still leading the series, 3–2, we returned to Chicago determined to close out the finals in game 6. The game was scheduled for Father's Day, which was an emotional time for Michael, and his offensive game suffered as a result. But our defense was insurmountable. Harper returned for the game and closed down Payton, and Michael did a brilliant job of holding Hersey Hawkins to a mere 4 points. The player who stole the game, however, was Dennis, with 19 rebounds and a lot of key put-backs on missed shots. At one point late in the fourth quarter, Dennis fed Michael for a backdoor cut that put the Bulls up 64–47 with 6:40 left. After the shot, Michael observed Dennis skipping downcourt, and they both erupted with laughter.

When the buzzer sounded, Michael gave Scottie and me a quick hug, darted to center court to grab the ball, then retreated to the locker room to get away from the TV cameras. When I got there, he was curled up on the floor hugging the ball to his chest, tears streaming down his face.

Michael dedicated the game to his father. "This is probably the hardest time for me to play the game of basketball," he said. "I had a lot of things on my heart, on my mind. . . . And maybe my heart wasn't geared to where it was. But I think deep down inside, it was geared to what was most important to me, which was my family and my father not being here to see this. I'm just happy that the team kind of pulled me through it because it was a tough time for me."

That was a poignant moment. But when I look back on that season, it's not the finale that stands out in my mind. It's a game we lost to the Nuggets in February that ended our eighteen-game winning streak. They call that kind of game a "bookie's dream" because we had flown to Denver from L.A. the day before and hadn't had time to adjust to the altitude change.

The Nuggets were a sub-.500 team, but they shot 68 percent in the first quarter and built up a surprising 31-point lead. Many teams would have rolled over at that point, but we refused to surrender. We did everything: We went big, we went small, we moved the ball, we shot threes, we sped up the tempo, we slowed it down, and midway through the fourth quarter we went ahead on a pirouetting break-away dunk by Scottie Pippen. Michael led the comeback, scoring 22 points in the third quarter, but this wasn't a one-man show. It was an inspiring act of perseverance by everyone on the team. And even though we lost in the closing seconds, 105–99, the players walked away feeling they had learned something important about themselves. They learned that, no matter how dire the situation, they would find the courage somehow to battle to the very end.

That night the Bulls found their heart.

12

AS THE WORM TURNS

To dare is to lose one's footing momentarily.
Not to dare is to lose oneself.

SØREN KIERKEGAARD

Zen teacher Lewis Richmond tells the story of hearing Shunryu Suzuki sum up Buddhism in two words. Suzuki had just finished giving a talk to a group of Zen students when someone in the audience said, "You've been talking about Buddhism for nearly an hour, and I haven't been able to understand a thing you said. Could you say one thing about Buddhism I can understand?"

After the laughter died down, Suzuki replied calmly, "Everything changes."

Those words, Suzuki said, contain the basic truth of existence: Everything is always in flux. Until you accept this, you won't be able to find true equanimity. But to do that means accepting life as it is, not just what you consider the "good parts." "That things change is the reason why you suffer in this world and become discouraged," Suzuki-roshi writes in *Not Always So: Practicing the True Spirit of Zen.* "[But] when you change your understanding and your way of living, then you can completely enjoy your new life in each moment. The evanescence of things is the reason you enjoy your life."

Nowhere is this truer than in the game of basketball. Part of me longed for the great ride we had in 1995–96 never to end, but even before the next season started, I could sense change in the air. Little did I know that the next two seasons would provide me with some tough lessons on dealing with impermanence.

The summer of '96 was a period of great upheaval in the NBA— the sports equivalent of musical chairs. Close to two hundred players switched teams as a result of a free-agency boom that year. Fortunately, Jerry Reinsdorf opted to keep the Bulls roster virtually intact so that we could make another run for a championship. The only players we lost were center James Edwards, who was replaced by Robert Parish, and journeyman Jack Haley, a friend of Rodman's from the Spurs whose primary job was being Dennis's minder.

The price tag for keeping the team together wasn't cheap: The Bulls payroll that year was $58 million plus, the highest ever in the NBA. The biggest line item, of course, was Michael Jordan's salary of $30 million. In 1988 Michael had signed an eight-year, $25 million deal with the Bulls that seemed like a big paycheck at the time but had long since been surpassed by several lower-level stars. Jordan's agent had proposed a two-year, $50 million deal to Reinsdorf, but Jerry opted for a one-year deal instead and soon regretted it. The next year he would have to up Jordan's salary to $33 million. Reinsdorf also worked out one-year deals with me and Dennis Rodman.

One of the biggest changes I noticed was a shift in Dennis's level of interest in the game. During his first year with us he was driven to prove—to himself and others—that he could still play great basketball without losing control of his emotions. But now he seemed bored with the game and drawn to other amusements. In my amateur opinion, Dennis was suffering from attention-deficit/hyperactivity disorder, or ADHD, a condition that limited his ability to concentrate and caused him to get frustrated and act out in unpredictable ways. That's why he was so enchanted with Las Vegas, haven of endless distractions.

Now that Dennis had become a national star, the media world was offering him all sorts of opportunities that threatened to divert his attention away from the game even further. In addition to endorsement deals and club appearances, he was costarring in the movie *Double Team* with Jean-Claude Van Damme and hosting a reality show on MTV called *The Rodman World Tour*. The event that garnered the most publicity, though, was the book tour for his best seller *Bad as I Wanna Be*, for which he appeared in a wedding dress and announced that he was marrying himself.

Another change that would eventually have a significant impact was the advancing age of our lineup. Rodman was thirty-five; Michael would be turning thirty-four in February 1997; and Scottie and Harper were in their early thirties. In general, the team was in excellent condition and played much younger than its years, but injuries were beginning to slow us down. Both Luc and Harp were recovering from off-season surgeries. And Scottie, who had played for Dream Team III in Atlanta during the 1996 summer off-season, was suffering from a sore ankle. I couldn't think of any top guards who'd done well in the NBA after age thirty-four. When would time run out for Michael Jordan?

Still, I was grateful that we hadn't been decimated by free agency like so many other teams. We could build on what we'd already achieved and deepen our relationships with one another. I told the team that this might be our last run together, so we should make it something special. Michael had a similar point of view. When reporters asked him what he thought the impact of all the one-year contracts might be, he sounded like a Zen monk: "I think what we're showing is that we're going to play for the moment. . . . We're going to come out here and play each and every game like it's our last."

It certainly looked that way in the opening weeks. We had our best start ever: 12-0, including a 32-point blowout against the Miami Heat. But Dennis seemed detached, even bored in some of the games. And soon he started acting out, challenging refs and making inflammatory remarks about them to the media. In December we suspended him for two days for his offensive comments about NBA commissioner David Stern and other league officials. Dennis's erratic behavior and his disappointing performance were especially troubling because we were already missing center Luc Longley, who had injured his shoulder while bodysurfing in California. We'd arrived in L.A. on a Saturday for a Sunday-night special at the Forum. Sunday afternoon I got a call from Luc: "Coach, I screwed up. A rogue wave caught me while bodysurfing and I separated my left shoulder. Sorry, mate." I gave him a pass and told him to get the medical attention he needed. We'd cover for him while he mended.

Things went from troublesome to worse. During a game in Minneapolis in January, Dennis was struggling for a rebound with the Timberwolves' Kevin Garnett when he collided with a courtside photographer and ended up kicking him in the groin. The NBA suspended him for eleven games, which cost him more than $1 million in lost income and fines. By the time he returned, Michael and Scottie had lost patience with him. "All I know is that Dennis doesn't give a damn about most things," said Scottie. "I'm not sure he's capable of learning any lessons from his suspensions. I don't expect him ever to change because if he did, he wouldn't be the Worm, the personality he has invented for himself."

The Bulls went 9-2 with Rodman out, and the players were adjusting to the idea of going for the championship without him. "We can be better with Dennis, we know that," Michael said. "But we can survive without Dennis, we know that, too. Our will to win is just as great without Dennis." When asked what advice he'd give Rodman on his return, Michael said, "I'd tell him to wear pants all the time."

Most of the players liked Dennis because he was our court jester. In Native American culture he would be known as a *heyoka*, which means "backward-walking man." *Heyokas*—also called tricksters—not only walked backward but also rode backward, wore women's clothes, and made people laugh. Dennis had a way of making everybody lighten up when things were tense. How could you get down on yourself when there's this crazy guy on the team who had dyed his hair with a big yellow happy face?

But Dennis also had a dark side. Once when he didn't show up for practice, I went to his house to see how he was doing. When I arrived, he was splayed out on his bed—nothing but a mattress on the floor—in a daze, watching videos. He'd gone on a bender the night before and was almost incoherent. I decided I needed to stay in much closer touch with him than I'd done in the past, especially since we'd let go of Jack Haley, who used to keep tabs on him between games. I suggested to Dennis that he start working with the team's psychologist, and he agreed to give it a try. But he refused to go to the man's office, so they held their first session in a shopping mall.

Other coaches had treated Dennis as if he were a child and tried to force him to submit to their will with rigid discipline. But that tactic had failed miserably. My approach was to relate to him as an adult and hold him accountable for his actions the same way I did everyone else on the team. He seemed to appreciate this. Once he told reporters that what he liked about me was that I treated him "like a man."

Shortly after Dennis returned from his third suspension of the season, Steve Kerr and Jud Buechler came to me and asked if the players could welcome Dennis back into the group with a special trip. Their idea was to borrow a bus the day after our game in Philadelphia on March 12 and return for a light practice the next day before our game that night with the New Jersey Nets. I agreed because I thought it would help weave Rodman back into the team faster—not to mention the fact that the Nets had the worst record in the league.

So the next day Dennis and his band of happy warriors set off in a bus they'd rented, which was plastered with promo photos for Howard Stern's movie *Private Parts*. The next morning I was eating breakfast with the coaching staff at the Four Seasons in Philly when the bus rolled up right in front of us and unloaded the players who were laughing, messing around, generally having a good time. I was thinking, *This is going to be the worst practice we've ever had*. I was right. The players were so out of it they could barely stand up, so I called off practice after forty minutes and told them to rest up for the game, which we lost, 99–98. But in the end it was worth it. Making Dennis feel as if he were part of the team again was more important than another *W* in the record books.

After Dennis and Luc returned to the lineup, the Bulls roared back. Scottie was in his prime, orchestrating the action so well that Michael later dubbed him "my MVP." Michael was more relaxed and settling into a less energy-draining style of play, with more medium-range jumpers and less one-on-one aerial theatrics. But most of all the players had the look of champions. No matter what calamities befell them, they felt confident that they would find a way to deal with them together. There's a Zen saying I often cite that goes, "Before enlightenment, chop wood, carry water. After enlightenment, chop wood, carry water." The point: Stay focused on the task at hand rather than dwelling on the past or worrying about the future. This team was getting very good at doing that.

Unfortunately, the Rodman reprieve didn't last long. In late March he sprained his left knee and was sidelined until the end of the regular season. The team was headed for a big road trip to the East Coast at the time, and I was worried that if Dennis was left to do rehab on his own in Chicago, he might backslide again. So we devised a plan for him to stay at his agent's house in Southern California and finish rehab there.

It seemed like a reasonable idea. We assigned Wally Blase, a young assistant trainer, to escort Dennis to his agent's house in Orange County and make sure he did his exercises every day. Before they took off, I called them both into my office and instructed them to go directly to California without any side trips. Then I gave Wally an eagle feather to seal the deal and told Dennis jokingly, "Take care of Wally and make sure he wears a condom."

"All right, bro," Dennis replied.

This was pre-9/11, and our security team figured out a way to get Dennis and Wally on the plane without going through the gate. So Wally's first inkling that this was not going to be a routine trip came when they were buckling up and the pilot announced that they would be landing in Dallas–Fort Worth in two hours and twenty minutes. *Dallas–Fort Worth! Yikes!* thought Wally. They hadn't even left Chicago and they'd already broken the first rule. Wally asked Dennis what was going on. "Don't worry about it, bro," he said. "I talked to my agent. We need to visit my mom in Dallas and take a look at the house I just bought her."

Rodman's plan sounded plausible. But when they arrived at the baggage terminal, two white stretch limos filled with scantily clad women were there to greet them. After visiting Mom, they cruised the Dallas clubs all night with the ladies, then returned to their hotel suite. Wally fell asleep on the couch.

The next morning Dennis woke Wally up at eight thirty. "Get up, bro," he said. "You can sleep when you're dead." They went to the gym, where Dennis worked out like crazy. Over breakfast Wally asked him when their flight left for California. "Not today, bro," Dennis replied. "Ever been to a NASCAR race?" It was the grand opening of the Texas Motor Speedway that day, and a top model Dennis had the hots for was going to be there. So they rented a helicopter and flew to the speedway to avoid traffic. When they landed, Dennis said, "Let's go meet the king, Richard Petty," and dragged Wally off to the VIP suite in the infield.

By the third day Wally was losing it. He told Dennis that he was going to lose his job if they didn't get to California soon. But Dennis wasn't ready to leave Dallas. "C'mon, bro," he said. "Yesterday was a bush-league race. Today's the real race." So they headed to the speedway again. Exasperated, Wally called his boss, head trainer Chip Schaefer, and reported that they were still in Dallas. "Don't worry about it," said Chip. "At least he hasn't gotten into any trouble."

The next day they finally made it to Southern California, and Wally thought things might slow down. But as soon as they landed, Dennis wanted to take a look at his new Lamborghini. While they were at the garage, Dennis handed Wally the keys to his other car, a yellow Porsche. "Have you ever driven a Porsche?" he asked. Wally shook his head. "Don't worry about it," Dennis said, and the two of them took off through the streets of Orange County as if they were competing in the Daytona 500.

It was one excellent adventure after another. One day they went to *The Tonight Show* and had their picture taken with Rodney Danger-field and the band No Doubt. Another day they met with movie producer Jerry Bruckheimer to discuss a possible role for Dennis in *Armageddon*. Another day they went to an Anaheim Ducks game and had their pictures taken with some of Wally's hockey idols. "It was like the movies *Get Him to the Greek* and *Almost Famous* all rolled into one," says Wally.

By the end of it, Wally and Dennis were so tight we often took Wally on road trips to be Dennis's buddy. The next year, during a break in the championship finals in Utah, Dennis said he was tired of boring Salt Lake City and rented a jet for them to go to Vegas. What Dennis didn't tell him was that he'd planned this jaunt as a birthday party for Wally and had invited a bunch of his friends, including actress Carmen Electra, singer-songwriter Eddie Vedder, and hockey legend Chris Chelios. "It was the night of my life," says Wally.

Wally, who's now head athletic trainer for the Atlanta Hawks, understood Dennis immediately. Yes, he's messed up and insecure, Wally says, but he's also "one of the nicest human beings you will ever meet." Dennis's greatest achievement, in Wally's view, was his ability to create the "perfect scenario for a professional athlete." "He's the only pro athlete that people *expected* to go out and party with strippers," he says. "Joe Namath did it and was chastised in New York, and Michael Jordan got caught gambling on a golf course, and everybody was hell-bent for leather. But with Dennis, moral ineptitude was part of his deal, and he created this persona that made people say, 'Oh yeah, that's perfectly normal.' It's genius when you think about it."

That may be true, but I think the secret of Dennis's appeal was the playful way he bucked the system. This made him an inspirational model for people, young and old, who felt themselves to be on the outskirts of society. I got many letters from special-education teachers who told me that their students who had ADHD loved Dennis because he was successful in life despite his debilitating condition. To them, he was a true champion.

What a strange year! Even though we were missing several of our stars for part of the season, we managed to finish with a 69-13 record, tying the 1971–72 Lakers for the second-best record ever for an NBA team. But Dennis and Toni were still recovering from injuries, and the team lacked the cohesiveness we'd enjoyed earlier in the year. One positive addition: In the final weeks of the season, we picked up six-eleven forward/center Brian Williams, aka Bison Dele, to give us more muscle inside. Williams played a key role backing up Luc and Dennis throughout the playoffs.

The first two rounds were uneventful. We swept Washington 3–0, and pushed past Atlanta in five games after losing home-court advantage in game 2, the first time any team had beaten us at home during the playoffs in two years.

The next round—the Eastern Conference finals against the Miami Heat—turned out to be a clash of two radically different basketball cultures. The team had been taken over by Pat Riley during the 1995–96 season and, with Alonzo Mourning at center and Tim Hardaway at point guard, had the makings of a classic Riley team. Much has been made of my rivalry with Pat over the years, particularly in the New York tabloids. But the main difference between us is philosophical, not personal. Riley has had a great deal of success with his bruising, old-school approach to the game. Like Riley's Knicks, the Heat were physical, aggressive, and primed to foul you on every play as long as they could get away with it. Our approach, on the other hand, was freer and more open. We played intense defense but specialized in stealing the ball, cutting off passing lanes, and pressuring ball handlers into making mistakes.

At first it looked like it was going to be a walkover. We breezed past Miami in the first game, 84–77, led by Jordan, who had a spectacular 37-point, 9-rebound performance. A key factor in the game was the defensive shift we made at halftime, putting Harper on Hardaway and Michael on three-point specialist Voshon Lenard. Next we wrestled our way to a 75–68 victory in game 2, the lowest-scoring playoff game in NBA history. In game 3 we devised a way to counter Miami's strong-arm defense by spreading out the triangle offense, making it difficult for the Heat to clog up the lane. And we danced to a 98–74 win.

During an off day, Michael decided to play forty-six holes of golf, and he had one of his worst starts ever in game 4, hitting only 2 of 21 shots from the field, as Miami glided to a 21-point lead. Michael nearly put us over the top in the fourth quarter, though, scoring 20 of our 23 points, but we ran out of time and lost, 87–80.

The most important moment came late in the third quarter when Mourning slammed Scottie and gave him a knot on his forehead as big as a golf ball. Michael was enraged and declared that game 5 was going to be a personal grudge match for him. "When my teammate got a knot on his head," he said, "I got a knot on my head."

Michael started making Miami pay right away in game 5, scoring 15 points in the first quarter. But the rest of the team had to step up when Scottie sprained his foot in the first quarter after another collision with Mourning and was out for the duration. Toni, who had struggled early in the series, replaced Scottie and hit 6 points in the first quarter to widen the Bulls' lead. I was particularly pleased by the reserves, who outscored Miami's bench, 33–12, led by Brian Williams, who put down 10 points, and Jud Buechler, who made some key stops on defense. The final score: Bulls 100, Heat 87.

Riley was humbled by the loss. "Dynasties get better as they get older," he said, adding that he thought the Bulls were "the greatest team in the history of the game since the Celtics, when they won 11 in 13 years." This was the fourth time one of his teams had been knocked out of the playoffs by the Jordan-led Bulls. "We all have the misfortune of being born at the same time as Michael Jordan," he added.

The Utah Jazz weren't convinced. This was the team's first trip to the championship finals, but the Jazz had some potent weapons: power forward Karl Malone, who had beaten out Jordan for the MVP award that year, and point guard John Stockton, one of the craftiest ball handlers in the game. The Jazz also had a wily outside shooter, Jeff Hornacek, who'd averaged 14.5 points per game that year. Our biggest concern was the Stockton and Malone trademark screen-roll, which had often bedeviled our team in the past. But I also wanted to contain Malone's inside game. Karl's nickname was "the Mailman" because he supposedly always delivered. He was big, aggressive, and difficult to manage under the boards, even for Rodman. So I put Luc Longley on him early in the series, hoping that he could slow him down with his size.

In game 1, however, it wasn't Malone's drive that decided the game but his restless mind. With the score tied 82–82 and 9.2 seconds to go, Malone was fouled as he battled for a loose ball under the basket. As he went to the line, Scottie whispered in his ear, "The Mailman doesn't deliver on Sundays." Karl missed the first shot. Clearly rattled, Karl bounced his second attempt off the rim into Jordan's hands. I expected the Jazz to double-team Michael on the last play, but instead they let forward Byron Russell go one on one against him, not a good idea. Jordan faked out Russell and put in a jumper to win the game, 84–82.

We breezed past the Jazz in game 2, but Utah exploded when it returned home for game 3, led by Malone's 37-point, 10-rebound performance. His secret? He revealed that he took the scenic route to the stadium through the mountains on his Harley. The next game, I gave Rodman his first chance during the series to shut down the Malone machine. In true form, Dennis poked fun at Malone before the game, saying he was planning "to go rent a bike and ride in the hills and try to find God or somebody." But it didn't do much good. Malone scored 23 points, pulled down 10 rebounds, and made two key free throws with eighteen seconds to go. At which point Pippen said, "I guess the Mailman does deliver on Sundays here." Later we learned that our equipment manager had mistakenly served our players Gaterlode, a high-carbohydrate drink, instead of Gatorade throughout the game, which explained why the team was so sluggish in the closing minutes. Each of the players, it was estimated, had ingested the equivalent of about twenty baked potatoes.

The next game involved one of the most inspiring acts of perseverance that I've ever witnessed. The morning of game 5, with the series tied 2–2, Michael woke up with what appeared to be a stomach virus but later turned out to be food poisoning. It was so debilitating that he skipped the shootaround that morning and spent most of the day in bed. We had seen Michael play through all kinds of ailments before, but this was the most disturbing. "I've played many seasons with Michael, and I've never seen him as sick," said Scottie. "It was to the point where I didn't think he was going to be able to put his uniform on."

Michael was severely dehydrated and he looked as if he might pass out at any moment, but he persisted, scoring 38 points on 13-for-27 shooting, including the game-winning three-pointer with twenty-five seconds left. This was a remarkable feat, but what most people don't understand about this game was that it couldn't have happened without a remarkable team effort. Scottie masterfully orchestrated the coverage to make sure Michael didn't have to worry about defense and could focus whatever energy he could muster on creating shots. But Scottie didn't even mention that after the game. "The effort that he came out and gave us was just incredible," he said of Michael's performance. "The leadership. He just kept everybody patient and made big shot after big shot. . . . He's the MVP in my eyes."

The next game, back in Chicago, was another struggle. We fell back early and were behind most of the game, but the team refused to quit. Scottie and Michael both had exceptional games, but this time it was the reserves that made some of the most inspiring plays: Jud Buechler nailing a critical three-pointer at the close of the third period. Toni making a dazzling spinning layup on Hornacek while hobbling around on a sore foot. Brian Williams standing up to Malone and pushing him off his spots. The most beautiful moment, however, was the shot Steve Kerr, who had been struggling all series, took to end the game.

The Jazz were leading by 9 points early in the fourth period, but with eleven seconds left, the scored was tied, 86–86, and the ball was in Michael's hands. The Jazz were determined not to make the same mistake they had in game 1. So as Michael dribbled up the left side against Byron Russell, Stockton moved over to double-team him, leaving Kerr open at the top of the key. At first Michael tried to split the defenders, but as soon as he went into the air, he realized it wasn't going to work. "It was unbelievable how he kept hanging in the air," Hornacek said later. "Stockton and Byron Russell were on him and I was on Kukoc, and Kukoc cut to the basket, so I had to go with him. I couldn't give him a layup. And Michael looked at Toni forever, Michael just hanging there, and then somehow he switched and threw it out to Steve."

Kerr squared up just beyond the free-throw line and shot a picture-perfect jumper to break the tie, and Kukoc made a final dunk to win the game—and the championship.

This had been a grueling journey filled with injuries, suspensions, and other challenges. But the exquisite harmony—and resilience—of the team during the closing minutes made it all worthwhile. Afterward, Michael, who scored 39 points and was named the finals MVP, said he wanted to split it with Scottie. "I'll take the trophy," he said, "but I'm going to give Scottie the car. He deserves it as much as I did."

Michael used the postgame press conference to put pressure on Jerry Reinsdorf, who had been noncommittal with the media, to bring everybody back for another run next season. My one-year contract was expiring, and several teams had already expressed interest. In addition, Scottie was heading into the final year of his contract, and there were rumors that he might be traded. To up the ante, Michael, whose contract was also running out, said he wouldn't return if Pippen and I weren't on board.

Three days later tens of thousands of fans crowded into Grant Park to celebrate our victory. The highlight was Kerr's tongue-in-cheek account of how his famous shot "actually" happened.

"When we called time-out with twenty-five seconds to go," he recalled, "we went into the huddle and Phil said, 'Michael, I want you to take the last shot,' and Michael said, 'You know, Phil, I don't feel comfortable in these situations. So maybe we ought to go in another direction.' Then Scottie said, 'You know, Phil, Michael said in his commercial that he's been asked to do this twenty-six times and he's failed. So why don't we go to Steve.'

"So I thought to myself, 'I guess I've got to bail Michael out again. I've been carrying him all year, so what's one more time?' Anyway, the shot went in, and that's my story and I'm sticking to it."

Michael and Scottie were falling over laughing, and the crowd loved it. But as I looked around the audience, I noticed there was one person sitting right behind Kerr who didn't even crack a smile. That person was Jerry Krause.

13

THE LAST DANCE

When patterns are broken, new worlds emerge.

TULI KUPFERBERG

When I was with the Knicks, Dave DeBusschere taught me an important lesson. In 1971–72 the Knicks brought in Jerry Lucas to back up Willis Reed, who had been struggling with injuries. Jerry was a versatile six-eight forward/center, a great rebounder, and an adept passer with a nice outside shot. Dave didn't have a high opinion of Jerry before he arrived. He thought he was an oddball egoist who seemed more concerned about bolstering his scoring and rebounding averages during games than about winning. But when Lucas joined the Knicks, Dave figured out a way to work with him. When I asked him how he could switch so quickly, he replied, "I'm not going to let my personal feelings get in the way of us reaching our team goal."

For the last two years of my tenure with the Bulls, that's how I felt about Jerry Krause. Though Jerry and I had our differences, I respected his basketball intelligence and enjoyed working with him on building the Bulls' championship teams. But our relationship had been slowly going south since our disagreement over Johnny Bach three years earlier. Moreover, the negotiations with him over my contract had deteriorated into a cool standoff during the 1996–97 season. As with most relationships, both of us contributed to the collapse. I was driven by the need to protect the team's privacy and autonomy at all costs, while Jerry was desperately trying to regain control of the organization. This kind of conflict is not unusual in the sports world, but unfortunately for us, our differences were being played out on a large public stage.

Looking back, I think my struggle with Jerry taught me things about myself that I couldn't have learned any other way. The Dalai Lama calls it "the enemy's gift." From a Buddhist perspective, battling with enemies can help you develop greater compassion for and tolerance of others. "In order to practice sincerely and to develop patience," he says, "you need someone who willfully hurts you. Thus, these people give us real opportunities to practice these things. They are testing our inner strength in a way that even our guru cannot."

I wouldn't exactly call Jerry my "enemy." But our conflict certainly tested my inner strength. Though Jerry and I agreed on most basketball-related issues, we had opposing views on how to manage people. I tried to be as open and transparent as possible; Jerry tended to be closed and secretive. To a certain degree, he was a victim of the system; it's hard to make good deals in the NBA without being cautious about sharing information. But Jerry wasn't a very skilled communicator, so when he talked to the players, he often came off as inauthentic or, worse, duplicitous. I felt compassion for Jerry because I knew at heart he wasn't the coldhearted Machiavellian the media portrayed him to be. He just wanted to show the world that he could build a championship team without relying on Michael Jordan, and he was eager to make that happen.

During the middle of the 1996–97 season, Bulls owner Jerry

Reinsdorf proposed that Krause and my agent, Todd Musburger, work out the basic terms of a new contract for me. We asked for an increase that would make my salary comparable to what other top coaches, such as Pat Riley and Chuck Daly, were making at the time. But despite my record, Krause had a hard time seeing me at that level, and the negotiations fell apart. To his credit, Jerry Reinsdorf realized that it wasn't fair for me to have to go through the playoffs—the time when most coaching positions are filled—not knowing whether I'd have a job the following season. So he agreed to let other organizations contact me, and soon I had interest from several other teams, including Orlando.

But I wasn't ready to give up on the Bulls. Shortly after the playoffs, Reinsdorf flew to Montana, and we worked out a one-year deal that worked for both of us. He wanted to bring everyone back to try to win one more ring. Later that summer he also hammered out one-year deals with Jordan (for $33 million) and Rodman ($4.5 million, plus incentives for up to $10 million), pushing the players' payroll (minus Scottie) up to $59 million for the 1997–98 season. Now the only question mark that remained was Pippen.

Scottie wasn't having a good summer. He had injured his foot during the playoffs and required surgery, which would put him out of action for two to three months. He was also in the final year of his seven-year contract and was getting increasingly resentful of the low salary he was being paid relative to other players in the league. In 1991 Scottie had signed a five-year extension to his contract for $18 million, which had seemed like a good deal at the time. However, since then wages had skyrocketed in the NBA; and now there were more than a hundred players making more than Scottie, including five members of his own team. So even though many considered him to be the best player in the NBA not named Jordan, he would have to wait another year, until his contract ran out, to cash in on his performance. In the meantime, there was still an outside chance that he might be traded.

To make matters worse, Krause had threatened to take legal action against Scottie if he played in his annual summer charity game and risked further damage to his foot. This infuriated Scottie, who said he felt that Krause was treating him as if he were his personal property. Krause asked me to intervene with Scottie, but I was reluctant to aggravate the situation. So Scottie went ahead with the charity game and, to get back at Krause, postponed surgery until the start of training camp.

I wasn't happy with this turn of events. Nor was Michael. We had both stood up for Scottie over the summer, but by delaying surgery he was putting the whole season in jeopardy. Scottie did so much to help the team gel, it was hard to imagine getting very far without him for as much as half of the regular season while he was recovering.

During our annual media day before the start of the season, Krause decided to talk to reporters and made the faux pas of his life. I presumed the reason Jerry came to the sessions was to clarify for reporters that my leave-taking was a mutual decision between him and me. In the process, however, he said that "players and coaches don't win championships; organizations do." The next day he tried to correct the mistake, saying that what he'd meant to say was that "players and coaches *alone* don't win championships," but the damage had already been done. Michael in particular was outraged by Jerry's dismissive remark and turned it into a rallying cry for the team throughout the season.

Later that day Krause asked me to come to his office and told me, "I don't care if you win eighty-two games. This is your last year." There it was. When Reinsdorf had visited me in Montana, we had talked about this being my last season, but it wasn't until Krause said those words that I really believed it. It was disturbing at first, but after I'd given it some thought, it felt incredibly liberating. At least now I had some clarity.

I dubbed the season "the Last Dance" because that's what it felt like. No matter what happened, most of the players whose contracts were up—including Michael, Scottie, Dennis, Luc, Steve, and Jud—wouldn't be wearing a Bulls uniform the next year. The finality of it gave the season a certain resonance that bonded the team closely together. It felt as if we were on a sacred mission, driven by a force that went beyond fame, glory, and all the other spoils of victory. We were doing this one for the pure joy of playing together one more time. It felt magical.

That's not to say it was easy. The team had gotten another year older. Rodman was thirty-seven; Pippen, thirty-three; and Michael and Harper would be turning thirty-five and thirty-four, respectively, during the year. We needed to husband our energy during the regular season so we would be in good shape when the playoffs rolled around. But that was going to be difficult without Scottie on the floor. We needed to figure out a way to manage until he returned.

Without Pippen to direct the action, the team was having a difficult time finding its rhythm and got off to a rugged start. Our big problem was finishing close games, which used to be our specialty. The low point came in Seattle at the end of November when we lost, 91–90, to the SuperSonics and dropped to eighth place in the Eastern Conference with an 8-6 record. Our opponents were starting to smell blood.

During our trip to Seattle Scottie's anger boiled over. He told reporters that he was so fed up with management that he no longer wanted to play for the Bulls. After the game he got drunk on the bus to the airport and launched into an ugly tirade against Krause, who was sitting up front. I tried to contain Scottie's outburst by pointing to the beer bottle in my hand and indicating that he'd had too much to drink.

When we returned to Chicago, I hooked Scottie up with our team psychologist to help him deal with his anger. I still worried, though, about his frame of mind. On Thanksgiving he called me late at night to discuss his situation. He told me he was dead serious about being traded, and I tried to get him to think about the problem from a different angle. I was concerned that if he pushed too hard with his demand at that moment, he might get blackballed in the league as a troublemaker and jeopardize his chances of signing with one of the top teams the following season. As far as I could tell, the best move for Scottie careerwise was to finish out the season with the Bulls. I advised him not to let his anger with management poison his desire to come back and help lead the team to a sixth championship. He answered that he didn't want to give management a chance to break his heart.

I could tell this was going to take time. In the end I decided that the best strategy was to have the players bring Scottie around, just as they had done after his 1.8-second meltdown four years earlier. I asked Harper, Scottie's best friend on the team, to let him know how much his teammates needed his help. I also nixed the idea of having Scottie travel with the team to prevent another embarrassing confrontation between him and Krause on the road. What's more, Scottie's rehab was progressing more slowly than expected because his muscles had atrophied so much. His vertical leap was down from thirty inches to seventeen inches in mid-December, which meant that it would take another month for him to return to form. Which was fine. I figured that the more time Scottie spent working out with his teammates, the more likely he would get in touch with the joy he had always felt playing the game. By late December I could see that he was softening to the idea of coming back to the Bulls.

In the meantime, the team was trying to right itself. In mid-December we were 15-9, after beating the Lakers at home, 104–83, but the team still hadn't gelled and was relying too heavily on Michael. During a film session I made what I intended as a joke after watching a clip of Luc messing up a play. "Everybody makes mistakes," I said. "And I made one coming back here with this team this year." At which point Michael said, "Me too," in a somber tone. Shortly after that, Luc, who was obviously hurt by our comments, said, "It's easy to be a critic." When Tex jumped on him and accused him of having a bad attitude, Luc said, "I wasn't talking about the coaching staff. Michael is the one being critical." To which Michael replied, "The only thing that upsets me is when we lose. I think you should resolve to make yourself better next time. Change."

The room fell silent. "It's over," Michael added. "We're not going to lose anymore."

Actually, he wasn't far off. Right after that, we began to rebound and went on a 9-2 run. One move that made a big difference was turning Toni Kukoc into a starter when we played teams with big forwards. This allowed him to act as a third guard, much like Pippen did, and take advantage of his creative ball-handling skills. Toni was a maverick, always looking for the play no one else could imagine. Sometimes this worked brilliantly. However, Toni didn't have the mental toughness or physical ability to navigate the rugged NBA eighty-two-game schedule as the primary scorer or ball handler. And without Toni to anchor it, our bench was much weaker.

The big surprise was Rodman. He had struggled in 1996–97, and I worried that he might be losing interest in the game again. But during Scottie's rehab, we asked him to step up and give the team an energy boost, and he suddenly started playing MVP-level basketball on both ends of the court.

Michael likes to tell the story of how he and Dennis bonded during this period. The key was their mutual love of cigars. "When Scottie got hurt, that left me and Dennis as leaders of the team," recalls Michael. "So I went to Dennis and said, 'Look, I know your antics. I know you like getting technicals. I know the image you try to project. But I need you, man, to stay in the game. I don't need you to get kicked out. Scottie is not here. That means you're going to have to lead from upfront, as opposed to being behind Scottie and me.'" For the most part Dennis lived up to the challenge. Then during one game, he got angry and was thrown out. "Now I'm steaming," says Jordan. "I'm pissed because we had this conversation and he left me hanging. That night he came knocking at my hotel room door and asked for a cigar. In the whole time we'd been together, he'd never done that. But he knew he had let me down. And that was his way of saying, 'I'm sorry.'"

Scottie returned to the lineup on January 10 against the Golden State Warriors, and the team transformed overnight. It was like watching a great conductor return after a leave of absence. All of a sudden, everyone knew what notes to play and how to harmonize. From that point on, we went on a 38-9 run and tied the Utah Jazz for the best record in the league, 62-20.

As the regular season wound down, I thought it was important for us to have some closure as a team. This was the end of an era, and I wanted us to take some time to acknowledge our accomplishments and the strength of our connection. My wife, June, suggested that we perform a ritual that she had used with children whose parents had died in the hospice program where she worked. So I scheduled a spe-

cial team meeting before the start of the playoffs and asked everyone
to write a short paragraph about what the season and our team had
meant to them.

We met in the tribal room. It was just the inner core of the
team: the players, the coaches, and the training staff. Only about half
of the people wrote something ahead of time, but everyone spoke.
Steve Kerr talked about the thrill of becoming a father while he was
with the team and bringing his four-year-old, basketball-crazed son
into the Bulls locker room to meet Michael, Scottie, and Dennis.
Head trainer Chip Schaefer quoted the famous passage from 1 Corin-
thians 13:

> If I speak in the tongues of men and of angels, but have not
> love, I am only a resounding gong or a clanging cymbal. If I
> have the gift of prophecy and can fathom all mysteries and all
> knowledge, and if I have a faith that can move mountains, but
> have not love, I am nothing.

Michael wrote a short poem for the occasion. It was very moving.
He praised everyone's dedication and said he hoped that the bond
we'd formed would last forever. Then he added: No one knows what
the future holds, but let's finish it right.

It was touching to hear a group of hardened NBA players revealing
themselves to one another in this tender way. After each person spoke,
I asked him to put his message in a coffee can. Then we turned the
lights out, and I set fire to their words.

I'll never forget that moment. The quiet aura in the room. The fire
burning in the darkness. The intense intimacy we felt sitting silently
together and watching the flames die down. I don't think the bond
among us had ever been stronger.

During the final week of the regular season, we lost two games, including a home game to the Pacers. That raised some questions in my mind as we entered the playoffs, even though we had locked up home-court advantage in the Eastern Conference. My main concern was fatigue. Michael and Scottie were playing big minutes, and I wasn't sure our bench was strong enough to give them the breathing room they needed late in games. Our strategy at the outset was to play tough defense, conserve energy, and set Michael up to take over in the closing minutes. One bright spot was the reemergence of Kukoc, who had struggled the previous year with a bad case of plantar fasciitis but was playing so well now that Sam Smith suggested that the Bulls' Big Three should now include Toni instead of Rodman. As for Dennis, I worried about his inconsistency and lack of focus, especially now that we no longer had Brian Williams to back him up. To strengthen our inside defense, we'd traded forward Jason Caffey and brought back Dickey Simpkins, a bigger, more aggressive player— and a former Bull—who we hoped would help Dennis and Luc clog the lane.

We swept the New Jersey Nets in the first round after a sluggish start in the first two games, which *Chicago Tribune* columnist Bernie Lincicome characterized as "dead men dribbling." In the next series, the Charlotte Hornets gave us a surprise in game 2, beating us with a strong fourth-quarter push led by former teammate B.J. Armstrong. Being one-upped by B.J. inspired the team—and Michael in particular—to explode and finish off the Hornets in five games.

Our next opponent, the Pacers, would not go down so easily. They were a powerful contender, coached by Celtics great Larry Bird and featuring one of the best shooters in the league, Reggie Miller, along with a tough front line led by center Rik Smits. During one of their Breakfast Club sessions, Michael, Scottie, and Harp came up with a creative defensive strategy for neutralizing the Pacers' backcourt. They suggested having Pippen cover point guard Mark Jackson because he had done so well against him in the past and putting Harper on Miller because he was good at breaking through screens. Michael, in turn, would guard the small forward (either Jalen Rose or Chris Mullin), which would free him from expending a lot of energy chasing down Reggie on defense.

I gave the scheme the go-ahead and it worked well, forcing the Pacers into 46 turnovers in the first two games, as we cruised to a two-game lead in the series. After the second game, however, Larry complained to the media about the physical play of Pippen. Ergo, the next time we met, Scottie got into foul trouble early in the game. Then Larry foiled our defensive scheme by substituting the quicker Travis Best for Jackson. As a result, we had to change our plan and put Harp (or Kerr) on Best and Michael on Miller. In the fourth quarter Reggie manipulated his way through enough screens to get some free space and score 13 points en route to a 107–105 victory.

The closing seconds of game 4 reminded me of the 1972 Olympics final, i.e., totally chaotic. We were leading 94–93 with 4.7 seconds left when Scottie was fouled and missed two free throws. Then Harper and Miller got into an altercation, and Ron pulled Reggie down onto our bench and started hitting him. Both players were later fined, and Rose, who jumped up to join in the scuffle, was suspended for one game. (I was fined too, for comparing the refs to the '72 Olympics officials who nullified the U.S. team's win with a bad call.) When everything settled down, Reggie pushed Michael out of his way with both hands, grabbed an inbound pass, and hit a three-pointer with 0.7 seconds left to win the game.

In game 5 we resorted to our deadliest weapon—our defense—

and shut down the Pacers 106–87 in Chicago to go ahead 3–2 in the series. "Tonight was unexpected dominance," said Michael. "When everybody's focused and playing our game, we can really play the game of basketball." So far, so good. But two days later the Pacers tied the series again in Indianapolis, in another game tainted by dubious officiating. With 1:27 left, Scottie's old nemesis, Hue Hollins, called him for illegal defense, a technical foul that allowed Miller to tie the game, 87–87. Then, with the Pacers ahead by two in the closing seconds, Michael drove to the basket and fell. To us it looked like a tripping foul, but the refs looked the other way. Game over.

Could this be the end of the Bulls dynasty? I've always been wary of playing seventh games. Anything can happen, and it usually does. If we lost, it might also mean that this would be Michael's last game. Before the game I talked to the players about the prospect of defeat. We could lose this game, I said, but what's important is playing with the right kind of effort, and not being overtaken by the fear of losing. Michael understood that. To him losing was not an option. During a team huddle, he said, with a cold, determined look in his eye, "We are not going to lose this game."

Nothing came easy. Michael was struggling, hitting only 9 for 25 from the field. But when his jump shot wasn't working, he manufactured points by driving to the hoop in a crowd and drawing fouls. He ended up with 28 hard-won points, 10 of which came at the line. He also pulled down 9 rebounds and made 8 assists.

Michael's drive was contagious—especially with the bench. Toni scored 21 points; Kerr had 11; and Jud Buechler grabbed 5 rebounds in eleven minutes. In fact, our work on the boards was the key to the game. We hit only 38.2 percent from the field that night, but we outrebounded the Pacers 50–34, which gave us a lot of second opportunities to score. And Rodman, who was having an off night, contributed a mere six to the total.

During the middle of the fourth quarter, the team missed 10 straight points and fell behind 77–74—and I thought we might be history. But then the whole team started getting creative, scrambling for the ball and looking for anything that might break the game open. Michael fired a pass to Longley, and Scottie, who was not having a good night offensively, pulled down Luc's miss and hit a jumper with less than five minutes left that put us ahead for good, 81–79. We went on to win 88–83.

"It's about heart, and I think you saw a lot of heart out on the basketball court," an exhausted Michael said afterward. "It was a great effort. It's truly a championship team in terms of finding ways to win and making it happen."

The next series—the championship finals against the Utah Jazz— wouldn't be a dream vacation either. First of all, we didn't get home-court advantage because the Jazz had swept us during the regular season. That meant we'd have to win two games on the road against them, unless we won three in a row at home, which had never been done before in the postseason. The key to beating the Jazz was to sabotage their great screen-roll game by pressuring the point guards, John Stockton and Howard Eisley. Karl Malone was a machine on offense, but he didn't excel at creating his own shots the way Michael did. Malone relied on the point guards to set things in motion for him. If we could cut off the point guards, we'd stifle Malone.

In game 1, I pulled Harper late in the game because he seemed tentative on offense. And Kerr couldn't contain Stockton in the closing minutes, so we lost, 88–85, in overtime. We edged out the Jazz, 93–88, in the second game, then returned to Chicago to make history. For game 3 we decided to have Pippen double-team Stockton as he moved the ball across half-court, and Scottie's size and wingspan made it difficult for John to initiate the offense. We won 96–54, and the Jazz walked off with the record for the fewest points scored in a playoff game by one team. Veteran Jazz coach Jerry Sloan said, "I don't know if I've ever seen a team play any better defensively since I've been in the business."

We won the next two games at home, giving us a 3–1 edge in the series. Scottie was so dominant in game 4 that Sam Smith called for him to be named finals MVP over Jordan. But first we had to win, and that was proving harder than we imagined. There was so much hype in Chicago about game 5, which could be Michael's grand finale, that the players had a difficult time focusing on the game, and we lost, 83–81.

It all came down to game 6 in Utah. Actually, it came down to 18.8 seconds in that game—one of the most dramatic moments in the history of sports. I didn't want to play another game 7, especially in the Delta Center, where the boisterous home crowd held powerful sway over the refs in big games. But things didn't look good when we arrived at the stadium for game 6. Scottie had serious back spasms and would be out much of the game. Harper had a stomach flu. Longley was playing limited minutes because of foul trouble. Dennis was averaging 6.75 rebounds in the series, well below his 15.0 average during the regular season. Kukoc and Kerr were performing well, but I didn't think they could offset the loss of Pippen. Before the game I asked Michael if he could play the full forty-eight minutes. "If you need it I can," he said.

Scottie left the game in pain after the first seven minutes and was out for the rest of the first half. Somehow we held it together and finished the half down by only 5 points. Scottie returned after the break and played for nineteen minutes, mostly as a decoy on offense. As the fourth quarter began, Utah was leading 66–61 and slowly losing ground to the Bulls, who tied the score at 77 with five minutes left.

But we had a problem: Michael's legs were tiring, and he couldn't get any lift on his jump shot. I urged him to drive to the basket instead, because the Jazz didn't have a center on the floor to jam up the middle. If he was forced to go to his jumper, I advised, he should make sure he completed the follow-through, which he hadn't been doing. With 41.9 seconds left, John Stockton hit a twenty-four-foot jumper that put the Jazz ahead 86–83. I called time-out and told the players to run a variation on one of my favorite plays—which involved clearing out space on one side of the floor for Michael so he could create his own shot. Scottie tossed in the ball to Michael at half-court and M.J. drove past Byron Russell on the right side and put in a high-arching layup to make it 86–85 Utah.

As expected, the Jazz didn't call a time-out and started to launch one of their standard plays. Michael anticipated where the pass was going and slipped around Karl to steal the ball from him.

That's when everything started to slow down. Michael, who often had an otherworldly sense of what was happening on the floor, moved the ball up court and sized up the situation. Kerr and Kukoc were on the floor, so Utah couldn't risk double-teaming him. That left Russell all by himself to guard Michael as he calmly let the clock run down like a big cat studying its prey. Then Russell made a stab for the ball, and Michael moved right as if he were driving to the basket, gave Byron a little push, and pulled up short and sent him flying to the floor. Slowly, ever so slowly, Michael squared up and lofted a beautiful shot to win the game.

Afterward Michael recounted what was going through his mind in those closing seconds. It sounded like a poem on mindfulness.

"When I got that [steal], the moment became the moment," he said. "Karl never saw me coming, and I was able to knock the ball away. When Russell reached, I took advantage of the moment. I never doubted myself. It was a two-point game, a three-point game, we kept hanging close. When I got the ball, I looked up and saw 18.8 seconds left. I let the time tick until I saw the court the way I wanted it. John Stockton was over on Steve Kerr, so he couldn't gamble and come off. And as soon as Russell reached, I had a clear path. I knew we could hold for 5.2 seconds."

I couldn't believe what had just happened. I thought I had witnessed Michael's greatest moment during his famous flu game the year before. But this was on a different level. It was as if the whole thing had been scripted. Even though Michael would return to basketball years later to play for the Washington Wizards, this is the shot everyone thinks of as his final bow. A perfect ending if ever there was one.

After all the celebrations were over, Michael invited the members of the team and their guests to a party at one of his restaurants in Chicago. When dinner was over, the team retired to the cigar room to smoke stogies and reminisce about our time with the Bulls. The stories ranged from the mundane to the profane. Then each of us gave a toast to another member of the team. I celebrated Ron Harper for his selfless act of switching from an offensive star to a defensive specialist, thereby setting up our run for the second three-peat. Scottie gave the final toast, to Michael, his partner and fellow leader. "None of this could have happened without you," he said.

There had been a lot of speculation after the finals about what would happen to the Bulls. Would Reinsdorf try to bring the team together again for one more run? The only way that could happen was if Michael pulled some kind of miracle deal comparable to his last shot. But in my mind I was already gone. And I told Michael that he shouldn't link his decision to me.

I had one more meeting with Reinsdorf at our championship party. He offered me a chance to stay with the Bulls, but without any guarantee that he'd bring back Michael and Scottie. He and Krause had decided to rebuild the team, a process that didn't interest me. Besides, I was desperately in need of a break. June and I were planning to move to Woodstock, New York, where we'd lived before I joined the Bulls. So I graciously turned him down. Michael waited for the lockout to end in January 1999 before officially announcing his departure.

As I walked out of the Berto Center on my last day, there were some reporters waiting outside. I chatted with them briefly, then climbed on my motorcycle and sped away. It was a bittersweet moment. I felt a great sense of relief, leaving behind all the drama of the past year. But I also knew it was going to be a challenge to let go of my deep attachment to this team that had given me so much.

The Buddhist teacher Pema Chodron talks about letting go as an opportunity for true awakening. One of her favorite sayings is "Only to the extent that we expose ourselves over and over to annihilation can that which is indestructible be found in us."

That's what I was searching for. And I knew it wasn't going to be easy. But as a new future unfolded before me, I took comfort in the knowledge that letting go is a necessary, if sometimes heart-wrenching, gateway to genuine transformation.

"Things falling apart is a kind of testing and also a kind of healing," writes Chodron. "We think that the point is to pass the test or to overcome the problem, but the truth is that things don't really get solved. They come together again and fall apart again. It's just like that. The healing comes from letting there be room for all of this to happen: room for grief, for relief, for misery, for joy."

I felt all those emotions during my final year in Chicago. And before long I would be headed off on another wild ride that would test me even more.

14

ONE BREATH, ONE MIND

Feelings come and go like clouds in a windy sky.
Conscious breathing is my anchor.

THICH NHAT HANH

I was in the middle of nowhere—a small village on Iliamna Lake in Alaska—when I heard the news. My sons, Ben and Charlie, were with me. We were on a fly-fishing trip in a secluded wilderness area, and the fishing wasn't going very well. So that afternoon we knocked off early and boated up the Iliamna River to see the falls. When we arrived back at the village, a throng of children surrounded us.

"Are you Phil Jackson?" one of the boys asked.

"Yes," I replied. "Why?"

"I hear you got the job with the Lakers."

"What? How do you know that?"

"We got a dish. It's on ESPN."

That's how my adventure began. Actually, it didn't come as a total surprise. My agent, Todd, and I had discussed the deal before I left for Alaska. I'd given him the go-ahead to negotiate with the Lakers since I would be unreachable by phone. Still, it was a bit of a shock to get the news from an Inuit boy in a place as far away in spirit from the glitzy, high-stakes culture of Los Angeles as any I could imagine.

This was not a simple move for me. After the 1997–98 season,

June and I had relocated to Woodstock, New York, a town where we'd lived before. Our hope was to revitalize our marriage, which had suffered during the past stressful year with the Bulls. What's more, June had grown weary of her role as an NBA wife. Now that all of our children were out of the house, she was looking forward to creating a new, more fulfilling life. So was I—or so I thought. I explored other interests, including giving speeches on leadership and working on my friend Bill Bradley's presidential campaign. But in the end, I couldn't find anything that captured my imagination as much as leading young men to victory on the basketball court.

Toward the end of the 1998–99 season, I started getting calls from teams interested in talking to me and I had meetings with the New Jersey Nets and the New York Knicks. Neither of these conversations went anywhere, but they whetted my appetite to get back in the game. Needless to say, this was not the kind of reaction June was expecting. She thought I was ready to put basketball behind me and move into a field with a less demanding travel schedule. But that was not to be, and over the summer we decided to separate.

Soon after, as I moved back to Montana—my true place of refuge—the Lakers called. The team was loaded with talent, including rising stars Shaquille O'Neal and Kobe Bryant, and two of the best outside shooters in the league, Glen Rice and Robert Horry. But the Lakers had struggled in the playoffs because of weak group chemistry, and the players lacked the mental toughness to finish off big games.

Mulling over whether or not to accept the job, I remembered sitting in my hotel room during my cross-country trek and watching the Lakers get swept by the San Antonio Spurs in the Western Conference semifinals. It had been painful to watch. The Spurs' big men, Tim Duncan and Dave Robinson, were forcing Shaq to take off-balance fadeaway jump shots instead of his power move to the middle and then beating Shaq downcourt to break through the Lakers' defense. Watching those games, I'd found myself visualizing ways to counter the Spurs' strategy and transform the Lakers into the team they were destined to be.

That's the message I wanted to deliver in late June at my first news conference as the newly appointed head coach of the team. The event was held at the Beverly Hills Hilton, and while I was preparing my remarks, Kobe dropped by my room, carrying a copy of my book, *Sacred Hoops*. He asked me to sign the book and said he was really excited about working with me because he was a big Bulls fan. It was a good sign.

"This is a team that is talented, young, and on the verge," I told reporters that day. "It's been on the verge, and it hasn't gotten over the top. It's a similar situation that happened ten years ago in Chicago, and we hope to have the same type of success."

The key, I said, was to get the Lakers to trust one another enough to work together effectively and make the transition from a *me* team to a *we* team, the way the Bulls had in the early 1990s. "When you have a system of offense, you can't be a person that just is taking the basketball and trying to score," I explained. "You have to move the basketball, because you have to share the basketball with everybody. And when you do that, you're sharing the game, and that makes a big difference."

After the news conference, Jerry West drove me out to Westchester to visit Jerry Buss at his new Spanish-style palazzo on the bluffs overlooking the ocean. Dr. Buss, who has a Ph.D. in physical chemistry but made his fortune in real estate during the 1970s, had the good luck to buy the Lakers (plus the Forum and the Los Angeles Kings) in 1979, the year Magic Johnson arrived and led the team to five championships over the next decade. Since then, the team had not lived up to its promise.

Dr. Buss was smart but very low-key, dressed in jeans, a plain shirt, and his trademark sneakers. He said he was proud of the great success the Lakers had enjoyed in the past, but he wanted to win one more championship.

"I think you can win three, maybe four championships," I said.

"Really?" he replied, stunned.

He was impressed by my chutzpah. He said later that he'd never heard a coach set such a high bar for himself at the start of the season. But the truth is, I wasn't bluffing.

It was a strange summer. Not long after I returned to Montana after my meetings with the Lakers' organization, my daughter Chelsea came to visit with her boyfriend and shattered her ankle in an off-road motorcycle accident that put her in a cast for eight weeks. Since getting around was difficult, she decided to take a leave from her job in New York and recuperate in Montana, where my son Ben and I could take care of her. June also came out for several weeks to lend a hand.

One day Shaq dropped by the house unannounced. He'd ventured to Montana in order to perform at a rap concert in nearby Kalispell. I wasn't home when he arrived, so June invited him in. When I drove up, Shaq was bouncing on a trampoline down by the lake and creating quite a sensation in the neighborhood. All of a sudden, dozens of boats filled with curious onlookers crowded into the bay near our house to gawk at this giant leaping through the air. Shaq did not disappoint. After the trampoline exhibition, he started doing comical backflips off the dock, then took off on a madcap Jet Ski tour of the bay.

Since he was already wet, I asked Shaq to help me move a large tree that had toppled in our yard during a recent storm. It was impressive watching him work. "We're going to have a lot of fun, Coach," he said when we were finished. That's what Shaq was all about: fun.

When the time came to pack up and drive to L.A., I felt anxious about my new life. I worried about what would happen to my kids now that I was becoming a single dad and moving to a new, unfamiliar city. To ease the transition, my daughters Chelsea and Brooke put together a mix tape for me of songs about starting over. It had been more than twenty-five years since I'd driven through the back roads of California. As I crossed the Sierra Nevada range, Willie Nelson's soulful version of "Amazing Grace" came on, and I was so overwhelmed with emotion that I pulled over, stopped the car, and cried. Looking out over the sunlit California peaks, I felt as if I were putting a dark chapter of my life behind me and heading toward something bright and new. And my kids understood. This was their way of saying, "Move forward, Dad. Live life. Don't close yourself off."

My first days in L.A. were magical. A friend found me a beautiful, airy house on the beach in Playa del Rey, not far from the airport and the Lakers' future practice facility. My new home had plenty of room for guests. To my delight, Brooke, who had just graduated from the University of Colorado, moved in a few weeks later to help me get settled, then stayed on to pursue a graduate degree in psychology. And during my first week in town, Bruce Hornsby, a songwriter friend who had introduced me to the Grateful Dead, invited me to a concert at the Greek Theatre in Griffith Park, where he was performing with Linda Ronstadt, Jackson Browne, and other music-world icons. It was a warm September evening, and the crowd was friendly and easygoing. Very California. I felt right at home.

One of my first jobs was to attend the NBA's annual business meeting in Vancouver. While I was there, I finally got to meet Dr. Buss's daughter, Jeanie, the team's executive VP of business operations, who hosted a dinner for the Lakers executives. She was smart and attractive, with beautiful eyes and a playful sense of humor. The next day I bumped into her at the airport. She was heading home to celebrate her birthday with friends, but her flight had been delayed, so we ended up chatting in the lounge. She told some amusing stories about Dennis Rodman's disastrous stint with the Lakers in 1999, which sounded like a bad reality show gone Theatre of the Absurd.

I still felt pretty raw emotionally and wasn't sure if I was ready for a new relationship. But then it happened. The next day I came into the office and found a slice of Jeanie's birthday cake sitting on my desk. When I dropped by her office to thank her, she blushed and I sensed this gift was more than a collegial gesture. So I invited her to dinner that night. Things were definitely looking up.

As we gathered at the University of Santa Barbara for training camp, I saw the Lakers as a stage 3 team with a decidedly "I'm great, you're not" point of view. One of the team's biggest strengths was Shaq's dominance at center. The triangle offense was designed for powerful centers who could dominate the lane, post up effectively, and catalyze the offense with sharp passing. Shaq could do all those things as well as or better than the centers we'd had in Chicago, but he was also an explosive scorer who attracted double- and triple-teams, which opened up all sorts of possibilities. *Los Angeles Times* columnist Mark Heisler wrote that Shaq represented an evolutionary step: "the first 300-pound seven-footer the NBA had ever seen who wasn't fat." Shaq had ballooned up to 350 pounds over the summer, but when he was in shape, he was stronger, faster, and more mobile than any other center in the league. He was also extremely gifted at running fast breaks. However, he wasn't as strong at rebounding or playing defense as I had expected, and I noticed that he was averse to moving out of the lane to cover screens, which made him vulnerable to good screen-roll teams, such as the Jazz, the Spurs, and the Trail Blazers.

Kobe was one of the most creative shooting guards I'd ever seen, capable of dazzling moves comparable in many ways to those of his idol, Michael Jordan. I admired Kobe's intense desire to win, but he still had a lot to learn about teamwork and self-sacrifice. Though he was a brilliant passer, his first instinct was to penetrate off the dribble and dunk over whoever was in his way. Like many younger players, he tried to force the action rather than letting the game come to him. I was toying with the idea of having him play point guard, but I questioned whether he'd be able to contain his ego long enough to master the triangle system.

Rice was another gifted player. A former All-Star small forward with the Charlotte Hornets, he had a precision jump shot that used to drive Scottie Pippen mad. Earlier in his career Glen had also been a quick, aggressive defender, but he'd fallen out of practice since joining the Lakers. The lineup also included Horry, a willowy six-ten power forward who was later dubbed "Big Shot Rob" because of his talent for shooting last-minute game-winning shots. Rob had won two rings with Houston before being traded, first to Phoenix, then to L.A. But his scoring average had tapered off and I was concerned that he might not have enough strength and size to battle the bigger power forwards in the league.

The team also had some promising backup players, including Rick Fox and Derek Fisher, both of whom would become important leaders later on. Rick was a former University of North Carolina star who was big and mobile enough to play both forward positions. He'd been drafted by Boston but languished there for several years during the post–Larry Bird era. Rick was known for making senseless errors, which the players called "Ricky Ball," but he was also a clutch shooter, a strong defender, and a selfless team player. Fisher, a six-one, two-hundred-pound point guard from the University of Arkansas at Little Rock, was smart, aggressive, and versatile, with a good outside shot and natural leadership abilities.

Our biggest weaknesses were at point guard and power forward. We pushed hard to make a deal with Houston for Scottie Pippen, but we lost out to the Portland Trail Blazers, our strongest rival in the Western Conference that year. Luckily, we were able to acquire Ron Harper, whose contract had run out with the Bulls, and A.C. Green, a veteran power forward who not only was a strong defender but was also well versed in the triangle, having played for former Bulls coach Jim Cleamons on the Dallas Mavericks. We also picked up backup center John Salley, who had won rings with the Bulls and the Pistons.

The reason we recruited so many experienced players was to reverse the Lakers' sorry history of caving under pressure because of immaturity and lack of discipline. In 1998 the Lakers missed 15 of their first 18 shots on the way to their most embarrassing defeat in team history, a 112–77 blowout by the Jazz in game 1 of the Western Conference finals. Horry said the game reminded him of *The Wizard of Oz* because the team played with "no heart, no brain, no courage." To which coach Del Harris added, "And no wizard."

I also assembled an experienced coaching staff, primarily made up of veterans I'd worked with in Chicago, including Cleamons, Frank Hamblen, and Tex Winter (much to Jerry Krause's dismay). I also retained Lakers assistant coach Bill Bertka.

Our plan was to begin at the beginning, teaching the players the rudiments of the system, starting with basic passing and shooting drills. The team soaked up everything we threw at them. When I asked the players to form a circle in the center of the court on the first day of training camp, it reminded Chip Schaefer, an athletic-performance coordinator I'd brought over from the Bulls, of that old

E.F. Hutton television commercial. "Everyone was just hanging on every word, even the veterans," recalls Chip. "Everybody's just, 'Shhhhh. I want to hear everything this guy has to say.'" Later, during practice, Chip noticed Rick Fox grinning from ear to ear. "He said, 'I feel like I'm back in junior high again,'" says Chip. "But it wasn't like, 'Oh my God, I'm back in junior high school.' He was beaming because there's something about fundamentals that basketball players love."

Fish takes a broader view. "We'd been through a couple of years of frustrating playoffs," he says. "Although we had a lot of talent, we still hadn't figured out a way to maximize our potential. So when Phil and the staff were hired, it brought everybody to attention and got us to focus in a way I hadn't seen in the first three years we played together. Whatever Phil said, whatever he wanted us to do and however he wanted us to do it, everybody seemed to have that kind of kindergarten impressionable spirit. And it made us into a machine, an efficient group that can be compared to some of the best teams in history."

My experience was somewhat different that first day. Although I was pleased by everyone's eagerness to learn, I was vexed by how short the players' attention spans were. Before training camp I'd sent them a three-page letter on the triangle offense, mindfulness meditation, and other topics I planned to discuss during camp. But when I started delivering my first serious talk, they had a difficult time focusing on what I was saying. They looked at the ceiling; they fidgeted; they shuffled their feet. This was an issue I'd never encountered with the Bulls.

To remedy the problem, psychologist George Mumford and I designed a program of daily meditation practice for the players, slowly increasing the time spent in each session from three minutes to ten minutes. I also introduced the players to yoga, tai chi, and other Eastern practices to help them balance mind, body, and spirit. In Chicago we'd used meditation primarily to increase awareness on the court. But with this team our goal was to bond the players together so that they would experience what we called "one breath, one mind."

One of the basic principles of Buddhist thought is that our conventional concept of the self as a separate entity is an illusion. On a superficial level, what we consider the self may appear to be separate and distinct from everything else. After all, we all look different and have distinct personalities. But on a deeper level, we are all part of an interconnected whole.

Martin Luther King Jr. spoke eloquently about this phenomenon. "In a real sense, all of life is interrelated," he said. "All persons are caught in an inescapable network of mutuality, tied in a single garment of destiny. Whatever affects one directly affects all indirectly. I can never be what I ought to be until you are what you ought to be, and you can never be what you ought to be until I am what I ought to be. This is the interrelated structure of reality."

The thirteenth-century Japanese Buddhist teacher Nichiren took a more pragmatic view. He wrote in a letter to his disciples who were being persecuted by feudal authorities that they should chant together "with the spirit of many in body but one in mind, transcending all differences among themselves to become as inseparable as fish and the water in which they swim." The unity that Nichiren prescribed was not a mechanical uniformity, imposed from without, but a connection that respected the unique qualities of each individual. "If the spirit of many in body but one in mind prevails among the people," he added, "they will achieve all their goals, whereas if one in body but different in mind, they can achieve nothing remarkable."

That was the kind of unity I wanted to foster with the Lakers. I didn't expect to turn the players into adepts, but I thought that meditation practice would help them break out of their me-oriented view of themselves and give them a glimpse of a different way of relating to others and the world around them.

When I first started coaching the Bulls, they had already started transforming themselves into a one-mind-oriented team. The Lakota ideal of the warrior appealed to them because they had been through so many battles with their major rival, the Detroit Pistons. But that approach didn't resonate as strongly with the Lakers. They had many enemies, not just one, and the most troubling of all, from my perspective, was the culture that fed them.

By the time most future NBA players are middle schoolers, they become immersed in a universe that reinforces egoistic behavior. As they grow older and continue to succeed, they become surrounded by legions of agents, promoters, groupies, and other sycophants who keep telling them they're "da man." It doesn't take long before they start to really buy into it. What's more, L.A. is a world devoted to celebrating the notion of the glorified self. Everywhere the Lakers went—not just the superstars but the other players as well—they were greeted as heroes and offered endless, often lucrative, opportunities to bask in their wonderfulness.

My intention was to offer them a safe, supportive refuge from all that craziness and put them in touch with their deep—but as yet undeveloped—longing for real connection. That was the essential first step on which the team's future success would depend.

15

THE EIGHTFOLD OFFENSE

Greatness is a spiritual condition.
MATTHEW ARNOLD

Rick Fox describes my approach to coaching as a play in three acts. The way he sees it, during the first twenty or thirty games of each season I'd sit back and let the characters reveal themselves. "Most coaches come into a season with an idea of what they're going to do and impose that on the players," he explains. "But I always felt that Phil came to the table with an open mind. 'Let's see how each individual expresses himself. Let's see how the group responds under fire and whether it's capable of solving problems.' He never appeared too concerned about the team at that point. Never any panic. Never overanalyzing anything because that would be premature."

Act 2 would take place during the twenty or thirty games in the middle of the season, before and after the All-Star game. "That's when he would nurture the team, when guys were starting to get bored," Rick adds. "Phil would spend more time with each of us then. He'd give us books. I always felt that he drove me the hardest during that time."

Then, during the last twenty or thirty games leading up to the playoffs, act 3 would begin and, according to Fox, my whole demeanor would change—the way I'd look, talk, and move my body—

as if I were saying, "This is my time." In the run-up to the playoffs, I'd often restrict the media's access to the players and take a more assertive role in promoting the team. "Phil gave us new confidence and an identity we didn't have before," says Rick. "But he would also take the pressure off of us and put it on himself. He would turn whole cities against him. And everyone would get upset at him and wouldn't be thinking about us. It was like, 'Look at this mess I've created over here,' and we would be able to do what we were doing without the spotlight being on us."

As the players used to say, "Sounds good." Of course, things didn't always turn out so neatly.

Before my first season with the Lakers started, I met with Shaq, Harper, and Kobe, and I told them that this was going to be Shaq's team and the offense would run through him. But I added that Kobe would be the floor leader, not unlike the relationship between Kareem and Magic in a previous era. I didn't feel that Kobe was ready to be cocaptain yet, so I put Ron in that spot and asked him to serve as Kobe's mentor while he learned how to be a leader. I wanted to spell everything out at the beginning so there wouldn't be any ambiguity about roles—especially with Kobe.

We didn't really get a chance to try out this structure, though, because Kobe broke his right hand during the first preseason game and was out until December. We picked up Brian Shaw, a big, versatile journeyman guard, to help cover for Kobe while he was out, and the team started to come together, going 12-4 in the first month. Our first loss was to the Trail Blazers, who did a good job of trapping our guards, sabotaging our offense, and fouling Shaq as soon as he got the ball. Afterward I asked Scottie, who was now with the Trail Blazers, what he thought of our team, and he quipped, "I think your triangle looks more like a square."

Later that month during a game against the Nets, I called a play we referred to as a "home run," but Horry missed it and the play fell apart. When I asked Robert what had happened, he said, "I didn't hear your call." At which point I made a reference to the Bible, knowing that Horry came from a religious family. "The sheep know their master's voice," I said. "It's all about recognizing the master's voice and responding to his call." Salley asked me what I meant by that politically incorrect statement, and I told him that it referred to a parable about the sheep knowing the master's voice that Jesus used as a metaphor to explain his disciples' understanding of the will of God. For weeks after that incident, the players would kid me when I called them to the circle at the start of practice, saying, "Yes, master."

Kobe returned on December 1 and the team continued its streak into January. But the offense wasn't flowing as smoothly as it had before. Kobe was having a difficult time staying in the triangle and would frequently go rogue, which annoyed his teammates. Many of them told me they didn't like playing with Kobe because he didn't respect the system. I'd been through this before with Michael, but Kobe, who had recently turned twenty-one, wasn't as mature and open-minded as Jordan.

If children are fated to live out the unfulfilled dreams of their parents, Kobe was a textbook case. His father, Joe "Jellybean" Bryant, was a six-nine forward for the legendary 1970s Philadelphia 76ers. Bryant Sr. once claimed that he played the same kind of game as Magic Johnson, but the NBA wasn't ready for his playground style. So after stints with two other teams, he finished his career in Italy, where Kobe grew up.

The youngest of three children (and the only boy), Kobe was the golden child in the family who could do no wrong. He was a bright, talented overachiever with a natural gift for the game. He spent long hours practicing, imitating the moves of Jordan and others he studied on tapes his relatives sent from the United States. When he was thirteen, the family moved back to Philadelphia, and he soon developed into a star at Lower Merion High School. John Lucas, then head coach of the 76ers, invited Kobe to scrimmage with the team over the summer and was surprised by the young player's courage and level of skill. Not long afterward, Kobe decided to forgo college and jump right into the pros, even though he had high enough SAT scores to take his pick of schools. Jerry West said Kobe's predraft workout at age seventeen was the best he'd ever seen. Jerry made a trade with the Hornets to draft Kobe thirteenth overall in 1996—the same year he lured Shaq away from Orlando with a seven-year, $120 million free-agent deal.

Kobe had big dreams. Soon after I started with the Lakers, Jerry called me into his office to report that Kobe had asked him how he had averaged 30-plus points a game when his teammate, Elgin Baylor, was also scoring 30-plus points per game. Kobe was hell-bent on surpassing Jordan as the greatest player in the game. His obsession with Michael was striking. Not only had he mastered many of Jordan's moves, but he affected many of M.J.'s mannerisms as well. When we played in Chicago that season, I orchestrated a meeting between the two stars, thinking that Michael might help shift Kobe's attitude toward selfless teamwork. After they shook hands, the first words out of Kobe's mouth were "You know I can kick your ass one on one."

I admired Kobe's ambition. But I also felt that he needed to break out of his protective chrysalis if he wanted to win the ten rings he told his teammates he was shooting for. Obviously, basketball isn't an individual sport. To achieve greatness, you must rely on the good offices of others. But Kobe had yet to reach out to his teammates and try to get to know them. Instead of spending time with them after games, he usually went back to his hotel room to study tapes or chat with his high-school friends on the phone.

Kobe was also a stubborn, hardheaded learner. He was so confident in his ability that you couldn't simply point out his mistakes and expect him to alter his behavior. He would have to experience failure directly before his resistance would start to break down. It was often an excruciating process for him and everyone else involved. Then suddenly he would have an aha moment and figure out a way to change.

One of those moments happened in early February. That's when the team was struck by a puzzling malaise. After a less-than-stellar performance, I closed the locker room to all but the players and asked what had happened to cause them to suddenly stop playing together. It was a rhetorical question, but I let them know we'd take it up the following day after practice. We gathered in a small video room at Southwest Los Angeles Community College—our temporary practice space. There were four rows of five chairs, and in the first row sat Shaq, Fox, Fish, Harp, and Shaw. Kobe was in the last row with his hoodie pulled over his head. I reviewed the demands that the triangle offense placed on each team member, then concluded: "You can't be a selfish player and make this offense work for the team's good. Period." When I opened the floor to comments, there was complete silence, and I was about to adjourn the meeting when Shaq spoke up. He got right to the point, saying, "I think Kobe is playing too selfishly for us to win." That got everyone fired up. Some of the players nodded in support of Shaq, including Rick Fox, who said, "How many times have we been through this?" No one in that room came to Kobe's defense. I asked him if he had anything to say. Kobe finally addressed the group, and in a calm, quiet voice he said he cared about everyone and just wanted to be part of a winning team.

I wasn't pleased with the meeting. I worried that having everyone's complaints on the table without any resolution would have a negative effect on team harmony. In the days that followed, we lost four out of five games, including a 105–81 "massacre" by the Spurs in the Alamodome. One night that week I had a dream about spanking Kobe and giving Shaq a smack. "Shaq needs and Kobe wants—the mystery of the Lakers," I wrote in my journal.

The players started blaming one another for the breakdown, and I realized that I had to address the unrest head-on. The first thing I did was meet Shaq for breakfast to discuss what it means to be a leader. I started by relating the story of how Michael galvanized the Bulls with his confidence in himself and his teammates before the must-win game 5 against Cleveland in the 1989 playoffs. The Cavaliers had just beaten us at home to tie the series, and Michael had had an off night. Still, that didn't faze him. His uncompromising faith revved up the team, and we won the final game—not surprisingly, on a last-second miracle shot by Jordan.

I told Shaq he needed to find his own way to inspire the Lakers. He needed to express his confidence and natural joy for the game in such a way that his teammates—Kobe especially—felt that if they joined forces with him, nothing would be impossible. A team leader's number one job, I explained, was to build up his teammates, not tear them down. Shaq had probably heard this kind of spiel before, but this time I think it clicked.

With Kobe I took a different tack. I tried to be as direct as possible and show him in front of the other players how his selfish mistakes were hurting the team. During one film session, I said, "Now I know why the guys don't like playing with you. You've got to play together." I also indicated to him that if he didn't want to share the ball with his teammates, I would gladly work out a trade for him. I had no trouble being the bad cop in this situation. (See under: *Sometimes you have to pull out the big stick.*) I knew Harper would soften the blow later by explaining to Kobe—in far less strident terms—how to play more selflessly without sacrificing his creativity.

I also talked to Kobe about what it takes to be a leader. At one point I told him, "I guess you'd like to be the captain of this team someday when you're older—maybe like twenty-five." He replied that he wanted to be captain tomorrow. To which I said, "You can't be captain if nobody follows you."

Eventually it sank in. Kobe began looking for ways to fit himself into the system and play more collaboratively. He also made an effort to socialize more with his teammates, especially when we were on the road. And after the All-Star break, everything started to come together. We went on a 27-1 streak and finished the season with the best record in the league, 67-15.

The players seemed relieved that we'd put to sleep a problem that had haunted the team for the past three years. As Rick Fox put it, Kobe's me-first attitude "was a land mine that was about to explode. We all knew that somebody had to step on it, but nobody wanted to. So Phil did it, and we all walk a lot more freely now."

As we prepared for the playoffs, I thought it might be useful for the players to have a refresher course on selfless basketball, but this time from a different perspective—that of the Buddha. So I devoted one of our practice sessions to talking about the Buddha's thinking and how it applies to basketball. I probably lost some of the players early on, but if nothing else, the discussion took their minds off the pressure of the upcoming postseason.

In a nutshell, the Buddha taught that life is suffering and that the primary cause of our suffering is our desire for things to be different from the way they actually are. One moment, things may be going our way, and in the next moment they're not. When we try to prolong pleasure or reject pain, we suffer. On the bright side, the Buddha also prescribed a practical way for eliminating craving and unhappiness by following what he called the Noble Eightfold Path. The steps were right view, right thinking, right speech, right action, right livelihood, right effort, right mindfulness, and right concentration.

I thought the teachings might help explain what we were trying to do as a basketball team.

1. RIGHT VIEW—involves looking at the game as a whole and working together as a team, like five fingers on a hand.

2. RIGHT THINKING—means seeing yourself as part of a system rather than as your own one-man band. It also implies going into each game with the intention of being intimately involved with what's happening to the whole team because you're integrally connected to everyone on it.

3. RIGHT SPEECH—has two components. One is about talking positively to yourself throughout the game and not getting lost in aimless back talk ("I hate that ref," "I'm going to get back at that bastard"). The second is about controlling what you say when you're talking with others, especially your teammates, and focusing on giving them positive feedback.

4. RIGHT ACTION—suggests making moves that are appropriate to what's happening on the floor instead of repeatedly showboating or acting in ways that disrupt team harmony.

5. RIGHT LIVELIHOOD—is about having respect for the work you do and using it to heal the community rather than simply to polish your ego. Be humble. You're getting paid a ridiculous amount of money to do something that's really simple. And fun.

6. RIGHT EFFORT—means being unselfish and exerting the right amount of energy to get the job done. Tex Winter says that there's no substitute for hustle, and my addendum is, if you don't hustle, you'll get benched.

7. RIGHT MINDFULNESS—involves coming to every game with a

clear understanding of our plan of attack, including what to expect from our opponents. It also implies playing with precision, making the right moves at the right times, and maintaining constant awareness throughout the game, whether you're on the floor or on the bench.

8. RIGHT CONCENTRATION—is about staying focused on what you're doing at any given moment and not obsessing about mistakes you've made in the past or bad things that might happen in the future.

What worried me about this team was the ghosts of playoffs past. The players had a tendency to lose patience and panic when the pressure started building and they couldn't get by on talent alone. As one Buddhist teacher I know put it, they tended to put a head on top of a head when the game started going into a nosedive. In other words, they let their fear or anger persist and steal their focus from the task at hand.

With the Lakers I found that I had to be a model of calmness and patience, much more so than with the Bulls. I had to demonstrate that the key to inner peace is trusting in the essential interconnectedness of all things. One breath, one mind. That's what gives you strength and energy in the midst of chaos.

The first round of the playoffs against Sacramento was an enlightening experience. The Kings had a fast, explosive young team with a deft passing attack that was hard to stop when the players were in full motion. The player I worried about most was Chris Webber, who was too strong and quick for our power forward duo of A.C. Green and Robert Horry. That meant he could break free and help out Vlade Divac on Shaq. I was also impressed with the Kings' bench, led by

Predrag Stojakovic, a chilling outside shooter. Our best bet, I figured, was to slow the pace down and neutralize the Kings' running game.

That worked in the first two games, which we won handily, but when the five-game series moved to Sacramento's noisy bandbox stadium, the Kings capitalized on some generous officiating and Shaq's lackluster defense to pull the series even, 2–2. After the third game a Sacramento reporter asked me if these were the most energetic fans I'd ever seen, and I told him no. "I coached basketball in Puerto Rico, where if you won on a visiting floor, your tires were slashed and you might be chased out of town with rocks breaking the windows of your car." But here, I said, "We're talking about semi-civilized in Sacramento. These people are just maybe redneck in some form or fashion." I meant it tongue in cheek, but the remark launched a backlash in the state's capital that haunted us for years.

The final must-win game in the Staples Center was a trial by fire for the young Lakers. "If you don't win this one," I told the players, "then you don't deserve to move into the next round. You've got to play to win, not play to avoid losing." And they rose to the occasion. The refs finally started calling Webber for playing a zonelike defense on Shaq, which freed the big man to take over the game, hitting 7 of his first 8 field-goal attempts and finishing with 32 points and 18 rebounds, as we went on to win, 113–86. "We knew if we didn't play our A game, we'd make history tonight," Shaq said. "And we didn't want to make that kind of history."

In the next series we jumped to a relatively easy 3–0 lead over Phoenix, but we fell apart in game 4, allowing the Suns to score an embarrassing 71 points in the first half.

During halftime I didn't talk to the players at first; I let them sulk and bicker among themselves until about two minutes before game time. Then I stormed into the locker room and hurled a bottle of Gaterlode against the wall to get their attention. I rarely throw tirades, but they needed to hear how I felt about their inconsistency and lack of discipline at a time when they couldn't afford to get sloppy. After the game, which we lost 117–98, I made a more thoughtful speech. "You guys are a little tired of each other and don't want to work together as a cohesive unit," I said. "All of this is understandable at this stage of a long season. To win a championship, however, you've got to find a way to match each other's energy and to match your opponent's energy. You've just got to figure out what it takes to win night after night. Let's learn from this game and don't let it happen again." Two nights later the Suns couldn't make anything work, and we breezed to victory, 87–65.

I knew from the start that our opponents in the Western Conference finals—the Portland Trail Blazers—were going to be the team to beat in the playoffs. They had the most expensive roster in the league ($73.9 million), including center Arvydas Sabonis (bigger than Shaq at seven feet three inches and 292 pounds), fiery power forward Rasheed Wallace, left-handed point guard Damon Stoudamire, versatile spot shooter Steve Smith, and Pippen, who could do everything. They also had a dynamic bench, featuring guards Bonzi Wells and Greg Anthony, and six-ten swing man Detlef Schrempf. To tweak them, I dubbed the Blazers "the best team money can buy."

The player I was worried about, of course, was Scottie. He had a Ph.D. in the triangle offense and knew every possible way to disrupt it. To keep Scottie from harassing our guards, we put six-nine Horry in the backcourt and had Harper rove around the top of the floor as a small forward. We also tried using Kobe as a traditional point guard so we could exploit the mismatch between our big guards and Portland's five-ten Stoudamire. Both strategies worked better than expected. Our biggest advantage, though, was at center. Despite his height, Sabonis wasn't mobile enough to contain Shaq, so the Blazers often triple-teamed him and resorted to a hack-a-Shaq strategy late in games. The Blazers might be bigger and more athletic than us, said Kobe, but "Shaq will match up with about four of them on his own."

The first game was a walk. Our bench had a big second quarter and Shaq erupted for 41 points as we sailed to a 109–94 victory. But in game 2 Scottie started to drive on Glen Rice and penetrate our defense, racking up 17 points in the first half to lead the Blazers to a double-digit lead before he fell and dislocated two fingers. Miraculously, we were down by only three at halftime, but then our offense completely imploded in the third quarter, scoring only 8 points, a franchise low in the playoffs. This game was a warning bell for me. I tried to let the players figure out on their own how to find their inner resolve and reverse the collapse, but it didn't happen. One thing I did know, however, was that we had to stop Scottie's free-ranging attack. After the game I told Kobe that he would be covering Scottie.

We won the next two games in Portland to take a 3–1 lead in the series. The first was an inspiring come-from-behind victory featuring a go-ahead jumper by Harper with 29.9 seconds left. The highlight of the second win was Shaq's perfect nine-for-nine performance on the line, the best he'd ever done in the playoffs. But after that, when dreams of rings started floating in everyone's head, the Blazers scorched us in back-to-back games to tie the series, 3–3.

Nothing was working. We were down by 15 points at the half in game 6 and Fox went into a rage. "Here we go again," he said, referring to the Lakers' history of collapsing during the playoffs. "Everybody's got a blank look on his face. So what are we going to do about it? Are we going to let the referees dictate the terms of the game? Are we going to be passive and get blown out again? Or are we going to stand up on our own feet? Are we going to provide support for each other?"

Tex said to me, "You'd better tell him to shut up."

"No," I replied. "Somebody's got to say these things"—meaning a player on the team and not the coach.

Did I tell you how much I dislike seventh games? Well, this one was especially challenging. The Blazers were on a roll, and we were struggling to contain them. Then in the third period, they took off, scoring 18 points on seven possessions, and suddenly we were down 16 and floundering. To be honest, I thought we were dead in the water. So I called time-out and tried to inject some life into our dazed and confused troops.

Then something beautiful happened: The team found itself. The Blazers were killing us with high screen-rolls because Shaq was averse to coming out of his comfort zone and getting caught chasing after players such as Stoudamire or Smith. During moments like this, Shaq was in danger of falling into a downward spiral of self-defeat, which had crippled him during big games in the past. The perfect example of putting a head on top of a head. So I told him, in no uncertain terms, that this was his moment. He needed to move out of the lane and start breaking down the screen-rolls no matter what. He nodded in agreement.

The other thing we needed to do was to stop trying to feed the ball to Shaq, who was being swarmed to death and had only 2 field goals in the first three quarters. We had a lot of players open, and the Blazers were daring us to make the shots they were giving us.

"Forget about Shaq," I said. "There are four guys around him. Shoot the shot, just shoot it."

The attack came from all angles. Brian Shaw, who was subbing for Harper, took off, hitting some key three-pointers, setting up Shaq for a big score, and battling Brian Grant for an important rebound. Kobe starting clicking on some plays we orchestrated for him. And our defense, led by a newly emboldened Shaq, shut down the Blazers' top shooters. During one stretch, the Lakers outscored the Blazers 25–4.

Then, with less than a minute left and the Lakers up by four, Kobe drove toward the basket and surprised everyone by lofting a beautiful pass to Shaq two feet above the rim, which he grabbed and dunked. It was a gratifying moment to see these two men come together for a perfectly coordinated play that put the game out of reach. That pass symbolized how far Kobe and Shaq had progressed since that unsettling team meeting during the winter when their egos collided. After that they had worked out a mutually agreeable way to collaborate that culminated in this dramatic closeout shot. That moment was an important turning point for our new team.

The championship finals against the Indiana Pacers would not be as transformative as our battle with the Trail Blazers. But it had its own dangers. The Pacers were the best shooting team in the league and had a lot of ways to make our lives difficult.

Their biggest threat, of course, was shooting guard Reggie Miller, known for his uncanny ability to weave through picks and hit game-winning jumpers. But they also had small forward Jalen Rose, a one-on-one artist; center Rik Smits, an impressive jump shooter; point guard Mark Jackson, a strong post-up player; versatile power forwards Dale Davis and Austin Croshere; and a strong bench that included three-point whiz Sam Perkins and superquick guard Travis Best. In addition, Indiana had one of the best coaching staffs in the game, with Dick Harter, a defensive guru, Rick Carlisle, the offensive coordinator, and Larry Bird, the head coach.

We got off to a good start. In game 1, in L.A., Shaq overwhelmed the Pacers with 43 points and 19 rebounds and Miller went flat, hitting only 1 of 16 shots. The game was decided early. Then two days later we had a replay, beating the Pacers with another Shaq virtuoso performance and 21-point nights for both Rice and Harper. The downside: Kobe sprained his ankle in the first quarter, and it looked as if he might have to miss the next game too.

Indiana bounced back and won game 3 in Indianapolis. But that wasn't the big story. Rice's wife, Christina, complained to reporters after the game that I was short-timing Glen, and the media jumped all over it. She told *Los Angeles Times* columnist Bill Plaschke, "If it was me, I would have already been Latrell Sprewell II" (referring to then-Warriors star Latrell Sprewell's choking attack on his coach P.J. Carlesimo). This was an outrageous comment, but Glen and I had already talked about restricting his playing time in certain situations, and he was on board. He handled the media masterfully, supporting his wife but not publicly defending her charges.

Besides, I had something more immediate to worry about: Kobe's ankle. Before the start of game 3, Kobe pleaded with me to put him in the game, even though his ankle was killing him. But after watching him painfully stand up on his toes in the hallway outside our locker room, I decided it was too risky to chance it and had him sit this one out.

Kobe was still in a great deal of pain three nights later, for game 4, but he insisted he could play through it, and it turned out to be his big night. The game was tight most of the way and went into overtime, but Shaq fouled out in the first minute of OT, and Kobe took over, hitting 8 of our 16 points to set up a 120–118 win. Afterward Shaq rushed on court and hugged the man he was now calling his "big little brother."

I was impressed with Kobe. This was the first time I saw how impervious he was to excruciating pain. He wasn't going to let anything stop him. That night he reminded me of Michael Jordan.

Then, true to form, we dropped the next game in dramatic fashion, losing by 33 points, the worst defeat of the season. The game was such an all-around fiasco, it made me question whether this team had the right stuff to win a championship. But Fox put a more optimistic spin on the game, saying, "It makes snapping back a whole lot of fun when you take a beating like we did today."

After reviewing the game tapes, we decided to change some of our defensive assignments, putting Harper on Miller, Kobe on Jackson, and Rice on Rose. We also moved A.C. over to front Smits because Rik had trouble catching passes that were lobbed over a defender's head. As expected, Smits had a bad game, hitting one for eight from the field. But the rest of the team was shooting in the Staples Center as if they were still playing at home. It wasn't until the fourth period—with the Pacers ahead 84–79—that the game started to turn.

One of our best moves was a play we called the "fist chest," which involved having two players do a screen-roll on the wing while another filled the corner. The beauty of the play was that it drew three Pacers away from the lane to cover the screen-roll and the corner shooter. That forced them to either cover Shaq one on one (a big mistake) or leave the corner shooter with a wide-open three (even worse).

We ran the fist chest six times in the fourth period, and it helped open up the floor for us. We also had success with a number of other plays, including one we dubbed the "Shaw-Shaq redemption," featuring Brian Shaw feeding Shaq with a lob pass high on the backboard. Kobe also came alive, hitting shots, pulling down rebounds, and most of all feeding Shaq, as we went on a 15–4 run at the start of the period to take the lead.

We were up 110–103 with 3:02 left when Bird finally resorted to the hack-a-Shaq strategy. In the next twenty-one seconds, they fouled Shaq twice, and he hit only one of his four free throws. So I decided to pull him out until the two-minute mark, when the Pacers would be hit with a technical if they deliberately fouled him. In the meantime, though, Indiana kept clawing back and narrowed the lead to 110–109 with 1:32 remaining.

That's as close as they got. With thirteen seconds left, Kobe hit two free throws to seal the win, 116–111. As he walked off the court, he pointed to his ring finger then waved his index finger in the air, as if to say this was just the first of many championships.

After the game, Dr. Buss teased me about my lack of patience. "Why did you have to win in the first year and make it seem so easy?" he joked. "It's making the rest of us look stupid for not doing it before."

To be honest, I never expected to win our first ring so quickly. I thought it would take the players at least two years to learn the system and gel into a cohesive unit. But this team was on the fast track to glory. It was gratifying to see that the basic principles we'd developed with the Bulls could be so effective in transforming a very different kind of team into champions. Obviously, Shaq's dominance was a key factor in our victory, and so was Kobe's relentless creativity. But what pleased me even more was the synergy the two of them exhibited in the last part of the season, after they realized that they needed each other to achieve the only goal that mattered.

I too had a personal breakthrough that season. I learned to overcome my fear of the unknown and create a new life in a new city without losing what I loved most. This was a time for me to establish new, deeper relationships with my children—not just Brooke, who lived in the house, but also my other children, who visited regularly. It was also a time for me to continue to open up spiritually. During difficult moments, meditation had helped me cope with all the uncertainty and self-doubt that arise when you break from the past and throw yourself into a new life. I felt more alive than I had in years.

What gave me the most pleasure, though, was watching this group of talented but undisciplined players shape themselves into a force to be reckoned with. They still had a lot to learn, but I was impressed by how quickly they had shifted from a me-oriented stage 3 team to a we-focused stage 4. Slowly, ever so slowly, they developed the confidence to bounce back from adversity and tap into a source of inner strength many of them had never experienced before. They faced their demons head-on and didn't blink.

16

THE JOY OF DOING NOTHING

Sitting quietly, doing nothing, spring comes,
and the grass grows by itself.

ZEN PROVERB

Sometimes when I'm filling out forms, I list my profession as "magician." I'm not trying to be mischievous. It's just that when I think of the ego-balancing act NBA coaches have to perform, making magic may be the best way to describe what we do.

That was certainly true in the fall of 2000, when we regrouped in L.A. to start the new season. The year *after* winning a championship is always the hardest. That's when everybody's ego rears its head and the uncanny chemistry the team felt just a few months earlier suddenly dissolves into thin air.

Rick Fox compares winning an NBA championship to getting your first Oscar. "It defines who you are," he says. "For the rest of your life you mean something." But it also changes your expectations. "You win a championship and you all go away and get patted on the back for several months," he adds. "Then you return for the new season, and you're saying, 'This is what I want to happen for me.'"

Most players try to conceal their personal agendas. But they're not hard to detect, especially when everybody starts playing together.

One of the beauties of the triangle offense is that it exposes each player's mind-set without his ever having to say a word.

The first thing I noticed was a loss of drive. The players had put their hearts and souls into winning the championship, and now many of them were on cruise control. But I decided not to ride them too hard in the early part of the season. Now that they were champions, I told them, it was time for them to start figuring out how to solve problems on their own.

Still, something was missing. We'd lost some of our savviest players in the off-season: Glen Rice left for New York as a free agent, A.C. Green got picked up by Miami, and John Salley retired. To fill the holes we'd acquired some solid players, including two former Bulls—forward Horace Grant and center Greg Foster—and J.R. Rider, a shooting guard who was capable of hitting 20-plus points a game, if he could stay focused. I also talked Ron Harper into postponing retirement for another year and made Rick Fox a cocaptain as well as the starting small forward. But as we trudged through the first two months of the season, losing more games than I thought we should, I could sense that this one was going to be an emotional roller-coaster ride. The team had lost its esprit de corps.

One player whose agenda wasn't hard to figure out was Kobe Bryant. He had worked hard over the summer—claiming to have taken 2,000 shots a day—and he'd made another quantum leap in performance. The fans loved his spectacular new moves, and his popularity soared, as he threatened to overtake Shaquille O'Neal in the all-important sale-of-eponymous-jerseys statistic. Kobe was off to an exhilarating start, leading the league in scoring and shooting close to 50 percent from the field. In early December he outscored rival Vince Carter 40–31 in a win over the Raptors in Toronto, and a local broadcaster proclaimed, "The Lakers were known last year as Shaq's team. Not anymore."

But Kobe was building his résumé at the expense of the rest of the team. Early in the season I'd asked him to keep playing the way he had the year before, running the offense through Shaq and sticking with the system until the final minutes of the game. Kobe responded by nearly doubling the number of shots he took each game and adopting an erratic style of passing—or more often, *not* passing—that infuriated his teammates, especially Shaq. Kobe's selfishness and unpredictability gave the other players a sinking feeling that he didn't trust them anymore, which further eroded team harmony.

The previous year Kobe had embraced the triangle offense. He couldn't wait to test drive the system that had turned Michael and the Bulls into champions. But at the start of this season he told me he thought the offense was boring and too simple, and it prevented him from displaying his gifts. I understood, but I told him we needed to win the most games with the fewest mishaps, including injuries and end-of-the-season fatigue. I don't think he bought it.

For me part of the challenge was that the Lakers were a very different team from the Bulls. We hadn't had a dominant center like Shaq in Chicago, so we'd adjusted the system to make the offense accommodate Jordan. With the Bulls we'd also had a great floor leader, Scottie Pippen, the man I've always said helped Michael to become Michael. By default the role of orchestrator on the Lakers fell to Kobe, but he wasn't interested in becoming Shaq's Pippen. He wanted to create shots for himself.

Rick Fox describes Kobe during this period as "willful and determined, like a bull in a china shop." In his first years with the Lakers, Rick often competed with Kobe for playing time. "Kobe's an alpha male," he says. "He looks at the world with the eye of someone who says, 'I know more than you,' and if you were in his way, he was going to push and push until you pushed back. And if you didn't push back, he was going to eat you."

Rick compares Kobe's competitive drive to that of M.J., whom Fox worked with at Jordan's basketball camps when he was a college student. Rick says: "There are no other individuals I've known who act like they do. To them, winning at all costs is all that matters. And they demand that everyone around them act the same way, regardless of whether they can or not. They say, 'Find somewhere inside yourself to get better, because that's what I'm doing every day of the week, every minute of the day.' They have no tolerance for anything less. None."

But Fox noticed a difference between Michael and Kobe. "Michael had to win at *everything*," he recalls. "I mean he couldn't drive from Chapel Hill to Wilmington without making it a race. Whether you wanted to compete or not, he was competing with you. But I think Kobe competes with *himself* more than anything else. He sets barriers and challenges for himself, and he just happens to need other people to come along with him. He's playing an individual sport in a team uniform—and dominating it. Once he steps off the court, though, he's not interested in competing with you in the way you dress or how you drive. He's obsessed with chasing the goals he set for himself at age 15 or 16."

Which is exactly what was making Kobe so difficult to coach. In his mind he had it all figured out. His goal was to become the greatest basketball player of all time. And he was certain he knew what he had to do to get there. Why should he listen to anybody else? If he followed my advice and cut back his scoring, he'd fall short of his ultimate goal.

How was I going to get through to this kid?

The player who was the most irritated by Kobe's self-serving style was Shaq.

After the playoffs, I'd told Shaq to have a good time over the summer and come back relaxed and ready to go. He got the first part of the message, but unfortunately he had trouble with the "ready to go" part. He arrived in training camp overweight and out of condition, and it took him almost half the season to get back in fighting shape. He looked exhausted, as if he were still trying to recover from the previous season, when he led the league in scoring and won all three MVP awards.

But early in 2000–2001 his shooting percentage declined, and his free-throw touch—which had never been great—disappeared. In early December Shaq broke Wilt Chamberlain's futility-at-the-line record by going 0 for 11 against Seattle. It got so bad that fans started sending me amulets and crystals to bring him luck. Even his three-year-old daughter started giving him tips. Tex Winter tried to work with Shaq but gave up after two days, saying that he was "uncoachable on free throws." So we brought in Ed Palubinskas, an Australian free-throw champion Shaq's agent had discovered, and his work paid off handily. By the end of the season, Shaq had improved his percentage on the line from 37.2 percent to 65.1 percent.

In late December, after a game against the Suns in which Kobe scored 38 points and Shaq struggled to get 18, O'Neal told general manager Mitch Kupchak and me that he wanted to be traded. Kupchak, who had replaced Jerry West after West had resigned unexpectedly over the summer, didn't take the request seriously. Mitch believed that Shaq was simply expressing his frustration with Kobe's attempts to hijack the offense.

This was the start of what evolved into a full-fledged feud between Shaq and Kobe over the question of who would lead the team. Clearly the alliance they'd formed the year before was falling apart.

I had encouraged the two of them to get to know each other better, in the hope that this would strengthen their bond. But Kobe balked at the idea of getting too close to Shaq and was appalled by the big guy's attempts to turn him into his "little brother." As Kobe explained, they came from different cultures and had little in common. Shaq was an army brat from the South by way of Newark, New Jersey, and Kobe was the worldly son of a former NBA player from Philadelphia by way of Italy.

They also had strikingly different personalities. Shaq was a generous, fun-loving guy who was more interested in getting you to laugh at his jokes than in winning the scoring title. He couldn't understand why Kobe always wanted to make everything so hard. "That's what drove Kobe crazy about Shaq," says Fox. "In the most serious moments, Shaq had to have fun. If he wasn't having fun, he didn't want to be there."

Kobe, on the other hand, was cool and introverted and could be bitingly sarcastic. Even though he was six years younger than Shaq, he seemed older and more mature. As former Lakers coach Del Harris said, "You ask what Kobe was like as a kid. That's just it, he was never a kid." But I think it was easy to mistake Kobe's worldliness and intense focus for maturity. As far as I could see, he still had a lot of growing up to do—and because of his nature, he'd have to do it the hard way.

Shortly after Shaq made his halfhearted trade appeal, a cover story on Kobe by Ric Bucher appeared in *ESPN the Magazine* in which Kobe hinted at being interested in moving to another team. The article referred to a conversation I'd had with him early in the season, asking him to turn down his game. Kobe's answer to me, in the story, was "Turn my game down? I need to turn it up. I've improved. How are you going to bottle me up? I'd be better off playing somewhere else." He also took a shot at Shaq. "If Shaq were a 70 percent free throw shooter," Kobe said, "it would make things so much easier. We have to know our strengths and weaknesses. I trust the team. I just trust myself more. Yeah, we won last year with the offense going through Shaq. But instead of winning the series in five and seven games, this year we'll have sweeps."

Recognizing how inflammatory these remarks might be to his teammates, Kobe tried to soften the blow by giving them a heads-up before the article appeared. But that didn't keep Shaq from going ballistic. "I don't know why anybody would want to change except for selfish reasons," he told reporters after our next practice. "Last year we were 67-15 playing with enthusiasm. The city was jumping up and down. We had a parade and everything. Now we're 23-11, so you figure it out." Then he dropped the bomb. "Clearly if the offense doesn't run through me," he said, "the house doesn't get guarded. Period."

It was tempting to inject my own ego into this dispute. In fact, that's what most of the media pundits thought I should do. But I was wary of turning what I considered a ridiculous sandbox fight into something more serious. I'd seen that happen too many times in Chicago when Jerry Krause would bluster his way into a volatile situation and end up making things worse. I generally prefer taking a page from the playbook of the other Chicago Jerry—Jerry Reinsdorf. He once said that the best way to handle most flare-ups is to sleep on them. The point is to avoid acting out of anger and creating an even stickier mess. And if you're lucky, the problem may resolve itself.

I'm not averse to taking direct action if that's what is called for, but like Reinsdorf, I've discovered that you can solve many difficulties with what Lao-tzu called non-action. This approach is often misinterpreted as passivity, but actually it's just the reverse. Non-action involves being attuned to what's happening with the group and acting—or non-acting—accordingly. In the foreword to his adaptation of Lao-tzu's *Tao Te Ching*, Stephen Mitchell compares non-action to athletic performance. "A good athlete can enter a state of body-awareness in which the right stroke or the right movement happens by itself, effortlessly, without any interference of the conscious will," he writes. "This is the paradigm for non-action: the purest and most effective form of action. The game plays the game; the poem writes the poem; we can't tell the dancer from the dance." Or as Lao-tzu proclaims in Mitchell's work:

> *Less and less do you need to force things,*
> *until finally you arrive at non-action.*
> *When nothing is done,*
> *nothing is left undone.*

With Shaq and Kobe I decided not to force the issue. Rather than try to strong-arm them into making nice, I let their conflict play itself out over the next few weeks. I didn't think it was worth escalating the fight and distracting the team from what I saw as the real problem: getting the players to regain the focus and self-discipline they'd had during our first championship run.

The day after the *ESPN the Magazine* article appeared I asked the media to back off the story. "This is our business," I said. "It isn't your business." Of course, I knew even as I said it that this was a futile request. We were in L.A., after all, the storytelling capital of the world. How could reporters resist a story about two young superstars clashing over who was going to be top dog?

At the same time, I didn't try to suppress the story or pretend it didn't exist. As Brian Shaw says, I let it "manifest" itself. "Phil allowed Shaq to be who he was and he allowed Kobe to be who he was," says Brian, "but at the same time, he let it be known that he was driving the bus. So when it got off course, he was going to be the one to steer it back in place. But as long as we stayed on the road, we could go ahead and take it wherever we wanted to."

During the next few weeks, Shaq and Kobe took their soap opera to absurd extremes. If Kobe noticed Shaq sidling up to one reporter, he'd refuse to talk to him or her, then promise an exclusive to someone else. And if Shaq saw that Kobe was getting his feet taped by one trainer, he'd insist on having his feet taped by another trainer. And so it went.

I was impressed by the way the rest of the players handled the situation. Most of them refused to take sides. Robert Horry made fun of the whole affair, calling it "a so-called feud between two big hot dogs." Brian Shaw, who had played with O'Neal in Orlando, said it reminded him of the clash between Shaq and rising star Penny Hardaway, except that Penny was okay playing Robin to Shaq's Batman, and Kobe wasn't. Brian liked to say that the Lakers weren't Shaq's team or Kobe's team; they were Dr. Buss's team, because he was the one writing the checks.

Rick Fox said the Shaq-Kobe split was reminiscent of the standoff between Larry Bird and Kevin McHale when Fox joined the Celtics in the early nineties. Larry was serious about everything, while Kevin took a more playful attitude toward the game. McHale made jokes at practice and often tossed crazy shots in the layup line, which drove Larry nuts. Everybody on the team was expected to pick sides between Larry and Kevin. It was a nightmare.

Fortunately, the Shaq-Kobe split didn't reach that point. By the time the All-Star game rolled around in mid-February, both players were sick of the spat and told reporters that they'd moved on. "I'm ready to stop answering these stupid questions," Shaq said. Meanwhile Kobe took the view that many of his teammates shared. "The things that don't kill you only make you stronger," he said.

Now that he's matured and is raising two headstrong daughters, Kobe laughs at what it must have been like dealing with him during that crazy season. "Both of my girls," he says, "they're at the stage where they feel like they know everything. It reminds me of me. I can imagine the headaches I gave Phil." But, he adds, "even though there were times when it seemed like I wasn't learning anything, I was learning."

From Kobe's perspective I used the rift between him and Shaq to strengthen the team. "Phil had two alpha males that he had to get going in the same direction," Kobe says now. "And the best way to do that was to ride my butt because he knew that's how he could get Shaq to do what he wanted him to do. That was fine with me, but don't act like I don't know what's going on."

In that sense, he's right. I pushed Kobe hard that season because he was more adaptable than Shaq. In fact, Tex, who was Michael Jordan's toughest critic, thought I should lighten up on Kobe. But I thought he needed strong direction on how to mature and grow. Kobe had all kinds of weapons. He could pass; he could shoot; he could attack off the dribble. But if he didn't learn to use Shaq the right way and take advantage of his enormous power, the team would be lost. Even though I knew it would inhibit Kobe's freewheeling style somewhat, I thought the best strategy for us was to get the ball to the big guy and have the defense collapse around him. It's not unlike football, where you have to establish your ground game before you can launch your aerial game. In basketball, you need to go inside first before you can go to your shooters and cutters for easy baskets.

Kobe understood this, but he had other forces driving him. "It was tough for Phil to rein me in," reflects Kobe, "because by nature I'm a number one. I had to go against my nature to become a number two. I knew I could lead a team, but it was a challenge for me because I'd never heard of a number two stepping into a lead role later on and winning."

But eventually, Kobe says, he reenvisioned the problem. "The way I looked at it," he explains, "I saw myself as a Navy Seal type of guy who goes in and does his job quietly. He doesn't get the accolades that he should have gotten, but the true basketball purists know what he's done."

After the All-Star break we went on a long road trip that I hoped would help bring the team closer together. As part of my annual give-each-player-a-book program, I presented Shaq with a copy of *Siddhartha*, Hermann Hesse's fictional account of the life of the Buddha. I thought the book might inspire Shaq to reexamine his attachment to material possessions. In the story the young prince Siddhartha renounces his luxurious life to seek enlightenment. The point I wanted Shaq to understand was that everyone has to find his or her own spiritual path—and accumulating more toys was not the way to get there. It was my way of nudging him to explore the road to inner peace—by quieting his mind, focusing on something other than his own desires, and becoming more compassionate toward his teammates, especially Kobe, who was dealing with some attachment issues of his own.

I was amused by the book report Shaq turned in a few weeks later. The gist was: This book is about a young man who has power, wealth, and women (much like me), and gives them all up to pursue a holy life (not so much like me). I would have been surprised if Shaq all of a sudden went on a search for enlightenment after reading the book, but I think the message about compassion hit home with him. He has a generous soul.

Kobe was a different story. The book I selected for him was *Corelli's Mandolin*, a novel set on a small Greek island occupied by the Italian army during World War II. During the course of the story, the islanders have to accept the fact that they no longer control their own destiny and must come together and adapt to the new reality. In the end, they win by losing. I hoped that Kobe might resonate with the message and its parallels to his own struggles with the Lakers. Unfortunately, he wasn't interested.

Still, life has a way of teaching us the lessons we need to learn. In the second half of the season, Kobe suffered a number of injuries—a sprained right ankle, a sore right hip, a sore right shoulder, and a sore right pinkie—that made him come face-to-face with his own vulnerability. Although earlier in the season Kobe had angered some of the veterans by saying that the team had "too many old legs," in March he was struggling and revealed to Brian Shaw that the players he most identified with were the old-timers, Harper, Grant, and Shaw himself. In her book about the 2000–2001 season, *Ain't No Tomorrow*, Elizabeth Kaye explores how Kobe's injuries softened his attitude toward his teammates and himself. "For the first time, on the court," reports Kaye, "Kobe could not simply power his way through everything. 'There are cracks and holes that I've always been able to get through,' he told Shaw, 'that I can't quite get through right now. I can't elevate the way I want to.'

"'That's how I feel every single day,' Shaw told him. 'So now this is where you grow up. This is where you say, okay, I have to rely less on my athletic ability and more on my smarts.'"

Luckily, not all the players were hobbled by injuries during the latter part of the season. After missing sixty-two games with a stress fracture in his foot, Derek Fisher returned, fired up and brimming with newfound confidence. His timing couldn't have been better. With Harper injured and Kobe out with the flu, we needed someone who could ignite the offense and lead the team out of its midseason doldrums.

When he charged out on the court for his first game—against the Boston Celtics at home—I could tell that this was a different Derek. He came out blasting, scoring a career-high 26 points, plus 8 assists and 6 steals. Not only that, his fearless attack on both ends of the court galvanized the team. That was the turning point in the season.

But we still had a few more hurdles to get over. The following week, just before a game in Milwaukee, a story appeared in the *Chicago Sun-Times* by columnist Rick Telander in which I mentioned a rumor I'd heard about Kobe sabotaging his team's games in high school early on so that he could make a dramatic comeback and dominate in the end. Not only was this an irresponsible, off-the-cuff remark, it turned out to be untrue. Kobe wasn't amused, and the Lakers soon got a call from his attorney threatening to sue me for slander. I apologized to Kobe in person, then later in front of the whole team. Still, I'd crossed a line and I knew it. What I didn't know then was that it would take years for me to fully win back Kobe's trust.

To make matters worse, during the Milwaukee game Kobe resprained his bad ankle, then missed the next nine games. This was a real blow coming so close to the playoffs. But while he was out, the team pushed it up another notch. In early April we went on an eight-game streak to close out the regular season. Midway through that streak, Kobe returned for a game against Phoenix at home, and it was clear that he had suited up as a "Navy Seal" that night. He spent most of the game giving the Suns a clinic on how to play righteous basketball, dishing off regularly to his teammates even after they flubbed their shots and playing aggressive defense, as we rolled to a 106–80 blowout. He told reporters after finishing with a (for him) mere 20 points, "It's not about scoring. It's about stopping people."

Basketball unfolds in strange ways. On many levels, this had been the toughest season of my career—tougher even than my last hurrah in Chicago. Who would have guessed that this team, which had looked like it was going to implode at any moment, would pull itself together at the end of the season and go on a winning streak to rival those of the best teams in the history of the game?

This was a team—despite all the turmoil—that knew it was destined for greatness, if only it could get out of its own way. During the heat of the meltdown, I talked a lot about the power of community. In L.A. it wasn't as easy to build community by traditional means because the players lived far away from one another and the city itself was seductive and distracting. But all the hardships we faced that season forced us to reunite.

In her book *The Zen Leader*, Ginny Whitelaw describes how joy arises when people are bound together by a strong sense of connectedness. "This joy may be more subtle than the 'jump for joy' variety," she writes. "It may feel like full engagement in what we do, and a quiet satisfaction arising. It may feel like energy that keeps renewing itself, much as pumping a swing seemingly gives us more energy than it takes."

This kind of joy is contagious and impossible to fake. The spiritual teacher Eckhart Tolle observes: "With enthusiasm you find you don't have to do it all yourself. In fact, there is nothing of significance you *can* do by yourself. Sustained enthusiasm brings into existence a wave of creative energy and all you have to do then is ride the wave."

As the playoffs began, the Lakers were riding that wave. I was struck by how poised and relaxed the players were in the closing minutes of games, compared to the previous year. Nothing seemed to faze them.

"The one thing people are starting to notice about our team now is how much composure we have," Fish told the *Los Angeles Times*'s Tim Brown. "We're not playing out of control; we're not turning the basketball over a lot. I think those are trademarks of not only Phil, but our whole coaching staff. Their personality." Fish was impressed by how the coaching staff continued to prepare the team meticulously for every game, no matter what was going on with Shaq and Kobe.

Clearly the players were beginning to internalize the coaching staff's chop-wood-carry-water attitude. A key moment occurred during the second game of the Western Conference finals against the San Antonio Spurs when I was ejected in the third quarter of the second game for stepping into a ref's space and supposedly impeding his ability to do his job. In the past, the team would have lost its bearings and gone into a slide, but this time the players turned up the defense and ended the game with a 13–5 surge to win, 88–81. "We've matured," said Fox afterward, "to the point where we maintained our composure. Outside of Phil."

After sweeping the Portland Trail Blazers in the first round, we faced the Sacramento Kings, who tried several different tactics to stop Shaq without much success. In game 1 Vlade Divac played him straight up, and Shaq scored 44 points and grabbed 21 rebounds. Then they put Scot Pollard on him for most of game 2, but that reduced Shaq's numbers by just 1 point and 1 rebound. Finally in game 3 on their home court, the Kings upped the pressure even more, swarming Shaq and hacking him relentlessly in the fourth quarter. Happily, that created a world of opportunities for other players, especially Kobe, who scored 36 points as we mounted a 3–0 lead in the series.

Later that night Kobe flew back to L.A. to spend time with his wife, Vanessa, who had been hospitalized with excruciating pain. He stayed with her until she stabilized, then flew back to Sacramento for game 4, during which he erupted for 48 points and 16 rebounds to lead the team to another sweep. His wild enthusiasm inspired his teammates. "I was prepared to do whatever," he said. "I was going to run and push myself to exhaustion. It doesn't matter."

By the time we arrived in San Antonio for the conference finals, we had won fifteen straight (including regular-season games), and the pundits were already speculating about our becoming the first team to sweep the playoffs. Getting past San Antonio wasn't going to be easy, though. They had two of the best big men in the game—David Robinson and Tim Duncan—and the best record in the league that season, 58-24. The last time we'd faced them, they had beaten us on our home court. But that was in March, before Fish's comeback. Ancient history.

Robinson and Duncan did a respectable job on Shaq, holding him to 28 points. But nobody on the Spurs seemed to know what to do with Kobe, who put up 45 points, the highest total by anyone against the Spurs in playoff history. An exuberant Shaq fist-bumped Kobe at the end of the game and gushed, "You're my idol." Later O'Neal told reporters, "I think he's the best player in the league—by far. When he's playing like that, scoring, getting everybody involved, playing good defense, there's nothing you can say. That's where I've been trying to get him all year."

When I'd first started working with Kobe, I'd tried to persuade him not to push so hard and to let the game flow more naturally. He'd resisted then, but not now. "Personally, I just tried to feed off my teammates," he said after that game. "That's one way that I am improving: learning how to use my teammates to create opportunities, just playing solid and letting the game and the opportunities come to me." He was sounding more and more like me.

When we returned to L.A. for game 3, we went on a 111–72 romp during which Kobe and Shaq combined for 71 points, or one fewer than the entire Spurs lineup. Then two days later we closed out the series. This time the hero was Fish, who made 6 of 7 three-point shots and scored a career-high 28 points.

Although we tried to play it down, it was hard to ignore that something big was happening. "It's become greater than Shaquille," said Fox after the game 3 win. "It's become greater than Kobe, greater than any effort by one or two people. I've never seen it before. It's as though we're starting to round into the team we thought we'd be."

None of this talk about making history intimidated the Philadelphia 76ers, the team we faced in the championship finals. They were a tough, fiery team led by guard Allen Iverson who that year at six feet, 165 pounds, became the smallest player ever to win the MVP award. Iverson dismissed talk of a sweep, pointing to his heart and saying, "Championships are won here."

After his whirlwind performance in the Staples Center in game 1, it looked as if he might be right. He scored 48 points, and the Sixers snuffed out our 5-point lead in overtime, ending our storied streak at 19. I was actually relieved when the media hoopla surrounding the streak died down. Now we could focus on beating the Sixers without distractions. Before the next game Iverson told reporters that the Sixers were going to "spread the war," hoping to intimidate Kobe and the rest of the team. But Kobe didn't back down when Iverson's jibes turned into a trash-talk shouting match at midcourt. And he silenced Iverson by scoring 31 points with 8 rebounds, as we banged out a 98–89 win.

That was just the beginning. Game 3 in Philadelphia was another street fight, but this time Shaq and Fish fouled out with a little over two minutes left and the Lakers up by 2. No problem. In the closing minutes, Kobe and Fox gutted it out, while Horry appeared out of nowhere to nail the win with another one of his trademark three-pointers and four free throws. "The 76ers have heart, but so what?" said Shaw. "You can have heart and lose. We have heart and we have injuries and we just play through it."

The rest of the series flew by. We won game 4 with "a whole lotta Shaquille O'Neal," as Iverson put it. Then we clinched the title two days later in a game that few would call a work of art. As often was the case, Horry summed up the moment perfectly. "It's closure," he said, referring to the difficult season. "So much turmoil. So many problems. So many people talking about what we weren't going to do. It's closure. That's what it boils down to."

I was relieved that this crazy season was finally over. Yet when I reflect back on it, I realize that I learned an important lesson that year about transforming conflict into healing. Gandhi once said, "Suffering cheerfully endured ceases to be suffering and is transmuted into an ineffable joy." If we had tried to squelch the strife instead of letting it play itself out naturally, this young, growing team might never have come together the way it did in the end. Without the pain, the Lakers would not have discovered their soul.

17

ONE-TWO-THREE—LAKERS!

To be trusted is a greater compliment than to be loved.

GEORGE MACDONALD

One day early in the 2001–02 season, Rick Fox told me he wasn't feeling high anymore, and it was driving him crazy. He wasn't talking about drugs; he was referring to the spiritual high he'd felt during our second championship run. Rick grew up in a Pentecostal family in the Bahamas, and he understood right away when I talked about basketball as a spiritual game. He said that when everybody was playing with one mind, it was a beautiful experience that made him feel higher than anything else he'd ever done. Then, all of a sudden, the feeling evaporated like a dream, and he longed to get it back.

I knew what he was talking about. I'd been there myself. The feeling Rick described is sometimes referred to as "spiritual addiction"—a sense of connectedness so powerful, so joyful, you never want it to stop. Trouble is, the more you try to hang on to the feeling, the more elusive it becomes. I tried to explain to Rick that his experience during the previous season, though profound, was just one moment in time; it was a losing battle to try to re-create it because everything had changed, including Rick himself. Sometimes basketball can be a joyride, as it was for us at the end of 2000–01, and sometimes it can be a long, hard slog. But if you look at each season as an adventure, it takes on a beauty all its own.

I knew on day one that 2001–02 wasn't going to be easy. Three-peats never are. The good news was that Kobe and Shaq were getting along. They weren't taking potshots at each other, and I often saw them laughing together at practice and after games. During a road trip to Philadelphia, Shaq and several other players attended a jersey-retiring ceremony for Kobe at Lower Merion High School, and Shaq hugged Kobe on stage afterward.

Not all the changes were so welcome; the team was in a state of flux again. In general, the Lakers' rosters were much more fluid than the Bulls' had been. There's a group portrait in Jeanie's office of the players who took part in all three championships during my first run as the Lakers' coach. The painting includes just seven players: O'Neal, Bryant, Horry, Fox, Fisher, Shaw, and Devean George. The rest of the roster was filled with an ever-changing rotation of players, some who played critical roles, others who never quite found their niche. This musical-chairs environment made it challenging to sustain a strong sense of team unity from one season to the next.

In the off-season we lost the last two ex-Bulls on the team: Ron Harper to a long-postponed retirement and Horace Grant to a spot on the Orlando Magic. We replaced them with two solid players: Mitch Richmond, a six-time All-Star guard, and Samaki Walker, a promising power forward from the San Antonio Spurs. But it was impossible to replace Ron and Horace's championship experience and steadying influence on the team.

If the second season felt like a soap opera at times, the third was reminiscent of *Oblomov*, the Russian novel about a young man who lacks willpower and spends most of his time lying in bed. Our biggest problem was boredom. That's true of many championship teams, but it was more pronounced with the Lakers. This team had been so successful so fast that the players had begun to believe that they could flip a switch whenever they wanted to and automatically rise to another level—the way we had done the year before.

Fox had an interesting theory about what was going on. He thought the players' egos were so inflated by the start of the season that they believed they knew more than the coaches did about what they had to do to win another ring. As he puts it, "The first year we all blindly followed. The second year we joyfully contributed. And the third year we wanted to drive the ship." Rick remembers having a lot more debates that year than before about the coaches' decision-making process. "I wouldn't call it anarchy," he adds, "but I started to see guys act out more and express their opinions more and try to figure out ways to get around the triangle." The result, he says, was that the team was often out of sync.

This didn't surprise me. I'd seen it before with the Bulls during their first three-peat season. As far as I was concerned, the Lakers were evolving into a more mature team, the inevitable result of our effort to empower the players to think for themselves instead of being dependent on the coaching staff for all the answers. I always welcomed debate, even if it disrupted team harmony temporarily, because it showed that the players were engaged in solving the problems. The big danger was when a critical mass of players jettisoned the principle of selflessness upon which the team was founded. That's when chaos ensued.

The mistake that championship teams often make is to try to repeat their winning formula. But that rarely works because by the time the next season starts, your opponents have studied all the videos and figured out how to counter every move you made. The key to sustained success is to keep growing as a team. Winning is about moving into the unknown and creating something new. Remember that scene in the first Indiana Jones movie when someone asks Indy what he's going to do next, and he replies, "I don't know, I'm making it up as we go along." That's how I view leadership. It's an act of controlled improvisation, a Thelonious Monk finger exercise, from one moment to the next.

But complacency and oversize egos weren't the team's only problems.

My biggest worry was Shaq's health. Before he left for the summer, he had promised to return at his rookie weight, 290 pounds. Instead, he showed up weighing more than 330 pounds, recovering from surgery on his left pinky, and with severe toe problems.

With Shaq, as with the rest of the players, I needed to suss out the most effective way to communicate. Fortunately, from the beginning Shaq and I were able to get through to each other with a minimum of bullshit. At times I'd be very direct. For example, just before the second game of the finals in 2001, I told him not to be afraid of going after Allen Iverson when he drove to the basket. Shaq was so taken aback by the implication that he was frightened of Iverson that he forgot to lead the team in the "1-2-3-Lakers" pregame chant. Still, that night O'Neal blocked 8 shots and, in effect, neutralized the Iverson threat. At other times, I'd motivate him indirectly through the media. During our midseason doldrums in 2000–01, I goaded Shaq into hustling more by telling reporters I thought the only players who were going all out were Kobe and Fox. Shaq felt stung by this comment, but after that he became much more aggressive on the floor.

Shaq had a great deal of respect for male authority figures because that's how he'd been raised by his stepfather, Phil, a career military man whom Shaq called "Sarge." In fact, during my first year with the team, Shaq started referring to me as his "white father." He was so hardwired to respect authority that he would often have other people tell me when he didn't want to do something. That first season I asked him to play forty-eight minutes a game instead of his typical forty. Shaq gave it a try for a week or two, going most of the way in several games, but then he decided he needed more rest. Instead of telling me himself, he appointed John Salley his messenger. On another occasion Shaq sent one of the trainers in to tell me that he wouldn't be coming to practice that day. When I asked why, the trainer said that Shaq, who had been training to become a police officer, had been up all night cruising the city looking for cars on the LAPD's stolen-vehicles list. At heart the big guy dreamed of being a real-life Clark Kent.

The Lakers staff called Shaq "the Big Moody" because he tended to get grumpy when he was struggling with injuries or disappointed in his game. Much of his frustration was directed at me. Early in the 2001–02 season I fined him for taking two days off when his daughter was born instead of the one day he'd requested. In response, Shaq told reporters, "That motherfucker knows what he can do with that fine." But in the next game, he scored 30 points with 13 rebounds against Houston.

Grandstanding in the press didn't trouble me as much as when Shaq lashed out in person at one of his teammates. That happened in a game against the San Antonio Spurs during the 2003 playoffs. Shaq was furious because Devean George had made a mistake at the end of the game that allowed Malik Rose to pick off an offensive rebound and put up the game-winning shot. Shaq started to go after Devean in the locker room after the game, but Brian Shaw made him stop.

Shaw was the team's truth teller. He had a good read on the team's prickly interpersonal dynamics, and I encouraged him to speak his mind. "My mother always told me growing up that my mouth would get me in trouble someday," says Brian, "because if I saw something that wasn't right, I had to point it out. I felt that as long as I was telling the truth, I'd be all right. You can't be mad at the truth."

When Brian saw Shaq attacking Devean, he called out to him, "If you'd used that much energy blocking out under the boards, you would have gotten yourself a rebound and we probably would have won the game. So instead of taking it out on Devean, why don't you take responsibility for where you came up short?" At that point, Shaq let Devean go and went after Brian, who tried to tackle him but ended up getting dragged around the locker room by Shaq until his knees were bleeding and the other players pulled him off.

"Shaq was mad at me because I hurt his feelings," says Brian. "But a couple days later, he came up to me and said, 'You know, you were right. It was my bad. I shouldn't have gone off like that.'"

Kobe was also going through a difficult transition that season. During the previous spring, he'd fallen out with his family over his marriage to Vanessa Laine, a then-eighteen-year-old recent high school graduate. Kobe's parents, Joe and Pam, who had been living with him in his Brentwood home, argued that he was too young to marry. But Kobe was eager to start his new life. "I do everything young," he told reporters. Joe and Pam, who had been regulars at Lakers games, returned to Philadelphia but didn't attend the championship finals that year in the family's hometown. It wasn't until two years later that Kobe and his parents reconciled. In the meantime he and Vanessa moved to a new house, a block away from her mother in Newport Beach, and had their first child, Natalia.

In his rush to make it in the NBA, Kobe had missed out on college and some of the growing pains that go along with being out in the world for the first time. After breaking with his parents, he started to establish himself as his own man, sometimes in surprising ways. Kobe had always avoided clashes with other players, but during the 2001–02 season, he became belligerent at times. Once he got into an argument with Samaki Walker while traveling on the team bus, then suddenly took a pop at him. Samaki laughed it off, saying, "It was good to see the intensity." Later, during a game in the Staples Center, Kobe reacted violently to Reggie Miller's trash talk, balling his fist and chasing Miller around the court until they crashed into the scorer's table. Kobe was suspended for two games.

Kobe had a lot of pent-up rage inside, and I worried that he might do something he might regret someday. But Brian, who had become Kobe's confidant and mentor, thought that these clashes were signs that Kobe was "branching out into manhood and establishing what he was going to stand for and what he wasn't." Watching Kobe, whom I had named cocaptain that year, go through these growing pains, says Brian, "you could see that he was obviously maturing, becoming more of a good teammate and one of the guys. There were times when he would still go off and say things, but for the most part he was much more comfortable in his own skin and a lot more confident about being who he is."

Improvising was the only way we could get through the 2001–02 season. Nothing that happened followed any pattern I'd seen before. We took off on a 16-1 run, the best start in franchise history, and the media began whispering that it looked like we could break the Bulls' 72-10 season record. That didn't last long. In December we sank into a puzzling lethargy that lasted through mid-February. Even though we held our own with our toughest rivals, we lost six times during that period to last-place teams, including twice to the rebuilding Bulls. We leveled off somewhat after that, but we were never able to flip that illusory switch everybody was talking about.

I knew this team was capable of playing much better basketball. The trick was trying to hold body, mind, and spirit together until we got to the playoffs. One of my biggest disappointments was figuring out how to get the most out of Mitch Richmond. Mitch was a terrific scorer who'd averaged 22.1 points coming into the season, but he had a difficult time adapting to the triangle offense. He also wasn't adept at jumping in and out of games off the bench because he needed a lot of time to warm up his legs. Fortunately, Shaw was able to fill in for Mitch as the third guard at the end of the season. Because the bench wasn't that strong, we had to rely heavily on the starters to play extra minutes, and the cracks were beginning to show. To prevent the starters from getting worn out too early, I decided to lighten up on the team during the final stretch. As a result, we entered the playoffs tied for second place in the Western Conference and still searching for our mojo.

We swept Portland in the first round, but we didn't look impressive doing it. It wasn't until we lost at home to the Spurs in the second game of the Western Conference semifinals, tying the series at 1–1, that we woke up and started playing like champions.

Shaq was suffering. To add to his toe problems, he'd sliced the forefinger of his shooting hand in game 1 and sprained his left ankle in game 2. Still, I thought he needed to be more aggressive and told him so. When reporters questioned me about him before game 3 in San Antonio, I said, "I had a heated conversation with Shaq, actually, about getting actively involved in chasing the ball down. . . . He said, basically, his toe [hurts]." Shaq had been avoiding the media that week, but when a reporter pressed him for a comment, he said, "Ask Phil, he knows every other fucking thing."

But Shaq came through in the game the way I expected. He scored 22 points despite his torn finger and pulled down 15 rebounds despite his troublesome feet. He also helped contain the Spurs' biggest threat, Tim Duncan, who missed 17 of 26 shots from the field.

Although Shaq rallied, this was Kobe's moment. With 6:28 left and the Lakers ahead, 81–80, Kobe scored 7 points in an 11–2 run that sealed the win. Afterward he sounded as if he'd just returned from a meditation workshop. "I was more centered and focused on all the stuff around me," he said. "If you get too emotionally wrapped up in a game, you overlook the little details. You have to step outside the circle."

That game showed me just how good this team could be in the fourth quarter. In game 4, we were behind by 10 points with 4:55 left, and Kobe came alive again, hitting 2 three-pointers, then making a rebound and put-back in the last 5.1 seconds to put the game away, 87–85. Two nights later we went on a 10–4 run in the final minutes to win the series, 4–1. This team was finally finding its identity as one of the great closers in the game. It was not a moment too soon.

The fans in Sacramento—home to our opponents in the Western Conference finals—loved to hate the Lakers. Ever since I'd joked a few years earlier that the state capital was a semicivilized cow town, the fans had been trying to get back at me, clanging cowbells and screaming obscenities behind our bench, among other diversionary tactics. Of course, it didn't help that we had eliminated the Kings from the playoffs for the past two years.

But this time the team's faithful had reason to be optimistic. Their boys had finished the season with the best record in the league (61-21) and had home-court advantage through the playoffs. The Kings were one of the best shooting teams I've ever seen. In addition to All-Star power forward Chris Webber, the team had a balanced lineup of shooters who could hurt you from all directions, including Vlade

Divac, Predrag Stojakovic, Doug Christie, and Hedo Turkoglu, plus a quick new point guard, Mike Bibby, who was fearless when it came to penetrating defenses and putting up clutch shots.

We won the first game in Sacramento, setting a record for consecutive playoff wins on the road (12). But the Kings struck back in game 2, taking advantage of Kobe, who was recovering from an attack of food poisoning. The big surprise came in game 3, which the Kings won handily behind Bibby and Webber, who combined for 50 points. Unfazed, Kobe joked with reporters after the game, "Well, we're not bored now."

The miracle shot happened in game 4. It looked bleak in the first half, when we fell behind by 20 points and couldn't get our offense moving. But we shifted the momentum in the second half, slowing down their fast-paced offense and eating away at their lead. With eleven seconds left, we had narrowed the lead to 2. Kobe drove to the basket and missed. Shaq grabbed the rebound and also missed. Kings center Vlade Divac batted the ball away and it ended up in the hands of Robert Horry, who was standing alone at the three-point line. As if everything were scripted, he squared up, released his shot, and watched it drop perfectly as the buzzer sounded. Lakers 100, Kings 99.

This was vintage Robert Horry, the kind of shot that young boys dream about. But we still had a long way to go before we could silence the cowbells. The Kings roared back and took game 5 on their home court, going ahead 3–2 in the seven-game series. But the Lakers didn't panic. At 2:30 A.M. on the morning of game 6, Kobe phoned his new best friend, Shaq, and told him, "Big fella, need you tomorrow. We'll make history." Shaq was still up, of course, mulling the upcoming game, and they revved each other up. "Facing elimination, this is nothing for us," Kobe later told reporters. "He felt the same way I did."

Shaq was unstoppable that night. He scored 41 points with 17 rebounds and completely dominated in the paint. The Kings threw everybody they could at him, and in the closing minutes both Divac and Scot Pollard fouled out, and all they had left was backup center Lawrence Funderburke, who was helpless against Shaq's inside moves. "You have to foul me to stop me—period," Shaq said later. Kobe was also on fire, scoring 31 points, including four critical free throws in the final seconds that nailed down the victory, 106–100.

The following Sunday a welcoming committee of Kings fans bared their butts as our bus arrived at Arco Arena for game 7. The players laughed. If nothing else, the prank helped take some of the edge off what may have been the toughest game they'd ever faced. This was an excellent road team, but playing a seventh game on an opponent's court is the most drop-dead-challenging test. The last time I had been in this predicament was as a player in 1973 when we had to beat the Celtics in a seventh game in Boston to win the Eastern Conference finals. That was one of the most unnerving—and exhilarating—moments of my career.

The Lakers were remarkably calm. Earlier that day we had meditated together at the hotel, and I'd been pleasantly surprised to see that everyone was seated and ready to go when I walked into the room. As we sat in silence, I could sense that the players were pulling themselves together, preparing mentally for the showdown that awaited them. These men had been through a lot together and knew instinctively that their connection with one another would be the force to dispel anxiety as the pressure mounted during the game.

They were right. This wasn't just a basketball game; it was a grueling marathon that lasted more than three hours. But in the end, it was the Lakers' collective composure that won the day. The lead changed seventeen times, and the game went into overtime when Bibby made two free throws to tie the score at 100, and Shaq missed a fourteen-footer at the buzzer. It was a brutal test of wills, and, as Fish told Bill Plaschke, we had to dig "deeper than we've ever dug before."

I was more animated than usual because I wanted to keep the players focused. Kobe said he thought the Kings were playing better basketball than we were. But we scrambled harder, which paid off in the final minutes of the game. Fox pulled down a playoff career record of 14 rebounds, and Horry grabbed 12 more. Meanwhile, the Kings were visibly shaken. Normally coolheaded, they misfired on 14 of their 30 free throws, while we hit all but 6 of our 33. And during the final two minutes of overtime, they squandered a 2-point lead by missing 5 shots in a row and turning over the ball twice.

The closeout was a group effort. Shaq hit a short jumper, then nailed two free throws, while Fish and Kobe each hit two from the line to put the game out of reach. Afterward the players were so weary they could barely celebrate, but they weren't surprised by the outcome. "We've been playing together for five years," said Horry. "If we don't understand what to do by now, something's wrong."

Shaq, who played a grueling fifty-one minutes, seemed less buoyant than usual after the game. But as our bus was pulling out of the parking lot, he spotted a crowd of Sacramento fans cursing at us and, lowering his pants, decided to give them a fond farewell, Sacramento style. One of our guys called it "a full moon rising."

In my mind that was the title game, but we still had the championship finals to get through. Our opponent, the New Jersey Nets, had one of the best point guards in the game, Jason Kidd, and an impressive power forward, Kenyon Martin, but they didn't have an answer for Shaq. They tried to have rookie Jason Collins cover him, but Shaq walked all over him, averaging 36 points en route to his third straight finals MVP award. Riding on Shaq's shoulders, we swept the Nets and became the first Lakers team to win three rings in a row since the club moved from Minneapolis in the early sixties. Now we could legitimately call ourselves a dynasty.

With this victory, I tied Red Auerbach's record for most championship titles won: nine. The media made a big deal about this, especially after Auerbach said it was hard to consider me a great coach because I'd never built a team or trained young players. I said that I was dedicating the victory to my mentor, Red Holzman, who would have been thrilled to see me tie his archrival, had he still been alive.

What mattered more to me, though, was what had happened to the team. When I started with the Lakers I thought we could accomplish great things if we could get to the point where the players trusted one another enough to commit to something larger than themselves. Midway through that long, hard season, when we were being embarrassed by the Memphis Grizzlies, I'm not sure I would have bet money on our chance of making history. But in the final hour, when it really mattered, the players dug deep and formed themselves into a championship team built on trust.

The player who understood this best—surprisingly—was Kobe Bryant. Not long before, he would have scoffed at the idea. But he had grown, and the team had grown with him. "We've been through so many battles," he said, "the trust naturally grows. The more wars you fight together the more you understand the people you're in battle with."

One breath. One mind. One spirit.

18

THE WISDOM OF ANGER

Holding on to anger is like grasping a hot coal
with the intent of throwing it at someone else;
you are the one who gets burned.

THE BUDDHA

t was supposed to be a peaceful summer. As I tooled through the
Rockies on my motorcycle in late June, I was glad to put the
2002–03 season behind me. It had been a tough year, marred by a
lot of injuries—from Shaq's toe to Kobe's knee to Rick Fox's foot.
We'd limped into the playoffs and barely survived a grueling first-
round series against the Timberwolves. The capper, injurywise, for
me took place during the semis against the San Antonio Spurs. That's
when I learned that one of my coronary arteries was 90 percent blocked
and I required an emergency angioplasty. As it turned out, the heart
procedure had a much happier ending than the contest with the Spurs.
For the first time in my four years with the Lakers we didn't even
make it to the Western Conference finals, let alone capture a ring.

Yes, I was more than ready to let go of that season. Since my surgery I'd been feeling better than I had in years, and I welcomed the
chance to contemplate the next chapter as I sailed across the mountains. Although the team had lost Robert Horry to the Spurs in the
off-season, we'd acquired Gary Payton and future Hall of Famer Karl

Malone. Malone was the quintessential power forward who could score 20-plus points and get 8 to 10 rebounds per game, while plugging up the lane with his sizable body. Payton was not only one of the best point guards in the league but also a tenacious defender (hence his nickname, "the Glove") who I hoped would slow down some of the league's pesky small guards. I had some concerns about how to mesh these big talents with Shaq and Kobe without creating a lot of bruised egos. Still, this was a good problem, and I was jazzed.

I took my time riding my BMW from L.A. across Arizona, up through Four Corners and into Durango, Colorado, where I caught up with a friend and a cousin. After crossing the breathtaking mountain pass into Ouray, my next stop was Eagle, Colorado, a small town near Vail. I was there to pick up a buddy from high school—we were heading to our fortieth reunion in Williston, North Dakota. When we left I had no idea that in a few days Eagle would make headlines and embroil me in a nightmare of pain and misinformation.

My friend and I had passed through Deadwood, South Dakota, and had just checked into a motel in my hometown of Williston when I got the phone call.

It was Mitch Kupchak calling to tell me that Kobe had been arrested in Eagle for alleged sexual assault. Without informing me or anyone else on our staff, Kobe had scheduled knee surgery with a specialist in Vail. Apparently, the night before the operation he had invited a nineteen-year-old woman to his hotel room in nearby Edwards for what he termed "consensual" sex. The following day the woman went to the police claiming that she'd been forcibly raped.

Watching the story unfold over the next few weeks, it was hard to assess what had actually happened. I had difficulty believing that Kobe was capable of committing such an act, and the evidence seemed superficial at best. On July 18, the day he was formally charged, he held a news conference with his wife, Vanessa, by his side. Kobe vehemently denied raping his accuser but admitted tearfully to having had an adulterous sexual encounter with her.

I was not without sympathy for Kobe and tried to reach him, without success, after I heard the news. This was a lot to handle for a young man who had just turned twenty-four—especially someone who often boasted to his teammates that he planned to be monogamous for life. Now he was being charged with a crime that could put him behind bars for years. What's more, Kobe had always been meticulous about his public image, and suddenly he was fodder for the tabloid media and late-night comedians.

For me, the incident cracked open an old wound that had never fully healed. Several years earlier, when my daughter Brooke was in college, she had been the victim of an assault while on a date with a campus athlete. I had never felt entirely clear about my response. Brooke expected me to get angry and make her feel protected. Instead I suppressed my rage—as I'd been conditioned to do since childhood. In truth, there wasn't much I could have done; the case was in the hands of the police, and meddling on my part would probably have done more harm than good. Still, burying my fury and maintaining a calm exterior didn't give Brooke any comfort; it left her feeling vulnerable. (In the end, after filing a report with the police, Brooke chose not to press charges.)

The Kobe incident triggered all my unprocessed anger and tainted my perception of him. I discussed my inner emotional wrestling match with Jeanie and was surprised by her pragmatic take on the situation. In her view, this was a legal battle, and Kobe was one of our star employees. We needed to provide him with the best support possible to help him fight this battle and win.

To me, the way forward wasn't so clear-cut. Although I knew it was my professional responsibility to help Kobe through this ordeal, it was hard for me to shake my anger because of what had happened to Brooke.

My struggle to come to terms with my anger reminds me of an old Zen story: One rainy evening two monks were walking back to their monastery when they saw a beautiful woman who was having difficulty navigating the puddles in the road. The elder monk offered to help and carried her over the puddles to the other side of the road.

Later that evening the younger monk approached the elder monk and said, "Sir, as monks we're not supposed to touch women."

"Yes, brother," replied the elder monk.

"So then, sir, why did you lift that woman by the roadside?"

The elder monk smiled and said, "I left her on the side of the road, but you are still carrying her."

Like the younger monk, I had a fixed idea in my head and it distorted my view of Kobe throughout the 2003–04 season. No matter what I did to extinguish it, the anger kept smoldering in the background. Which, unfortunately, set the tone for much of the weirdness that followed.

Of course, Kobe's alleged crime and my reaction to it weren't the only factors at play that year. When I returned to L.A. in September, there was a perfect storm brewing with the team. Not only did we have to deal with Kobe's legal issues, but he was also due to become a free agent at the end of the season. This, in turn, would force Dr. Buss to make some tough decisions about the future of the organization. The early signs indicated that Kobe wanted to move to another team where he could be the main man and not have to compete with Shaq for that honor. The team he seemed most interested in was our local rival, the Clippers. Early in the season he made an awkward attempt

to discuss his future with Clippers coach Mike Dunleavy—a viola-
tion of NBA rules. To his credit, Mike didn't let the conversation get
very far.

Meanwhile Shaq wasn't feeling the love. He came to training camp
asking for a two-year, $60 million extension on his contract, due to
run out in 2006. That would be a high price to pay for a star who was
already beginning to lose some of his edge. Dr. Buss, who had always
been generous with Shaq, balked at the price tag. So Shaq acted out
as only Shaq could. During an exhibition game against the Golden
State Warriors in Hawaii, he slammed down a dunk and shouted to
Dr. Buss, who was sitting courtside, "Now you going to pay me?"

Another aspect of the gathering storm was my contract, also scheduled to expire that year. Dr. Buss and I met before the season started
to discuss the general outline of a deal and agreed to hammer out
details later. Part of me wanted to take some time off from basketball
to clear my head and focus on other interests. To a large degree, my
decision would depend on the outcome of negotiations with Kobe
and Shaq. If the Lakers had to make a choice between the two stars,
I favored keeping Shaq because it would be easier to build a championship team around him than around Kobe. As the season progressed, however, it became clear that Dr. Buss didn't share my view.

Before the start of training camp, I met with Kobe and tried to get
a read on how he was doing. He'd lost weight and appeared tired and
gaunt. He'd also developed a hard edge that I hadn't seen before. I
assured him that I would make it as easy as possible for him to get
through the season. When I asked Kobe how he was feeling, he was
not especially forthcoming; his way of handling stress was to retreat
inside. Toward the end of our conversation, however, he told me, with
a determined look, that he wasn't going to put up with Shaq's bullshit
anymore.

He was serious. After Kobe's shaky debut in a late exhibition game,

Shaq suggested that Kobe needed to modify his game and rely more on his teammates until his leg got stronger. Kobe snapped back that Shaq should worry about his own position, not the guard spot. But Shaq wouldn't let it go. "Just ask Karl and Gary why they came here," he said. "One person. Not two. One. Period. So he's right, I'm not telling him how to play his position. I'm telling him how to play team ball." Shaq also said that if Kobe didn't like him voicing his opinion, he could opt out next year because "I ain't going nowhere."

A few days later Kobe hit back with a searing critique of Shaq's leadership in an interview with Jim Gray on ESPN. If this was going to be Shaq's team, Kobe said, he needed to set an example. That meant not coming to camp fat and out of shape and not blaming others for the team's failures. "'My team' doesn't mean only when we win," Kobe said. "It means carrying the burden of defeat just as gracefully as you carry a championship trophy." Kobe also said that if he decided to leave the Lakers at the end of the season, a major reason would be "Shaq's childlike selfishness and jealousy."

Shaq was furious and told Mitch Kupchak that he was going to mess Kobe up the next time he saw him. So Mitch and I decided to separate Shaq and Kobe when they arrived at the training facility the following day to prevent one of them from doing something stupid. I took Shaq and Mitch took Kobe. Later when I spoke to Kobe, he revealed that what really angered him about Shaq was his decision to have toe surgery too close to the start of the previous season, which Kobe believed had put our chances of winning a fourth ring in jeopardy. I'd never heard Kobe mention that before.

Fortunately, after the last round of heated exchanges, things quieted down for a while. It helped to have on the team veteran players like Karl and Gary who had little or no patience for this kind of juvenile one-upmanship. It also helped that we got off to a brilliant 19-5 start. Alas, our success was short lived. In December Karl injured his right knee in a home game against the Suns and was out for most of the season. We didn't have a strong backup for Karl, and we went into a period of malaise until we rebounded late in the season.

My strategy of giving Kobe space didn't seem to be working. The more liberty I gave him, the more belligerent he became. Much of his anger was directed at me. In the past Kobe had been passive-aggressive when he didn't want to do something I asked of him. Now he was aggressive-aggressive. He made sarcastic cracks in practice and challenged my authority in front of the other players.

I consulted a psychotherapist, who suggested that the best way to deal with someone like Kobe was to (1) dial back the criticism and give him a lot of positive feedback, (2) not do anything that might embarrass him in front of his peers, and (3) allow him to think that what I wanted him to do was his idea. I tried some of these tactics and they helped somewhat. But Kobe was in heavy-duty survival mode, and when the pressure became unbearable, his instinctive reaction was to lash out.

I realized there wasn't much I could do to change his behavior. But what I could do was change the way I reacted to his angry outbursts. This was an important lesson for me.

Managing anger is every coach's most difficult task. It requires a great deal of patience and finesse because the line between the aggressive intensity needed to win games and destructive anger is often razor thin.

In some Native American tribes, the elders used to identify the angriest braves in the village and teach them to transform their wild, uncontrolled energy into a source of creative power and strength. Those braves often became the most effective tribal leaders. That's what I've tried to do with the young players on my teams.

In Western culture we tend to view anger as a flaw that needs to be eliminated. That's how I was raised. As devout Christians, my parents felt that anger was a sin and should be dispelled. But trying to eliminate anger never works. The more you try to suppress it, the more likely it is to erupt later in a more virulent form. A better approach is to become as intimate as possible with how anger works on your mind and body so that you can transform its underlying energy into something productive. As Buddhist scholar Robert Thurman writes, "Our goal surely is to conquer anger, but not to destroy the fire it has misappropriated. We will wield that fire with wisdom and turn it to creative ends."

In fact, two recent studies published in the *Journal of Experimental Social Psychology* demonstrate a link between anger and creativity. In one study, researchers discovered that feelings of anger initially improved the participants' ability to brainstorm creatively. In another study, the same researchers found that subjects who were prompted to feel angry generated more creative ideas than those who experienced sadness or a nonemotional state. The conclusion: Anger is an energizing emotion that enhances the sustained attention needed to solve problems and leads to more flexible "big picture" thinking.

No question, anger focuses the mind. It's an advance-warning system alerting us to threats to our well-being. When viewed this way, anger can be a powerful force for bringing about positive change. But it takes practice—and no small amount of courage—to be present with such uncomfortable feelings and yet not be swept away by them.

My practice when anger arises is to sit with it in meditation. I simply observe it come and go, come and go. Slowly, incrementally, over time I've learned that if I can stay with the anger, which often manifests itself as anxiety, and resist my conditioned response to suppress it, the intensity of the feeling dissipates and I'm able to hear the wisdom it has to impart.

Sitting with your anger doesn't mean being passive. It means becoming more conscious and intimate with your inner experience so that you can act more mindfully and compassionately than is possible in the heat of the moment.

This is hardly easy, but acting mindfully is key to building strong, trusting relationships, especially when you're in a leadership role. Says Buddhist meditation teacher Sylvia Boorstein, "An unexpressed anger creates a breach in relationships that no amount of smiling can cross. It's a secret. A lie. The compassionate response is one that keeps connections alive. It requires telling the truth. And telling the truth can be difficult, especially when the mind is stirred up by anger."

From the moment of Kobe's arrest, I had a lot of practice working with my anger that year, and Kobe was my main teacher. In late January he showed up at the training facility with a bandaged hand and announced that he'd have to miss that night's game. It seems he'd accidentally put his hand through a glass window while moving boxes in his garage and required ten stitches in his index finger. I asked him to do some running during practice and he agreed but never did it. Afterward I asked him why he'd lied to me, and he said he was being sarcastic.

I wasn't laughing. What kind of adolescent game was this guy playing? Whatever it was, I didn't want any part of it.

After practice I went upstairs and told Mitch Kupchak we needed to talk about trading Kobe before the mid-February deadline. "I can't coach Kobe," I said. "He won't listen to anyone. I can't get through to him." It was a futile appeal. Kobe was Dr. Buss's wunderkind, and he was unlikely to trade him, even if it meant jeopardizing our shot at another ring.

A few days later Dr. Buss, who worried that his young star might jump to another team, visited Kobe in Newport Beach and tried to persuade him to remain with the Lakers. Obviously, I wasn't party to the meeting, but shortly thereafter, while we were riding on the team bus, Kobe told Derek Fisher, "Your man's not coming back next year." The "man" he was talking about was me.

I felt completely blindsided. Clearly, Dr. Buss had shared information with Kobe about the team—and my future—before consulting me. It was a harsh blow, and Kobe seemed to be reveling in it. Deep down, this turn of events made me question whether I could trust Kobe or Dr. Buss.

Later that day I called Mitch and told him I thought that he and Dr. Buss were making a big mistake. If they had to choose between Shaq and Kobe, I advised going with Shaq because Kobe was impossible to coach. And, I added, "You can take that to the owner."

A few days later my agent called to tell me that the Lakers were suspending contract negotiations with me. When the Lakers announced the news on February 11, reporters asked Kobe if my departure would affect his free-agency plans and he replied coldly, "I don't care." Shaq was stunned. He couldn't fathom how after all we'd been through, Kobe could throw me under the bus. I asked Shaq to refrain from stirring things up. The last thing the team needed was another verbal shooting match between the two players.

Jeanie was convinced that the Lakers were deliberately trying to undermine me, and she was probably right. Still, I found the announcement strangely liberating. Now I could focus on the task at hand—winning one more championship—without having to worry about the future. The die had been cast.

———

After the All-Star break, I met with Kobe to clear the air. Obviously, my laissez-faire approach with him had backfired and was having a negative effect on the team. Kobe had interpreted my efforts to give him a wide berth as indifference. So I decided to take another tack and work much more actively with him. My intention was to help him focus his attention on basketball so that the game would become a refuge for him in the way that it had been for Michael Jordan when he was being hounded by the media over his gambling problems.

But the team was in a perilously fragile state. I asked Kobe to stop making divisive comments that confused the young players and threatened to divide the team even further. Now that the issue of my contract had been settled, I added, we were free to focus on this year alone and not worry about anything else. "You and I can work this out, right?" I asked him. He nodded. I knew this wasn't the end of the friction between us. But it was a good beginning.

The question of Kobe's free agency was a dark cloud hanging over the team. Nobody knew which way he was going to turn. To complicate matters, he was away from the team a great deal, in both body and spirit. And when he was present, he seemed detached and often fell back on his old habit of trying to win games on his own. We hadn't exactly gelled into "Dream Team IV" as some sportswriters had predicted early in the season.

Kobe wasn't our only problem. Gary Payton was having adjustment issues of his own. Gary was used to having the ball in his hands most of the time, but now he had to share it with several other ball-hungry players. And he was struggling to find his rhythm. As the point guard for the Sonics, he was used to attacking off the dribble and posting up smaller guards. Now he had to work within the triangle offense, which he felt stifled his ability to express himself creatively. Not only that, he'd lost a step or two on defense, which caused columnist Mark Heisler to joke that his nickname should be changed from "the Glove" to "the Pot Holder."

Still, soon after Karl Malone returned to the lineup in March, the team started to win again and went on an 11-0 streak. During that period I began to give Fish more playing time late in games because he had a better feel for the system than Payton. I also made Kobe the team's floor general and put him in charge of directing the action.

But the rift between Kobe and rest of the team was growing. During the final week of the season, Kobe, who had never been shy about shooting, took just one shot in the first half of a game against Sacramento, allowing the Kings to take a 19-point lead and win handily. The media concluded that Kobe had intentionally tanked the game to improve his negotiating position with Dr. Buss. Kobe said he was just doing what the coaches had asked him to do—share the ball—but nobody bought it. One player, speaking anonymously, told the *Los Angeles Times*'s Tim Brown, "I don't know how we can forgive him."

This led to an ugly scene at practice the next day. Kobe burst into the training facility in a rage and polled every player, one by one, trying to find out who was responsible for the quote. It was a wrenchingly painful episode.

At the start of the season, one writer had called the Lakers "the greatest array of talent ever assembled on one team." Now we were slumping into the playoffs in second place in the Western Conference and feeling as if we were coming apart at the seams. The injuries were mounting. Malone had sprained his right ankle, Devean George had strained his calf, Fish had pulled a muscle in his groin, and Fox was hampered by a dislocated right thumb.

But the injuries weren't the worst of it. Given all the distractions, my greatest concern was that the team had yet to find its identity. As Fish said, "This year just seems like nothing ever really got settled.

Every time it seemed like we were kind of settling in and getting to know each other and playing good, something would happen that would take us back a couple steps. I think that was the biggest difference with this season. There was never really a point where we got comfortable as a team."

It wasn't until we fell behind 2–0 in the Western Conference semifinals against the San Antonio Spurs that we started to wake up. In game 3, at the Staples Center, we reverted to our standard winning formula—playing ironclad defense and feeding Shaq in the post—and overwhelmed the Spurs, 105–81. The next game featured a stunning performance by Kobe, who flew back from his arraignment in Colorado to score 42 points with 6 rebounds and 5 assists, leading the Lakers to a come-from-behind victory and a 2–2 tie in the series. Afterward an overjoyed Shaq dubbed Kobe "the best player ever"—including Michael Jordan. This wasn't the first time Kobe had lifted the team after flying back from one of his court appearances in Colorado. But it was the most inspiring. Basketball, he said, was "kind of like a psychologist. It takes your mind away from so many things. So many things."

The fifth game, in San Antonio, was when the magic really happened. We were up by 16 in the third quarter, but the Spurs clawed back and regained the lead in the closing minutes. With eleven seconds left Kobe put up a twenty-footer that gave us a 72–71 edge. That set up what should have been the final play with five seconds on the clock: an off-balance fallaway eighteen-footer by the Spurs' Tim Duncan that miraculously went in.

The Spurs started jumping up and down as if the game already had been won. I told the players at the time-out that even though there was less than half a second left on the clock, we were still going to win. Payton took the ball out of bounds, and Robert Horry, who knew our last-second shot set, took the passing lane away. As a result, Gary had to call another time-out. This time I told him to look for the open man, whoever it was, and he found Fish breaking free on the left side of the key. With nanoseconds left, Fish grabbed the pass and shot a miracle turnaround jumper. Swish. Game.

We put away the Spurs in game 6 and proceeded to take apart the Timberwolves in six games to win the Western Conference finals. But Malone reinjured his knee in the last game, which disrupted our momentum and put a big question mark over the upcoming championship finals against the Detroit Pistons.

Even before Malone's accident, I was nervous about the Pistons. They were a young, cohesive team that was peaking at the right moment, having just won the Eastern Conference finals against the team with the league's best record, the Indiana Pacers. Our players didn't take the Pistons that seriously because they didn't have a lot of big-name stars, but they were coached by one of the best, Larry Brown, and created tough matchup problems for us. Chauncey Billups, a strong, inventive playmaker, could easily outrun Payton or Fisher; Tayshaun Prince, a six-nine, long-armed defender, would give Kobe trouble; and we had no good answer for their power-forward double threat of Rasheed Wallace and Ben Wallace. Brown's strategy was to draw offensive fouls on Shaq by having his big men fall down when he backed in. Before each series I spent a lot of time visualizing new ways to neutralize our next opponent's attack. With the Pistons, I was drawing a blank.

It started with game 1 in L.A. The Pistons outmaneuvered us defensively and grabbed back home-court advantage, even though Shaq and Kobe combined to score 59 points. We rebounded in game 2 and squeaked out a win in overtime. But when the series moved to Detroit, we started to struggle and weren't able to recover. Malone's knee continued to cause him problems and the engine ground to a halt. The Pistons roared to victory in five games.

My biggest disappointment during this season was our inability to shut out all the distractions and mold this talented group of superstars into the powerhouse it should have been. There were some great individual performances—from Kobe, Karl, and others—but in the end we remained a collection of mostly aging veterans with tired legs, struggling to keep up with a young, hungry, energetic team that was not unlike the Lakers of a few years past.

To Fox, the reason we lost was simple. "A team always beats a group of individuals," he said. "We picked a poor time to be a group of individuals."

For Fish, the demise of the Lakers started much earlier, in the middle of our third championship run. As soon as success became a normal part of the team's culture, he says, "the players started to take more credit for what was happening. So there was less focus on what the coaching staff brought to the equation and more focus on whose team it was. Was it Shaq's team or Kobe's team? And which guys on our roster needed to step up and get better? All those things began to creep into the locker room, and it really changed the energy and the cohesion that was there those first few years."

The collapse happened quickly. Shortly after the playoffs ended, Dr. Buss confirmed what Mitch Kupchak had already told me. He said that the team was moving in a different direction and wouldn't be renewing my contract. And not surprisingly, he was planning to trade Shaq and hoped to re-sign Kobe. I told Dr. Buss that losing Shaq would probably mean handing over at least one championship to whoever got him. He said he was willing to pay that price.

My prophecy came true. In mid-July, the Lakers traded Shaq to Miami, and he led the Heat to a championship two years later. One day after the Shaq trade, the Lakers announced that Kobe had re-signed with the team. His trial in Colorado proceeded with jury selection on August 27 and was over by September 1. The judge dismissed the charges after the prosecution dropped the case. Apparently, their key witness, Kobe's accuser, refused to testify.

Coaching legend Cotton Fitzsimmons once said that you don't know what kind of coach a guy's going to be until he's been fired. I'm not sure what this says about me, but in any case, I was ready to take a break from basketball and find some other ways to nourish my mind and spirit. I had some work to do on *The Last Season*, a book I was writing about my time with the Lakers. After that, I was heading far away from L.A. on a seven-week head-clearing trip to New Zealand, Australia, and various points around the South Pacific.

Despite all the intense drama, I felt good about what I'd accomplished with the Lakers during the five years I had been with the team, even though I wished I could have rewritten the ending. And I was encouraged by the positive shift in my relationship with Kobe by the time I left. Coming to terms with anger is always treacherous and inevitably puts you in touch with your own fears, frailties, and judgmental mind. But the steps Kobe and I took that season, each in our own way, laid the foundation for building a stronger, more conscious connection in the future.

When I look back at this time, it feels like the end of an important chapter for me—in a good way. Coaching the Lakers was like having a wild, tempestuous fling with a beautiful woman. And now it was time to move on and try something new.

19

CHOP WOOD, CARRY WATER

Forget mistakes, forget failures, forget everything,
except what you're going to do now and do it.
Today is your lucky day.

WILL DURANT

'd just started my sabbatical in Australia when I got a call from Jeanie. She said the situation with the Lakers was dire. The team had gone into a tailspin and the new coach, Rudy Tomjanovich, had resigned. Could I come back and save the team?

I can't say I was surprised. Rudy was a good coach who had won two championships with the Houston Rockets, but he had inherited a no-win situation in Los Angeles. What's more, Rudy had just completed treatment for cancer and just wasn't up to the job physically or emotionally.

The team wasn't up to the job either. The roster had been decimated in the off-season. Not only did the Lakers trade Shaq, but they also lost Karl Malone to retirement, Rick Fox to the Celtics (he retired a few months later), and Gary Payton and Fish to free agency. There were a few new players who came over from Miami in the Shaq trade—forward Lamar Odom, guard Caron Butler, and center/forward Brian Grant, who had knee issues. Kobe was trying to carry this as-yet-formless bunch all by himself but couldn't.

I told Jeanie that returning to L.A. was out of the question. I wasn't prepared to give up the rest of my trip, included a tour of New Zealand by motorcycle with my brothers. Nor did I have any interest in trying to rescue a team that was long past salvaging. "How about next season?" Jeanie asked.

"I'll think about it," I replied.

I suppose I might have felt a momentary flicker of schadenfreude, but, in fact, the demise of the Lakers didn't make me happy. I'd worked hard to transform the team into a champion, and it was painful to watch my former assistant coach, Frank Hamblen, try in vain to hold things together at the end of the 2004–05 season. This was the first time the Lakers had failed to make the playoffs since the early 1990s.

When I returned home, I talked to a number of other teams with open coaching positions, including New York, Cleveland, and Sacramento. But none of those jobs appealed to me as much as the idea of rebuilding the Lakers from the ground up—something I hadn't had the chance to do the first time around. But before I said yes, I needed to get a read on whether Kobe and I could work together again.

I hadn't talked to Kobe since our tense end-of-the-season meeting a year earlier. Since then, I'd published *The Last Season*, in which I revealed my frustrations about trying to coach him during the turbulent 2003–04 season. I had no idea what kind of reception I'd get from him, but when I called I didn't sense any hard feelings. Kobe's only request was for me to be more discreet with the media and not share personal information about him with reporters. That seemed reasonable.

I think we both realized that in order to succeed we needed each other's support and goodwill. Prior to the 2004–05 season, Kobe had boasted that as long as he played for the Lakers, the team would never fall below .500. But that's exactly what happened: The Lakers tied for

last place in the Pacific Division with a 34-48 record. That turned
out to be a real wake-up call for Kobe. He'd never known such failure
before, and it forced him to acknowledge that he'd have to wholeheartedly join forces with others if he was going to win any more
championships.

I knew that if I accepted the job, my first crucial task would be to
restore the team's lost pride. To my mind the sports pundits and fans
had turned on Kobe and blamed him—unfairly—for breaking up
the Lakers' great championship lineup. I thought my return might
help put some of that noise to sleep. I was also intrigued by the possibility of building a new championship team centered on Kobe instead of Shaq. But to make that happen, Kobe and I would have to
forge a deeper, more collaborative relationship, and he'd have to grow
into a different kind of leader than he'd been in the past. That would
take time, I knew, but I didn't see any insurmountable obstacles in
the way. Kobe seemed as eager as I was to bury the past and move on.

When I met with Dr. Buss to hammer out the details of a three-year
deal, I needed his assurance that I'd be given a bigger role in personnel
decisions and not be kept in the dark, as had been the case during the
Shaq-versus-Kobe stand-off in 2003–04. Dr. Buss agreed but turned
down my other request—getting part ownership of the team. Instead
he offered me a salary increase and explained that he planned to hand
over control of the Lakers to his six children. As part of that move,
he'd brought in his son, Jim, to learn the business so that he could
eventually take over the basketball side of the Lakers. Meanwhile,
Jeanie would continue overseeing sales, marketing, and finance.

Jim Buss had been promoted to VP of player personnel when I
returned in the 2005 postseason. He was eager to draft Andrew
Bynum, a talented high-school center from New Jersey, and asked me

to take a look at him when he came to L.A. for a tryout. My only reservation about Andrew was his running gait, which would lead to serious knee problems later on. But otherwise I thought he had the potential to develop into a formidable big man. I gave the deal my okay, and we made him the tenth pick overall. At seventeen, he was the youngest player ever to be drafted by the NBA.

My biggest concern about recruiting players right out of high school has always been the temptations of the NBA life. Many young players get so seduced by the money and fame that they never develop into mature young men or live up to their promise as athletes. In my view, the key to becoming a successful NBA player is not learning the coolest highlight-reel moves. It's learning how to control your emotions and keep your mind focused on the game, how to play through pain, how to carve out your role on the team and perform it consistently, how to stay cool under pressure and maintain your equanimity after crushing losses or ecstatic wins. In Chicago we had a phrase for this: going from a basketball player to a "professional" NBA player.

For most rookies it takes three or four years to get there. But I told Andrew that we were going to fast-track him because of the key role we envisioned for him on the team. I explained that if he pledged to dedicate himself to the task, I'd pledge to support him all the way. Andrew assured me that I didn't need to worry about his maturity; he was serious about stepping up. And he stayed true to his word. By the next season he would be the Lakers' new starting center.

Andrew wasn't the only player on the team who required this kind of training. We had several young players who needed to be schooled in the basics—including Smush Parker, Luke Walton, Brian Cook, Sasha Vujacic, Von Wafer, Devin Green, and Ronny Turiaf. Instead of a deficit, I saw this as an opportunity to build the new team from the bottom up, with a core group of young players who could learn the system together and provide us with a lot of energy off the bench.

Given the team's makeup, I found myself being less authoritarian and a more patient father figure than usual. This was a team that was crawling its way up from infancy—a new experience for me—and I had to nurture the players' confidence with care.

One major hurdle to get over with my new team was the lack of consistent scoring options beyond Kobe. I'd originally hoped that Lamar Odom would fill that bill. A former number-four pick overall who averaged 15-plus points a game, Lamar was a graceful six-ten forward with a freewheeling style of play that reminded me of Scottie Pippen. He was great at pulling down rebounds and pushing the ball up court to break down the defense in the open floor. With his size, agility, and playmaking skill, Lamar created matchup problems for a lot of teams, and I thought we might be able to turn him into a strong "point forward" à la Pippen. But Lamar had trouble learning the intricacies of the system and his game often fell apart when we needed him the most. I found that the best way to use Lamar was to give him the freedom to react spontaneously to whatever was happening on the floor. Whenever I tried to box him in to a set role, his spirit seemed to deflate.

There were others whose performance didn't quite match my expectations. Shortly after I returned, we picked up Kwame Brown in a trade with Washington, hoping to add some muscle to our front line. We knew that Kwame had been a disappointing number-one pick overall for the Wizards, but, at six feet eleven and 270 pounds, he had a good one-on-one game and the strength and quickness to defend the top big men in the league. What we didn't know until much later was that he didn't have any confidence in his outside shot. At one point during a game against Detroit, Kobe came over to the bench, laughing. "You might as well take Kwame out of the game, Phil," he said. "He just told me not to pass him the ball because he might get fouled and have to shoot a free throw."

Another player who had looked promising at first but lacked mental toughness was Smush Parker. Although on paper veteran Aaron McKie and European newcomer Sasha Vujacic looked stronger than Smush, he outplayed them both in training camp and scored 20 points in three of the first four regular-season games, so we anointed him starting point guard. Smush was a slight, crafty player who was good at slipping through defenses to attack the basket and playing tough, full-court defense. His shooting was erratic, but his spirited play helped energize the offense and get us off to a strong start that season.

But Smush had had a difficult childhood that left him fragile emotionally and limited his ability to bond with others. When he was young, his mother had died of AIDS. If everything was going his way, Smush could be the most energetic player on the floor. But when the pressure mounted, he had a hard time holding himself together. He was a time bomb waiting to explode.

Meanwhile Kobe continued to excel. In the first part of the season I told him to let loose since the team had yet to master the system—and he responded by shooting for the history books. Kobe scored 40-plus points in twenty-three games during the regular season and averaged a career-high 35.4 points. The highlight was his 81-point game against the Toronto Raptors in January at the Staples Center. He got ticked off in the third quarter when the Raptors went ahead by 18 points and he erupted for 55 points in the second half to lead the team to a 122–104 victory. Kobe's 81 was the second-highest total in NBA history, behind Wilt Chamberlain's legendary 100-point game in 1962. What made Kobe's performance different was the variety of shots he took from all over the floor, including 7 three-pointers—which didn't exist in the NBA in Wilt's day. To put Kobe's performance in perspective, the highest total Michael Jordan ever hit in a game was 69.

Ever since Kobe was a rookie, the question of whether he would become "the next Michael Jordan" had been the subject of endless speculation. Now that Kobe's game had matured, this no longer seemed like a frivolous question. Even Jordan has said that Kobe is the only player who can be compared to him, and I have to agree. Both men have an extraordinary competitive drive and are virtually impervious to pain. Michael and Kobe have both played some of their best games under crippling conditions—from food poisoning to broken bones—that would sideline lesser mortals for weeks. Their incredible resilience has made the impossible possible, allowing each of them to make game-turning shots with packs of defenders hanging all over them. That said, their styles are different. Michael was more likely to break through his attackers with his power and strength, while Kobe often tries to finesse his way through mass pileups.

As their coach, it's the differences between them that intrigue me more than their similarities. Michael was stronger, with bigger shoulders and a sturdier frame. He also had large hands that allowed him to control the ball better and make subtle fakes. Kobe is more flexible—hence, his favorite nickname, "Black Mamba."

The two men relate to their bodies differently as well. Trainer Chip Schaefer, who worked extensively with both players, says that Kobe treats his body like a finely tuned European sports car, while Michael was less regimented in his behavior and given to indulging his taste for good cigars and fine wine. Still, to this day Schaefer marvels at how graceful Michael was as he moved up the floor. "What I do for a living is all about athletic movement, and I've never seen anybody else move like that," he says. "The only word for it is beautiful."

The differences between Michael's and Kobe's shooting styles are also pronounced. Michael was a more accurate shooter than Kobe. He averaged nearly 50 percent from the field during his career—an extraordinary figure—and was often in the 53 percent to 54 percent range during his prime. Kobe averages a respectable 45 percent, but his hot streaks tend to go longer than Michael's did. Jordan was also more naturally inclined to let the game come to him and not overplay his hand, whereas Kobe tends to force the action, especially when the game isn't going his way. When his shot is off, Kobe will pound away relentlessly until his luck turns. Michael, on the other hand, would shift his attention to defense or passing or setting screens to help the team win the game.

No question, Michael was a tougher, more intimidating defender. He could break through virtually any screen and shut down almost any player with his intense, laser-focused style of defense. Kobe has learned a lot from studying Michael's tricks, and we often used him as our secret weapon on defense when we needed to turn the direction of a game. In general, Kobe tends to rely more heavily on his flexibility and craftiness, but he takes a lot of gambles on defense and sometimes pays the price.

On a personal level, Michael was more charismatic and gregarious than Kobe. He loved being with his teammates and security guards, playing cards, smoking cigars, and joking around. Kobe is different. He was reserved as a teenager, in part because he was younger than the other players and hadn't been able to develop his social skills in college. When Kobe joined the Lakers, he avoided fraternizing with his teammates. But his inclination to keep to himself shifted as he grew older. Increasingly, Kobe put more energy into getting to know the other players, especially when the team was on the road. During our second series of championships, he became the life of the party.

Both Michael and Kobe have impressive basketball IQs, but I wouldn't call either of them "intellectual" in the conventional sense of the word. Michael attended the University of North Carolina and is gifted at math, but he didn't show much interest in the books I gave him to read while I was his coach. Nor did Kobe, for that matter, though now he picks my brain regularly for book suggestions, especially ones about leadership. Kobe could have attended any college he wanted, but he skipped that step because he was in too much of a hurry to conquer the NBA. Still, he must have wondered whether he made the right choice, because in the summer of 1997 he strapped on a backpack and took a course in advanced Italian at UCLA.

One of the biggest differences between the two stars from my perspective was Michael's superior skills as a leader. Though at times he could be hard on his teammates, Michael was masterful at controlling the emotional climate of the team with the power of his presence. Once he bought into the triangle, he knew instinctively how to get the players on board to make it work.

Kobe had a long way to go before he could make that claim. He talked a good game, but he'd yet to experience the cold truth of leadership in his bones, as Michael had. Soon that too would begin to change.

Midway through the 2005–06 season, the players began to feel comfortable playing within the system, and they were starting to win games—even when Kobe wasn't breaking any records. I was thrilled to see the team progress faster than expected. We finished the regular season with an 11-3 run and rolled into the playoffs with a 45-37 record, an eleven-game bump over the previous season.

The momentum kept building, and we sailed to an unexpected 3–1 lead in the first round over the division-leading Phoenix Suns. Our game plan was to have Kobe draw double-teams, then feed Kwame and Lamar down low, a strategy that seemed to be working. Our come-from-behind win in game 4 was remarkable. With 0.7 seconds left in regulation, aided by a key steal by Smush, Kobe tossed up a baseline shot to tie the game, then hit a fallaway seventeen-footer with 0.2 seconds remaining for the win in overtime. "This is the most fun I've ever had," he said after the game. "Because this is *us*. This is us, the entire team, enjoying the moment with the entire city of Los Angeles."

We didn't celebrate for long. Hours before game 5 we learned that Kwame was being investigated for alleged sexual assault in L.A. The charges were eventually dropped, but the reports distracted the players and kept us from putting the series away in game 5. Then the momentum shifted in the Suns' favor. In game 6 Smush was increasingly reluctant to shoot, so Kobe encouraged him to focus on putting pressure on point guard Steve Nash defensively and not to worry about scoring. Still, despite a heroic 50-point performance by Kobe, we went down in overtime. After the game Smush fell apart emotionally, having scored just 5 points on 12 shots. And the team headed back to Phoenix to face the Suns in game 7 on their home turf. It wasn't much of a contest. At the half I told Kobe to revert to our original strategy and feed Lamar and Kwame in the post. So he dialed his game back and took only 3 shots in the second half. Unfortunately, Lamar and Kwame were missing in action and scored a combined total of 20 points, despite endless opportunities. As the game devolved into a 121–90 rout, the Lakers' worst loss ever in a game 7, I was reminded of how important character is when it comes to winning big games. What this team needed was more heart.

Not only did the team have some weaknesses, but so did I—a serious hip problem. I had hip replacement surgery just before the start of our 2006–07 training camp. This restricted my ability to move up and down the floor to monitor each player's performance during practice, and I had to learn to coach games from a specially designed chair. Interestingly, though I worried that my limited mobility might diminish my authority, just the opposite occurred. I learned to be forceful without being overbearing—further lessons in the school of *less is more.*

The 2006–07 season started with a flourish, but things got rocky in the second half when several players—including Lamar, Kwame, and Luke Walton—were down with injuries. The lineup got so thin at one point that I had to use six-five guard Aaron McKie as our power forward and Andrew Bynum took over at center. In February the team went into free fall, losing thirteen out of sixteen games in a single stretch. By mid-March Kobe was fed up and took matters into his own hands. Which worked for about two weeks. He scored 50-plus points in five of seven games and we won all but two. However, the other players complained about never seeing the ball, and I asked Kobe to back off.

Usually I tried to work the tail end of a season so that the team peaked going into the playoffs. But there was no hope of that happening this time. The team's chemistry was shot, and we'd run out of magic tricks. We ended the season with a 4-8 run and I finally gave up on Smush, replacing him with rookie Jordan Farmar, who was quicker and more reliable at covering fleet-footed guards.

But we needed a lot more than speed to keep pace with Phoenix in the first round. If anything, the Suns were an even stronger team that year. They'd won the Pacific Division title three years in a row and had the best point guard in the business, Nash, who had previously won two straight MVP awards. The Suns certainly didn't lack confidence. Before game 1, the *Los Angeles Times* ran a story that included an excerpt from *Sports Illustrated* writer Jack McCallum's book *:07 Seconds or Less*, in which Suns coach Mike D'Antoni critiqued several of our players' defensive flaws. "Kwame is awful," he said. "Odom's a very average defender. Vujacic can't guard anybody. And Bryant in the open floor takes chances that aren't good."

I didn't agree with Mike's assessment, but I was impressed by the Suns' level of chutzpah going into the series. Still, I thought we could surprise them again, if only we could stay focused.

That turned out to be a big "if." Throughout the series I showed the players clips of the movie *Hustle & Flow*, because, in my opinion, they needed more of both to outmaneuver the Suns. Obviously, they didn't get the message. The team sleepwalked through the first two games in Phoenix, then came alive to win in game 3 in L.A., only to fall back into a doze and lose the series, 4–1. I was so frustrated by the team's low energy in the decisive game 4 that I threw a mock fit and sent everyone home early from practice the next day. But lack of hustle (not to mention flow) was only part of the problem. We needed a blast of more seasoned talent to turn this team into a viable contender. Some of the young players I'd hoped would evolve into champions just couldn't hold their own in the clutch.

I wasn't the only one losing patience. Kobe was furious that the team hadn't made any significant personnel moves since trading Shaq to Miami. After game 5, he told reporters he was tired of being "a one-man show," scoring 50 points a game and losing. "I'm not with that," he said. "I'm about winning. I want to win championships and win them now. So, [the Lakers] have some decisions to make."

It wasn't an empty threat. After the playoffs he asked me how much progress we were making to bring in new talent. I told him we had talked about free agents and were considering players who might be available, but so far no deals had been made. "I guess I'm going to have to do something about that," he said.

A few weeks later, enraged by a story in the *Los Angeles Times* by Mark Heisler in which a "Laker insider" claimed that Kobe was responsible for the post-Shaq mess, Kobe made his displeasure public in a radio interview with ESPN's Stephen A. Smith. He criticized Dr. Buss for not being up front with him about the direction he wanted to take the team and demanded to be traded. Later, when speaking to other reporters, Kobe confirmed his desire to move on and said that he'd be willing to waive the no-trade clause in his contract to make that happen. In fact, during a training session that off-season for the 2008 Olympic team, he gave reporters no indication of whether or not he'd be suiting up in purple and gold when training camp rolled around in October.

There was one strong trade possibility in the offing that had the potential to get Kobe to change his mind and stay. That was with Minnesota for center Kevin Garnett. My hope was that Garnett would be a good partner for Kobe and that his addition to the lineup would help calm Kobe down and motivate him to recommit to the team. What's more, bringing Garnett on board could set us up for another solid championship run. But the trade fell apart at the last minute when Boston made an offer that Minnesota and Garnett found more attractive. Years later Garnett admitted that he wasn't in favor of the L.A. deal, in large part because of Kobe's dissatisfaction with the team.

None of us was thrilled by the prospect of trading Kobe. It's almost impossible to get equal value when you trade a player of his stature. The best deal you can hope for is one that gets you two solid starters and maybe a good draft pick, but not a comparable star. Nevertheless, Dr. Buss met up with Kobe in Barcelona over the summer and agreed to entertain trade offers from other teams as long as Kobe stopped mouthing off about it in the media. After a month or two without any progress, Kobe and his agent requested permission to put together a deal themselves and had several conversations with the Chicago Bulls, but nothing ever came of those efforts.

Right before the start of the 2007–08 season, Dr. Buss, Jim Buss, Mitch Kupchak, and I held several meetings with Kobe and his agent to discuss possible trades. None of them made any sense from a business perspective, so Dr. Buss asked Kobe to hang in there while we waited for better offers to emerge. Explaining his rationale, he told Kobe, "If I had a diamond of great value—say four carats— would I give it up for four diamonds of one carat each? No, there is no equal value we can get from a trade that would match what you bring to the team."

I granted Kobe a few days off from practice to mull over his op- tions. I wasn't unsympathetic to his dilemma, even though I still be- lieved we could turn the Lakers around. No question, losing Kobe would be a blow to the organization and to me personally. Kobe and I had been through tough times together, and during the past two seasons we'd started to forge a stronger relationship.

The will-he-or-won't-he question hung over the team like a thick band of clouds, and the rest of the players were distressed by all the uncertainty. I counseled them not to worry because Kobe's decision was out of our hands. All we could do was rededicate ourselves to the team and prepare for the upcoming season. We needed to be ready for whatever happened, with Kobe or without him.

As with everything else in life, the instructions remain the same, despite changing circumstances: Chop wood, carry water.

20

DESTINY'S CHILDREN

Connection is why we're here. It's what gives
purpose and meaning to our lives.

BRENÉ BROWN

A funny thing happened while we were in limbo: A new, more
dynamic team began to emerge.

Opening night at the Staples Center was rocky. We lost
95–93 to the Rockets, and the crowd booed Kobe when he was introduced. But three days later we went to Phoenix and beat our nemesis,
the Suns, decidedly, 119–98. Our leading scorer that night was newcomer Vladimir Radmanovic with 19 points, and we had four other
players in double digits. Derek Fisher, who had rejoined the Lakers in
the off-season, viewed the win as a harbinger of things to come. As he
later put it, "That game planted just the small seed in our mind that
if we played the right way, we could be pretty darn good."

By mid-January, we had a 24-11 record and had beaten most of the
best teams in the league. One of the reasons for our early success was
the coming of age of Andrew Bynum, who had been working on his
footwork and passing skills with Kareem Abdul-Jabbar and Kurt
Rambis and had developed into a serious scoring threat. Kobe was

quick to notice and started using him in screen-rolls, which created a lot of easy shots for Andrew. In the first three months, he averaged a career-high 13.1 points and 10.2 rebounds a game.

Another reason for our success was the influx of energy from several young backup players, including Radmanovic, Jordan Farmar, Luke Walton, and Sasha Vujacic. Although this crew still had a lot to learn, they'd come a long way. Best of all, they were lively and enthusiastic and improved the team's chemistry. And when they were clicking, they added a new, fast-moving dimension to our attack that was hard to stop. In late November we also acquired another talented young player, Trevor Ariza, in a trade with Orlando. He was a quick, versatile small forward who could attack the basket and hit outside shots on the run.

The third—and probably most important—reason for our early breakthrough was the second coming of Derek Fisher. Fish was a veteran of our run of three straight championships, and his return to the Lakers after three years at Golden State and Utah gave us a mature, experienced leader who could run the offense and give the team a much-needed sense of order.

As I've mentioned, one of the keys to our approach is to give players the freedom to find their own destiny within the team structure. Fish wasn't a creative playmaker like Steve Nash or Chris Paul. But he took advantage of his strengths—mental toughness, clutch outside shooting, and coolheadedness under pressure—to create a role for himself that not only worked for him but had a profound impact on the team.

"It sounds more mystical than it really is," he says of the process he went through. "The coaches' goal was to set down some basic guidelines for us on how to play basketball together as a group. And then you were expected to create your own chart for everything else. It was an uncanny way of creating organization without over-organizing. It wasn't about what they thought you should be doing, the way many coaches do. They stepped back and let you find your own way."

In his first incarnation with the Lakers, Fish started out as a backup guard. But he was a diligent student of the game and he continued to add new skills to his repertoire until he worked his way into a starting role in 2001, after Ron Harper left. And though at first he had trouble breaking through screens on defense, he learned to use his formidable strength to muscle his way around big men. He also developed a deadly three-point shot that came in handy in the closing minutes when opponents would gang up on Kobe, leaving Fish wide open to do serious damage. By the time we reached the three-peat season, Fish had become the Lakers' third leading scorer behind Shaq and Kobe.

He also was one of the most selfless players I've ever coached and a role model for the rest of the players. At the start of the 2003–04 season, I asked him to give up his starting job to make room for Gary Payton, and he did so without complaint. Yet as the season progressed, I increased his playing time, especially at the close of games. The offense just flowed more smoothly when Fish was on the floor.

After that season, he became a free agent and landed a lucrative five-year deal with the Warriors, but he never found a comfortable role for himself there. Two years later they traded him to Utah, where he played a key role as a backup guard in the team's drive to the Western Conference finals. But when his daughter was diagnosed with eye cancer that year, Fish approached me about coming back to L.A., where she could get better medical care. Eventually he worked out a deal with Mitch Kupchak that involved getting out of his contract with the Jazz and signing a new one with the Lakers at a reduced salary.

When Fish showed up, I made him cocaptain. I also told him that

I wanted to give backup point guard Jordan Farmar 20-plus minutes per game because he was good at coming off the bench and igniting the attack with his quickness and speed. Fish was fine with that, and together they averaged 20.8 points per game. Once I asked Fish what he needed to improve his game. He replied that he'd like to get more shots, but he knew that he'd have to take what he could get because someone had to run the offense, and it wasn't going to be Kobe or Lamar.

Fish was the perfect leadership partner for Kobe. They had come up together as rookies and trusted each other implicitly. Derek was more patient than Kobe and more balanced in his approach to problem solving. While Kobe infused the team with his drive to win, Fish had a gift for inspiring players with his words and keeping them grounded and focused. "Every time Derek gave a speech," says Luke Walton, "I felt that there should be music playing in the background, like one of those epic sports movies. When he talked, I wanted to write it down because nobody could have said it better."

Sometimes Fish acted as a mediator between Kobe and me. Once when I got on Kobe in a team meeting for shooting too much and disrupting the offense, he stormed off in a rage, saying he wouldn't take part in the day's shootaround. But Fish skillfully intervened, talking privately with Kobe and getting him to cool down.

When he returned to the Lakers, Fish quickly realized that he and Kobe had to adopt a different style of leadership from the one that had worked for us during our first run. There were no other championship veterans on this team, no Ron Harpers or John Salleys or Horace Grants. So Fish realized that if they wanted to get through to our roster of young, inexperienced players, he and Kobe would have to put themselves in their shoes. "We couldn't lead this team from 10,000 feet," he says now. "We had to come back to sea level and try to grow with our guys. And as that process took place, we started to feel a real connectivity and brotherhood."

January was a turning point for the team. Midway through the month Bynum dislocated his left kneecap in a game against Memphis—a tough blow that put him out of commission for the rest of the season. But the next day, in a radio interview, Kobe paid a tribute to Andrew that put an end to speculation that Kobe might be traded. During the off-season Kobe had poked fun at Bynum's inexperience, but now he sounded like his biggest fan, claiming that the Lakers were "a championship caliber team with him in the lineup."

Two weeks later I learned from Kupchak that he'd worked out a deal with the Grizzlies to bring All-Star center Pau Gasol to Los Angeles. (In return, Memphis got Kwame Brown, Aaron McKie, Javaris Crittenton, and the rights to Pau's brother Mark, currently an All-Star center with the Grizzlies.) The Pau deal reminded me of the moment in 1968 when the Knicks acquired Dave DeBusschere in a trade with Detroit, a deal one writer called "the basketball equivalent of the Louisiana Purchase." Like DeBusschere, Pau was mature and intelligent with a deep understanding of the game and a willingness to take on a diminished role, if necessary, to improve the team's chances of winning. He was the right personality at the right time. As soon as he arrived, we transformed from a team struggling to eke out 100 points a game to a fast-paced scoring machine, averaging 110-plus and having a lot more fun doing it.

A star on Spain's national team, Pau grew up immersed in a more collaborative European style of basketball, which made it easy for him to adapt quickly to the triangle offense. Pau's game was ideally suited for the triangle: Not only was he a solid seven-foot, 250-pound post player with a wide range of midrange jumpers, hook shots, and strong up-and-under moves, but he also was an excellent passer and rebounder who was quick enough to ignite fast breaks. His main weakness was his lower-body strength. He often got pushed off the block by some of the stronger, more aggressive big men.

Before Pau came on the scene, we were going through a minor losing streak, and some of the younger players were starting to act out in ways that were having a negative effect on morale. But all those issues disappeared as soon as Pau showed up. For one thing, the trade removed two of the most rebellious players—Kwame and Javaris. But even more important, Pau's gracious demeanor shifted the emotional climate on the team. It was hard to complain when one of the finest talents in the league was playing alongside you, doing whatever it took to win.

Pau's arrival also allowed several players to expand their games in unexpected ways. Lamar Odom, for instance, had been struggling for years—unsuccessfully—to establish himself as a strong number two player. But Pau's presence on the floor took the pressure off and freed Lamar to revert to the looser, freewheeling style of ball he was more comfortable with.

Kobe's game changed for the better as well. Kobe was thrilled to have a big man on the team with "a pair of hands," as he put it, and the two players quickly developed into one of the best one-two combinations in the league. Pau's presence also gave Kobe the opportunity to focus more attention on playmaking and letting other players take shots. That made him a better team player overall and, by extension, a better leader. Kobe was ecstatic with the key acquisitions we'd made that season, notably Fish, Trevor Ariza, and Pau. "Got a new point guard, got a new wing, got a Spaniard, and then it was all good," he said. "I had a bunch of Christmas presents that came early."

Kobe's bitter discontent that had infected the team in the preseason was now ancient history. Best of all, the character and heart needed to create a brotherhood of champions had been restored.

All of a sudden, everything started to break our way. With Pau in the lineup, we went on a 26-8 run and finished the season with the best record in the Western Conference, 57-25. And Kobe was voted the league's MVP, in part because he had blossomed into a better all-around player. The only team with a better record was the Celtics, who had acquired Garnett and sharp-shooting guard Ray Allen in the off-season and danced to the third-best record in franchise history, 66-16.

Usually talent wins out in the playoffs, but sometimes victories are decided by happenstance. For us it was a little bit of both. We pushed past the Nuggets and Jazz in the first two rounds, playing some of the most spirited, integrated basketball I'd seen in years. Afterward, while we waited to see which team we'd face in the Western Conference finals, a strange turn of events tipped the odds in our favor. The defending-champion Spurs won a hard-fought game 7 in New Orleans, only to be held up at the airport after the game. The team was forced to sleep on one plane while they waited for another to arrive. As a result, their flight didn't arrive until 6:30 A.M. Pacific time. Coach Gregg Popovich refused to blame this nightmare trip for his team's lackluster performance in the next two games, but I'm certain it played a role. They built up a 20-point lead in the third quarter of game 1 but flagged in the fourth, and we stole the game away from them, 89–85. Three days later they looked exhausted as we ran over them in a 30-point rout. The Spurs bounced back and won game 3 in San Antonio. But Kobe took over in the next two games and we closed out the series in five.

That set up a long-anticipated showdown with Boston. The rivalry between the Lakers and Celtics is one of the most storied in sports. In fact, Dr. Buss was so obsessed with the Celtics that he had put winning more championships than them on his bucket list. At the time we trailed Boston by two, 16–14, and had a dreadful 2-8 record against them in head-to-head clashes in the finals. This was the first time the two teams had faced each other in the finals since 1987, when the Lakers triumphed, 4–2.

I wasn't sure if our team was ready to knock the Celtics off again. They had a powerful front line, led by Garnett, Paul Pierce, and Kendrick Perkins, and I worried that they might be able to outmuscle us under the basket, especially with Andrew Bynum out of the picture. I also was concerned that our team had been too successful too soon and hadn't been tested hard enough in the earlier rounds to stand up to a tough, physical team like Boston.

The Celtics took game 1 in Boston, 98–88, inspired in part by the return of Pierce in the fourth quarter after leaving the game in the third with what looked like a serious knee injury. Then they cruised to a 2–0 lead in the series three days later. I was impressed with the way they played Kobe. They didn't double-team him, but they had several defenders switch off and assist whoever was covering him. That often prevented him from penetrating inside and kept him exiled to the perimeter for most of the game. Garnett, who was the league's Defensive Player of the Year, did an excellent job on Lamar, sitting on his left hand and challenging him to make jump shots. This made Lamar increasingly insecure. Garnett felt confident enough to sag off Lamar at times and help Kendrick Perkins punish Pau when he moved into the lane.

We bounced back briefly, winning game 3 at home, but collapsed in the second half of the next game and blew a 24-point lead to fall behind 3–1 in the series. After staving off embarrassment in game 5, we returned to Boston to endure such a lopsided defeat in the final game (131–92) that it haunted us all summer.

The tone was set early in the first quarter when Garnett plowed down the lane, knocked Pau to the ground, and dunked the ball over him while he lay on the floor trying to keep from getting hit. Naturally, none of the refs called a foul.

After the game, Kobe and I sequestered ourselves in a locker room used by the Boston Bruins, who play in the same stadium. Kobe was in a depressed state and took his time before going into the shower room. While we were sitting there, Ron Artest, who was then playing for the Sacramento Kings, dropped by and told us that he would like to be part of the Lakers someday. Little did we know that Artest would play a critical role for us the next time we faced the Celtics in the finals two years later.

The nightmare continued after we left the stadium. By then the streets were filled with mobs of rowdy Celtics fans, cursing the Lakers and trying to turn over the team bus while we were stalled in traffic. One fan stood on the front bumper, glared at me, and gave me the finger. I was angry at the Boston police for not doing anything to break up the crowd. But in the end I was thankful for the disturbance because it galvanized everybody on the bus into committing themselves to returning to Boston and repaying the Celtics in kind.

There's nothing like a humiliating loss to focus the mind.

After we returned home, my former Knicks teammate Willis Reed called to console me about the Boston fiasco. I told him I thought our players needed to grow up and take responsibility for what had happened during the finals.

"I figured you just left your guys out there to die in game 7," he said, "so that they could learn something from that awful feeling."

"Yes," I said. "Because you can't really understand what that's like unless you go through it yourself."

From that point on, none of the players needed convincing. When they returned to L.A. in October for the 2008–09 training camp, there was a fire in their eyes that I hadn't seen before. "There's no experience that wrenches your gut like making the NBA finals and losing," says Fish. "We went into the off-season questioning everything because we had come so close, but we were still so far away. I think that loss forced us all to ask ourselves, 'Do we really want this?'"

The answer was decidedly yes. From day one this was a team possessed. "There wasn't anything that was going to hold us back," Fish adds. "No matter what we faced, no matter how many ups and downs, we knew we were tough enough—mentally and physically—to figure this out. And we did."

During training camp, we talked about what we'd learned in the playoffs that could help us in the future. The players said that they'd discovered just how good we could be but realized that we hadn't played with the kind of physical intensity we needed to win it all. When we were overrun by Boston, Pau got labeled as "soft," which we knew wasn't true. Still, if we wanted to win a championship, we had to change that perception.

I was impressed by the players' cool determination. The previous year they had taken a quantum leap forward in terms of mastering the system. Now, inspired by their mutual loss, they were deepening their commitment to one another so that they could become more integrated—and invincible—as a team.

This is what I often refer to as *dancing with the spirit*. By "spirit" I don't mean anything religious. I mean that deep feeling of camaraderie that arises when a group of players makes a commitment to stand up for one another to achieve something greater than themselves, no matter what the risks. This kind of commitment often involves covering for teammates' weaknesses or fouling when necessary or protecting another player from being harassed by the enemy. When a team is bonding like this, you can feel it in the way the players move their bodies and relate to one another on and off the court. They play the game with a joyful abandon, and even when they're squabbling, they do so with dignity and respect.

The 2008–09 Lakers were that kind of team, and their spirit grew stronger as the season progressed. This was not the most talented team I'd ever coached, nor the most physically dominant. But the players had a deep spiritual connection that allowed them, every now and then, to produce miracles on the court. What I especially liked about this version of the Lakers was that many of the players had grown up together and learned to play the game the right way. By this time, they also knew one another well enough to integrate their movements in ways that baffled their opponents.

One player who reflected the spirit of the team was Luke Walton. The son of Hall of Famer Bill Walton, Luke had been immersed in basketball wisdom since early childhood. After attending the University of Arizona, he was drafted by the Lakers in 2003 but had difficulty finding a role for himself because he didn't fit the standard profile of a small forward. He didn't have a killer jumper, nor was he gifted at creating his own shots. But he loved moving the ball and playing the game the right way. He was also gifted at shifting the flow of the action from one side of the court to the other, a critical move in the triangle offense. Many coaches don't place a high value on such skills, but I encouraged Luke to grow in that direction. Eventually, he blossomed into one of the best facilitators on the team.

Like many of the younger players, Luke was emotional and would often shut down and avoid talking to anyone for a few days if he hadn't played well or the team had lost because of a mistake he'd made. I tried to convey to him that the best way to get off the emotional roller coaster is to take the middle way and not get too high when you win or too low when your game fails you. Over time Luke matured and calmed down.

Some players require a gentle touch, while others, such as Luke, need something more provocative to wake them up. Sometimes I would get under his skin on purpose to see how he would react. At other times I'd throw him into difficult situations in practice to find out if he could handle the pressure.

"It was frustrating," recalls Luke, "because I didn't always know what Phil was doing or why he was doing it. And he's not going to explain it. He wanted you to figure it out on your own." After a couple of years Luke realized that he'd absorbed what we had been teaching him, and he started to play the game naturally in a more integrated way.

Another player who evolved into a more integrated player during this period was Kobe. Ever since Fish had returned, he'd been developing a more inclusive style of leadership that came to fruition during the 2008–09 season.

In the past Kobe had led mostly by example. He'd worked harder than anyone else, rarely missed a game, and expected his teammates to play at his level. But he hadn't been the sort of leader who could communicate effectively and get everyone on the same page. If he talked to his teammates, it was usually, "Give me the damn ball. I don't care if I'm being double-teamed."

That approach usually backfired. As Luke describes it, "I've got Kobe on the floor yelling at me to give him the ball. And I've got Phil on the bench telling me to make the right pass no matter what. So instead of just seeing what's happening on the court, I'm trying to take in Kobe yelling and Coach telling me not to pass to him. And it made my job a lot harder."

But then Kobe started to shift. He embraced the team and his teammates, calling them up when we were on the road and inviting them out to dinner. It was as if the other players were now his partners, not his personal spear-carriers.

Luke noticed the change. Suddenly, Kobe was reaching out to him in a much more positive way than before. If Luke was bummed about missing three straight shots, Kobe would say, "C'mon, man, don't worry about that shit. I miss three straight shots every fucking game. Just keep shooting. The next one's going to go in." Says Luke, "When your leader is telling you that, instead of giving you a death stare, it makes the next shot a lot easier to take."

The season started out on a 17-2 roll and didn't taper off until early February, when I decided to slow things down after beating Boston and Cleveland. I wanted to do everything possible to keep the players from burning out before the playoffs. Still, our biggest losing streak was a mere two games, against the Spurs and the Magic. We finished the season with the best record in the Western Conference, 65-17, which gave us home-court advantage over everyone except the Cleveland Cavaliers, if we had to play them.

To inspire the players, I started wearing my 2002 championship ring to playoff games. That ring had seen a lot of action. I'd worn it through two failed championship finals runs and three other playoff campaigns that went south. As I told *Los Angeles Times* reporter Mike Bresnahan, "I've got to get rid of that ring."

My biggest reservation was the team's lack of a sense of urgency. Everything had come so easily during the regular season, and we'd glided past the Utah Jazz in the first round, 4–1. I was concerned about how our team would handle an opponent that matched up well against us and played a more physical brand of basketball. That happened in the second round, against the Houston Rockets.

The Rockets didn't look all that imposing on paper. They were missing two of their best players—Tracy McGrady and Dikembe Mutombo—and we were confident we could contain their other major threat, center Yao Ming, with double coverage by Bynum and Gasol. But when Yao broke his foot in game 3 and was sidelined for the rest of the series, Rockets coach Rick Adelman responded by putting in a small lineup led by six-six Chuck Hayes at center, forwards Ron Artest and Luis Scola, and guards Aaron Brooks and Shane Battier. The strategy worked. In game 4 our lackadaisical defense broke down and Houston tied the series, 2–2. Lamar called it "our worst game of the year."

Even though the team's spirit seemed to be flagging, we roared back in game 5 at the Staples Center, beating the Rockets 118–78, the Lakers' biggest playoff victory since 1986. But then we lost our mojo again and fell apart in game 6. Kobe later dubbed the team bipolar, and he wasn't far off. It was as if the Lakers had two conflicting personalities, and we never knew which one—Dr. Jekyll or Mr. Hyde—was going to show up on any given night.

That changed—finally—in game 7 in L.A. We decided to start playing aggressive defense at the very beginning, and that raised our game to another level. All of a sudden, Pau was fighting back and making key blocks; Kobe was playing Jordanesque defense, cutting off passing lanes and grabbing steals; Fish and Farmar were teaming up to contain Brooks; and Andrew was an unshakable force in the lane, scoring 14 points with 6 rebounds and 2 blocks. In the end we held the Rockets to 37 percent shooting and outrebounded them 55–33 as we sailed to victory, 89–70.

Kobe took the long view after the game. "Last year at this time everybody was pegging us as unbeatable and we got mopped up in the finals," he said. "I'd much rather be a team that's there at the end of the finals, not now."

We had a few more lessons to learn before we reached that point, but I was grateful that we had woken up from our split-personality trance. Or had we?

Our opponent in the Western Conference finals—the Denver Nuggets—posed a different kind of threat. They were loaded with great shooters, including Carmelo Anthony, whom Kobe nicknamed "the Bear," and two players who had hurt us in the past: point guard Chauncey Billups and power forward Kenyon Martin.

The Nuggets came after us hard in game 1, and we survived by the skin of our teeth with a heroic, last-minute push by Kobe, who scored 18 of his 40 points in the fourth quarter. Then we let a 14-point lead dribble away in game 2 and lost, 106–103. I was disappointed by Bynum's lack of hustle and weak defense in that game, so I put Odom in the starting lineup in game 3 to give us a little more athleticism up front. That helped, but what impressed me more was the team's resilience in the final minutes of the game. During a break late in the fourth quarter, Fish gathered the team together and delivered one of his most inspirational speeches. "This is a moment in time when you can define yourself," he said. "This is a moment when you can step into that destiny."

His words had an impact. With 1:09 left, Kobe, who finished with 41 points, hit a three-pointer over J.R. Smith to put us ahead, 96–95. Then, in the final thirty-six seconds, Trevor Ariza snatched Kenyon Martin's inbound pass to seal the win.

The series was far from over, however. The Nuggets steamrolled over us in game 4 and were pushing hard in the next game. The turning point came in the fourth quarter of game 5, when we instituted a scheme to use the Nuggets' aggressiveness against them. Rather than having Kobe and Pau avoid double-teams, we had them lure defenders toward them, which created openings for Odom and Bynum inside. Then, as soon as the Nuggets tried to plug that hole, Kobe and

Pau went on the attack. We won the game, 103–94, and polished off the series in Denver two days later.

We had hoped to meet the Celtics again in the championship finals, but Orlando beat them in a hard-fought seven-game series in the Eastern Conference semifinals, then knocked off the Cleveland Cavaliers to face off against us. The Magic had a twenty-three-year-old center and Defensive Player of the Year, Dwight Howard, and a strong group of three-point shooters, led by Rashard Lewis. I was surprised by Orlando's success in beating the Celtics (without Garnett) and the Cavaliers (with LeBron James), but I still didn't think the team was ready for prime time.

Kobe didn't either. He made it look too easy in game 1 at the Staples Center, knocking down 40 points, the most he'd ever scored in a finals game, while our defense held Howard to 12 points en route to a 100–75 win. The basketball gods were with us in game 2 when Courtney Lee missed on a potentially game-winning alley-oop play in the closing seconds and gave us a second chance to nail down the win in overtime.

When we moved to Orlando for game 3, the Magic came alive, shooting an NBA-finals-record 62.5 percent on the way to a 108–104 victory. That set the stage for Fish's finest moment ever in the playoffs.

Fish, who had a knack for making big game-winning shots, did not shoot well in game 4. In fact, as we took the floor, down 3 points with 4.6 seconds left in regulation, he had missed his previous 5 three-point attempts. But that didn't prevent him from squaring up for another when his defender, Jameer Nelson, foolishly backed away to help guard Kobe instead of committing a two-point foul against Fish to take the game. That mistake allowed Fish to put up the three and sent the game into overtime. Then, with the score tied and 31.3

seconds remaining, Fish threw another dramatic three to put the Lakers ahead to stay, 94–91.

Pure character. Pure Fish.

If this were a movie, it would have ended there. But we still had one more big hurdle to get over.

Before game 5 even started, the media was in the locker room asking the players to imagine what it was going to feel like to win a ring. And when I strolled into the trainers' room, I noticed Kobe and Lamar quizzing each other about championship-finals trivia. So I closed the doors and tried to set a different mood.

Instead of giving my usual pregame talk, I pulled up a chair and said, "Let's get our minds right." We sat in silence for five minutes and got our breath in sync.

Then assistant coach Brian Shaw started to give his chalk talk on the Magic. But when he turned the board around, it was completely empty. "I didn't write anything down," he said, "because you guys already know what you need to do to beat this team. Go out there and play with the idea of playing for and with each other and we'll end these playoffs tonight."

It was a great way to set the tone for a final game.

Kobe led the attack from the start, scoring 30 points as we took the lead in the second quarter and never looked back. When the buzzer sounded, Kobe leaped into the air and celebrated with his teammates in center court. Then he came over to the sidelines and hugged me.

I don't remember exactly what we said to each other, but the look in his eyes touched me the most. This was our moment of triumph, a moment of total reconciliation that had been seven long years in coming. The look of pride and joy in Kobe's eyes made all the pain we'd endured in our journey together worth it.

For Kobe, this was a moment of redemption. He would no longer have to listen to all the sports pundits and fans telling him that he would never win another championship without Shaq. Chinese water torture is how he described their lack of faith in him.

For me it was a moment of vindication. That night I surpassed Red Auerbach's championship record, which was gratifying in its way. But more important to me was how we did it: together, as a fully integrated team.

The most gratifying thing of all was watching Kobe transform from a selfish, demanding player into a leader that his teammates wanted to follow. To get there, Kobe had to learn to give in order to get back in return. Leadership is not about forcing your will on others. It's about mastering the art of letting go.

21

DELIVERANCE

Fall down seven times. Stand up eight.

JAPANESE PROVERB

This was the moment we'd all been waiting for. After nine months and 104 games, the 2009–10 season came down to this: a rematch with the Boston Celtics in game 7 of the championship finals. As we arrived at the Staples Center that afternoon, there was no doubt that the players were plotting revenge for the debacle that had taken place two years earlier in the TD Garden.

It was bad enough that the Celtics had humiliated us on the court in the final game of the 2008 finals. They'd done it in classic Boston style, dunking coach Doc Rivers with Gatorade before the clock ran out so that we had to sit on the bench in misery while workers mopped the floor and a stadium full of besotted hometown fans screamed invectives at us. Then, when we thought it was all over, we had to endure a postgame ride from hell through an unruly mob determined to upend our team bus. This was the nightmare that had stuck in our minds for two years.

If it had been any other team, we might have been able to laugh it off. But this was the Celtics, the team that had haunted the Lakers ever since 1959 when Boston swept the then-Minneapolis Lakers in four games to win the NBA championship. The Celtics were so dominant in the 1960s that Jerry West stopped wearing anything green because it reminded him of the frustration the Lakers had endured during that decade.

The most embarrassing defeat came in 1969 when an aging Celtics team, led by Bill Russell in his final year as player-coach, bounced back from a 3–2 deficit to snatch victory from the Lakers on their home court. The Lakers had been so confident going into game 7 that owner Jack Kent Cooke had thousands of purple and gold balloons hung from the ceiling of the Forum, ready to be released during the postgame celebration. Alas, that was not to be. With less than a minute to go, West knocked the ball away on defense, right into the hands of Don Nelson, who tossed up a shot from the free-throw line that hit the back of the rim, bounced high into the air and fell miraculously back into the hoop to put the Celtics ahead for good, 108–106.

West, who played brilliantly throughout the series and was the first and only player from a losing team ever to be named finals MVP, was shellshocked. "I didn't think it was fair that you could give so much and maybe play until there was nothing left in your body to give, and you couldn't win," he told author Roland Lazenby years later. "I don't think people really understand that trauma associated with losing. I don't think people realize how miserable you can be, and me in particular. I was terrible. It got to the point with me that I wanted to quit basketball."

West didn't quit, though. Three years later he finally won a championship ring, not against the Celtics, but against my team, the Knicks. Still, the Celtics' curse hovered over the franchise like an undropped balloon until the mid-'80s, when the "Showtime" Lakers beat Boston two out of three times in the finals. The rivalry between the two teams was such an important part of Lakers lore that Magic Johnson once revealed that he cheered for Boston when the team wasn't playing against L.A. because, as writer Michael Wilbon wrote, "only the Celtics know how it feels to sit atop the basketball world for the franchise's entire existence."

History was not on our side going into game 7 in 2010. Over the decades the Lakers had faced the Celtics four times in finals series that came down to seven games and had lost every time. But on this go-round we were playing at home, and we'd beaten the Celtics decisively, 89–67, two days earlier in game 6. We also had a few more weapons in our arsenal than in 2008, notably center Andrew Bynum, who had been sidelined with a knee injury that year. And we'd acquired forward Ron Artest, one of the best defensive players in the league. My main worry was Boston's Rasheed Wallace, who was filling in for injured center Kendrick Perkins. Wallace wasn't as strong as Perkins on defense, but he was a formidable offensive threat who had done serious damage to us in the past. I wasn't taking anything for granted.

By Lakers' standards, 2009–10 had been a fairly uneventful season. The biggest setback took place before the season began when Trevor Ariza, who had played a big role in the 2009 championship run, left the team to become a free agent. Trevor was a quick, daring defender who often ignited our fast-breaking offense by making steals or forcing turnovers. He also was a clutch outside shooter from the corners and other points on the floor. But during the off-season, negotiations between Trevor's agent and the Lakers stalled, and Mitch Kupchak started talking seriously with Artest, whose contract with the Rockets was ending. Before the deal was complete, however, Ron announced on Twitter that he was joining the Lakers. Baffled by this turn of events, Trevor signed with Houston as a free agent and was later traded to New Orleans.

What I liked about Artest was his size (six feet seven inches, 260 pounds), his strength, and his lockdown defensive play. Ron, who had recently been voted the "toughest" player in the NBA in a survey of general managers, was forceful and crafty enough to neutralize strong, mobile forwards such as Boston's Paul Pierce. But Ron could be erratic on offense and wasn't as speedy as Trevor, which meant we'd have to shift our quick, fast-breaking attack into a slower, half-court offense.

I also had concerns about Ron's unpredictability. He was best known for the wild brouhaha he took part in as a Pacer during a 2004 game against the Pistons at Auburn Hills. The fight broke out after Ron fouled Ben Wallace as he was driving to the basket, and Wallace retaliated by shoving him in the chest. Midway through the brawl, a Detroit fan threw a cup at Ron and he charged into the stands and started whaling away, which resulted in a seventy-three-game suspension, the longest in NBA history not related to drugs or gambling. (Wallace and other players were also penalized, but not as severely as Ron.)

During our series against Houston in the 2008 playoffs, Ron, then playing for the Rockets, got ejected from game 2 after getting into a clash with Kobe over a rebound. He also missed two team buses en route to the Staples Center for game 7, and caught a third bus—transporting Houston management—wearing only his sweats.

Ron grew up in New York's rough Queensbridge projects, and sports tattoos of a *Q* on his right leg and a *B* on his left to remind him of his roots. He remembers hearing gun shots while playing at the Twelfth Street courts. And he once witnessed a young man getting killed during a game at a local recreation center when a brawl broke out and one of the players tore off a leg of the scorer's table and stabbed him with it. "I'm still ghetto," Ron once told the *Houston Chronicle*. "That's not going to change. I'm never going to change my culture."

Basketball was Ron's salvation. When he was twelve, he was good enough to play AAU ball. He joined Lamar Odom and another future NBA star, Elton Brand, on the Brooklyn Queens Express, a team that went 67-1 one summer. All three players went on to success in high school and college, and were selected in the first round of the 1999 draft. The Bulls chose Brand and Ron, as the first and sixteenth picks overall, respectively, and the Clippers took Lamar as the fourth pick overall. Since 1999 Artest had played for four other teams—the Bulls, Pacers, the Kings, and the Rockets—but now he was going to be playing with his childhood buddy, Lamar. For Ron, it was like coming home.

Despite his background and his proclivity for playing rough, Ron is a good-natured soul off the court who does a lot of unpublicized charity work for children. Once, when he was in China, he met a young fan who couldn't afford to pay for his textbooks, let alone a pair of Ron's signature basketball shoes. So Ron took his $45,000 watch and auctioned it off to pay for the boy's education.

Ron has a flair for the outlandish. During his stint with the Kings, he offered—unsuccessfully—to forgo his entire salary in order to keep his friend, guard Bonzi Wells, from jumping to another team. And in 2011 he changed his name to Metta World Peace, as he said, "to inspire and bring youth together all around the world." The word "metta" means "loving kindness" in Pali, and refers to a key tenet of Buddhist teaching: cultivating universal love. Clearly, Ron has come a long way since his first days at the Lakers when he told *San Diego Union-Tribune* reporter Mark Ziegler, "I don't know what Zen means, but I'm looking forward to being a Zen man. I hope it makes me float. I always wanted to float."

My major concern about Ron was whether he could learn the tri-angle offense fast enough. Like Dennis Rodman, Ron had a hard time staying focused. Dennis's solution was to work out in the gym day and night to burn off restless energy. But Ron had trouble stick-ing to a workout regimen, so he practiced jump shots instead. The only problem was that every day he would shoot with a different style. And that affected the way he performed in games. Sometimes he was blessed and everything dropped in. Other times there was no way of telling what was going to happen.

During a practice session I suggested to Ron that he select one style of shooting and stick with it, but he took it the wrong way. "Why are you always picking on me?" he said.

"I didn't know I was picking on you," I replied. "I'm just trying to help you along."

Neither of us was speaking in anger, but assistant coach Brian Shaw pulled me aside and said, "You're walking a dangerous line there, Phil." I was stunned. I thought I was trying to be supportive. How-ever, Brian worried that Ron might misinterpret my body language—moving in closer and talking in a low tone of voice—as a form of aggression.

After that incident, I realized that the best way to communicate with Ron was to couch everything in a positive way—not just with the words I used, but with my gestures and facial expressions as well. Eventually, he figured out the system and, with the help of Kobe and others, began integrating himself into the team's DNA.

Ron wasn't the only question mark in 2009–10. Another concern was Kobe's physical decline over the course of the season. In December he broke the index finger on his shooting hand during a game against the Timberwolves, but he decided to skip surgery and tough it out, a decision he later regretted. Not surprisingly, the injury had a negative impact on his shooting percentage; his numbers were down in several categories.

In February he aggravated his sprained ankle and agreed to sit out three games to let it heal. Kobe was proud of his iron-man resilience and hated to miss games. In fact, he had taken part in all 208 games in the previous two seasons. But he needed to recover, and the break gave the team a chance to practice playing together without him. They won all three games against leading opponents.

Just when Kobe started finding his rhythm again, his right knee, which had been bothering him for years, began to swell and forced him to miss two games in April. This injury would bother him throughout the playoffs and contributed to his mystifying shooting slump at the end of the season.

The only upside to Kobe's knee problem was its positive effect on our relationship. When his knee had started acting up the year before, I gave him the freedom to go light at practice—or even skip one here and there, if necessary, to help him maintain his leg strength. Kobe was touched by my concern for his well-being, and the bond between us grew stronger. We often bounced around ideas during practices and spent time scrutinizing game videos together on the team plane. Over time we developed the kind of intimate partnership that I'd enjoyed with Michael Jordan. But the connection was less formal with Kobe. With Michael, I'd often arrange meetings ahead to discuss strategy. Kobe and I talked all the time.

Kobe likes to say that he learned 90 percent of what he knows about leadership from watching me in action. "It's not just a basketball way of leadership," he says, "but a philosophy of how to live. Being present and enjoying each moment as it comes. Letting my children develop at their own pace and not trying to force them into doing something they're not really comfortable with, but just nurturing and guiding them along. I learned that all from Phil." I'm grateful for the thought.

As we headed into the playoffs, Kobe would have a number of opportunities to test his leadership skills. Throughout the regular season the team had been beset by injuries, affecting several players in addition to Kobe. Pau Gasol and Andrew Bynum each missed seventeen games due to various problems, and Luke Walton was out for most of the season with severe back pain. But we had good team chemistry for most of the year, and that allowed us to hold on to first place in the Western Conference with a 57-25 record, despite a 4-7 slump at the end of the season.

Our opponent in the first round was the Oklahoma City Thunder, a team that pushed us harder than we expected. To get inside their up-and-coming forward Kevin Durant's head, I told reporters that I thought the refs were babying him by giving him a lot of easy calls, as if he were a superstar. (He shot the most free throws during the season, in large part because of a move he used to hook his shooting arm under those of defenders, which has since been disallowed by the NBA.) Durant got defensive about the remark, which was what I wanted, but the NBA fined me $35,000, which was not exactly my plan. As it turned out, Durant had an unimpressive series, but I think Ron's defense on him had more to do with that than my gamesmanship.

The Thunder's strategy was to leave Ron wide open in the corners so that they could pull down the rebounds when he misfired and launch fast breaks. And Ron obliged, missing 20 of 23 three-point attempts in the first four games. The Thunder's fast-paced attack—and our slow transitional defense—allowed Oklahoma City to win two games at home and tie the series, 2–2.

Kobe had struggled during the first four games, but experienced a rebirth in game 5 after getting a significant amount of liquid drained from his aching knee. One of our best moves was having him cover the Thunder's free-wheeling point guard, Russell Westbrook, who had been running wild against our other guards. Kobe not only held Westbrook to 15 points on 4 for 13 shooting, he also galvanized our offense by acting as a facilitator and moving the ball inside to Pau, who scored 25 points, and Bynum (21). The final score: Lakers 111, Thunder 87.

In game 6, the puppet master was Artest, who held Durant to 21.7 percent from the field, one of the worst shooting percentages in play-off history. Still, the game was touch-and-go until the last second when Pau tipped in a Kobe miss to seal the victory, 95–94.

The next two rounds were not as nerve-racking. A big plus was that Kobe, whose knee had become less bothersome, suddenly started averaging close to 30 points a game. After finishing off the Jazz in four games, we faced the Phoenix Suns—the hottest team in the league since the All-Star break—in the Western Conference finals. They weren't as big as the Lakers upfront, but they had a strong 1-2 combination in Steve Nash and Amar'e Stoudemire, plus a strong bench and an energetic swarming defense.

The turning point was game 5 in L.A. The series was tied 2–2 and the score was close most of the way. Late in the game, with the Lakers ahead by 3, Ron grabbed an offensive rebound. But instead of letting the clock run down, he took an ill-conceived three-pointer and missed, allowing the Suns to fight back and tie the game with a three-pointer of their own. Fortunately, Ron redeemed himself with a few seconds left, picking off Kobe's wayward jumper and putting it in the hoop for the win at the buzzer.

Two days later we returned to Phoenix and closed out the series. Ron came alive again, going four for seven from three-point territory and scoring 25 points. It looked as if he were finally coming into his own—not a moment too soon.

As the championship finals got under way against Boston, I was worried about the Celtics' bruising defense. Their strategy was to plug the lane with big bodies, put pressure on our guards to give up the ball, and force Lamar and Ron to take jump shots. It was a sound plan—one that had worked against us in the past. But we were more resilient than we'd been in 2008 and we had a wider range of scoring options.

We came out strong in game 1, powered by Pau, who was eager to show the world that he wasn't the "soft" pushover that reporters had made him out to be in 2008. But the Celtics answered back in game 2 with a stunning performance by shooting guard Ray Allen, who scored 32 points, including a finals record 8 three-pointers. Fish took a lot of heat in the media for letting Allen run amok, but Kobe also had trouble containing point guard Rajon Rondo, who had a triple-double. All of a sudden, the series was tied, 1–1, and we were headed for three games in Boston.

Game 3 was payback time for Fish. First, he shut down Allen on defense, forcing him to go 0-13 from the field, one miss shy of a finals record. Then Fish commandeered the game in the fourth quarter, going on an 11-point surge to win back home-court advantage for the Lakers. He fought back tears as he entered the locker room after the game, overcome by what he'd just accomplished. Still, the Celtics didn't let up. They took the next two games to go ahead 3–2 in the series and set up a classic showdown in L.A.

Tex Winter used to say that our successful championship runs were usually triggered by one game in which we completely dominated our opponents from beginning to end. Game 6 was such a game. We took command in the first quarter and beat the Celtics decisively, 89–67, to tie the series again.

Boston's spirit was hardly broken, though. They came out strong at the start of game 7 and had a six-point lead at the half. Midway through the third quarter, the Celtics pushed their edge up to 13, and I decided to step out of character and call two time-outs. This time I couldn't sit back and wait for the players to come up with a solution; I needed to shift the energy immediately.

The trouble was, Kobe wanted to win so badly that he'd abandoned the triangle and reverted to his old gunslinging ways. But he was pressing so hard that he was missing his shots. I told him to trust the offense. "You don't have to do it all by yourself," I said. "Just allow the game to come to you."

This was a classic example of when it's more important to pay attention to the spirit than the scoreboard. Soon after, I overheard Fish formulating a plan with Kobe to have him get back inside the offense when Fish came off the bench and returned to the floor.

As soon as Kobe made the switch, things started flowing smoothly again and we began slowly eating away at the Celtics' lead. The key moment was Fish's three-pointer with 6:11 left in the game that tied the score, 64–64, and ignited a 9–0 run that put us ahead by 6. The Celtics pulled within 3 on Rasheed Wallace's three-pointer at the 1:23 mark, but Artest answered back immediately with another three-pointer, as we held on to win, 83–79.

The beauty of this game was its raw intensity. It was like watching two veteran heavyweights who'd been battling each other with everything they had step back into the ring one last time and push themselves until the last bell sounded.

When the game was over, emotions ran deep. Kobe, who called this win "by far the sweetest" of them all, leapt onto the scorer's table and reveled in the cheers of the crowd, his arms outstretched and a blizzard of purple-and-gold confetti snowing down on him. Fish, who was usually Mr. Stoic, teared up again in the locker room as he embraced a wet-eyed Pau Gasol. Magic Johnson, who'd taken part in five championship celebrations, told the *Los Angeles Times*'s Mike Bresnahan that he'd never witnessed such an outpouring of emotion in a Lakers' locker room. "I think they finally understood the history of the rivalry and how hard it was to beat the Celtics," he said.

For me, this was the most gratifying victory of my career. It had been a trying season marred by inconsistency and troublesome injuries, but in the end the players were a study in courage and teamwork. I was moved to see Pau overcome the "softie" stigma that had haunted him for two years and Fish fight back after being torched by Ray Allen. It was also endearing to watch Ron mature and play a key role in containing Pierce, then make all the right shots just when we needed them. "I didn't think that winning that trophy was going to feel as good as it feels," he said later. "But now I feel like somebody."

Beyond the thrill of capturing another ring, there was something deeply satisfying about putting the Celtics' curse behind us with a triumphant victory in our own house. Indeed, the fans played a big part in this win. Lakers fans are often mocked for their laid-back approach to the game, but on this day they were more engaged than I'd ever seen them.

It was as if they, too, understood instinctively the symbolic importance of this moment—not just to the team but to the L.A. community as a whole. In the city of dreams, this was the only *real* reality show in town.

22

THIS GAME'S IN THE REFRIGERATOR

We are all failures—at least the best of us.

J. M. BARRIE

Maybe I should have ended it there, with the crowd roaring and confetti raining down. But life is never quite so well scripted.

I had reservations about coming back for the 2010–11 season. For one thing, I was having trouble with my right knee and I was eager to get on with replacement surgery. Second, although most of the core team would be returning, we were likely to lose some key players to free agency, notably guards Jordan Farmar and Sasha Vujacic, both of whom would be hard to replace. Third, I had a secret longing to escape the grueling NBA travel schedule and the pressure of constantly being in the public eye.

During the Western Conference finals, I had lunch with Dr. Buss in Phoenix to discuss the upcoming season. He said that contract negotiations with the players' union weren't going well and he expected the owners to institute a lockout when the 2010–11 season was over. That meant that the Lakers needed to take some measures right away to trim expenses. He also confided that other owners were giving him grief about my salary, claiming that the terms of my contract forced them to pay their own coaches more. Bottom line: If I decided to come back, it would be at a reduced salary.

I told him I would give him an answer in July. Of course, I knew when I said it that it would be hard for me to say no to Kobe and Fish if we won the finals. And sure enough, not long after our victory over the Celtics, they both started pleading with me via text to stick around and "win a 3P again."

So I negotiated a one-year deal with Dr. Buss and began working with Mitch Kupchak on assembling a new roster. I dubbed the campaign the "Last Stand," which, alas, turned out to be a pretty accurate way to describe this snake-bitten season.

We were faced with replacing nearly 40 percent of the last season's roster. In addition to Jordan and Sasha—who would be traded to the Nets in mid-December—we were losing backup center Didier Ilunga-Mbenga as well as forwards Adam Morrison and Josh Powell. We replaced the outgoing players with a mixed group of veterans and young players, the most promising of whom were forward Matt Barnes and guard Steve Blake. But Barnes injured his knee and missed about a third of the season, and Blake caught the chicken pox at the end of the season, which diminished his playing time in the playoffs. What's more, Theo Ratliff, the thirty-seven-year-old center we brought in to back up Andrew Bynum was injured and didn't get much playing time. Still, I wasn't worried about our front line. The team's lack of youth and energy was a bigger concern. Jordan, Sasha, and Josh were always challenging the veterans to rise to their level of energy. Losing them meant that our practices weren't going to be as intense as before—not a good thing.

Another problem, of course, was Kobe's right knee. He'd had another round of arthroscopic surgery in the off-season and later said that his knee had lost so much cartilage that the doctors told him it was "almost bone on bone." Kobe continued to have trouble recuperating after games and hard practices. So we reduced the amount of time he spent practicing the day before games, with the hope that the additional rest would allow his knee to recover faster. That diminished the intensity of the practices, as well, but, more important, it isolated Kobe from the team, which created a leadership vacuum late in the season.

Despite all these issues, the team got off to a healthy 13-2 start and looked pretty strong until the new LeBron James-led Miami Heat picked us apart, 96–80, in the Staples Center on Christmas Day. Then we went on a road trip just before the All-Star game that ended with three disturbing losses to Orlando, Charlotte, and Cleveland.

During the game against the Cavaliers—the team with the worst record in the NBA at that point—Kobe got into foul trouble battling guard Anthony Parker, and Ron Artest tried to save the day but made a series of mistakes instead that put us down by 5 going into the half. Kobe and Fish were not pleased. They said that nobody could figure out what Ron was trying to do on the court, particularly on defense, which made it hard to stage a cohesive attack.

I called a team meeting during the All-Star break and we talked about ways to get the team back on track. Chuck Person, a new assistant coach, suggested that we try a system of defense that he claimed would help us guard against our old bugaboo—screen-rolls—and, in the process, tighten up the way we worked together as a team. The system was counterintuitive and required players to unlearn many of the defensive moves they'd been using since high school. Some of the other assistant coaches thought it was risky to introduce such a radically different approach in the middle of the season, but I thought it was worth the gamble.

The main downside was that Kobe wouldn't have enough time to practice the new system with the team because of his bum knee. I thought that would be a minor obstacle. Kobe was a quick study and good at adapting to challenging situations. But as we began to roll out the system in games, he often got frustrated with his teammates and started giving them directions that contradicted what they'd been learning in practice. This disconnect would haunt us later.

Nevertheless, the new system worked well at first and we went on a 17-1 streak after the break. But in early April we lost five games in a row, including one to arguably the best screen-roll team in the league: the Denver Nuggets. And to hang on to second place in the conference, we had to win the last game of the season—against Sacramento in overtime. We'd gone into late-season slides before and still triumphed, but this time felt different. We shouldn't have been struggling so hard at this point in the season.

It didn't help that our opponent in the first round of the playoffs was the New Orleans Hornets, whose star point guard, Chris Paul, had little difficulty penetrating our new defensive system and creating havoc all over the floor. The Hornets also had former Laker Trevor Ariza, who was determined to show us that we'd made a mistake letting him go. He did a good job of it, giving Kobe trouble on defense and knocking down several key three-pointers. Before we knew it, the Hornets had stolen the first game in L.A., 109–100, and we had to fight hard to scratch out a lead in the series, 2–1.

The Hornets weren't our only obstacle. After practice on the Saturday before game 4, Mitch met individually with the members of my staff and informed them that their contracts, which ran out on July 1, weren't going to be renewed for the next season. This included all the assistant coaches, trainers, massage therapists, weight and conditioning instructors, and the equipment manager—everyone except athletic trainer Gary Vitti, who had a two-year contract. Mitch's intention was to give the staffers time to find new jobs, in light of the expected NBA lockout. But the timing of the announcement—in the middle of a tight first-round series—had a disruptive impact on the players as well as the staff.

As if that weren't enough, later that night rookie Derrick Caracter was arrested for allegedly grabbing and shoving a female cashier at an International House of Pancakes and was charged with battery, public drunkenness, and resisting arrest. He was released on bail on Sunday and no charges were filed, but he didn't get to play in game 4, which the Hornets won to tie the series, 2–2.

Earlier in the series, we were studying the game videos as a group and observed that Chris Paul was sliding through the defense and forcing one of our big men to switch off and cover him, which was exactly what he wanted.

I turned the projector off and said, "Well, what do you think, guys? Our defense looks totally confused. We don't know what we're trying to do. And that's playing right into his hands."

Fish spoke up first. "I think there's something wrong here. I know we've been through a lot, and some of our guys have been out. Maybe it's our attitude or our lack of focus. But something's not right."

After hearing that, I took a seat facing the players and told them of a personal problem I'd been struggling with for the past two months—something that they'd obviously been picking up on a nonverbal, energetic level. In March I'd been diagnosed with prostate cancer. For weeks afterward I grappled with how best to proceed. Ultimately, I decided to wait until after the playoffs to have surgery; my doctor had assured me that we could control the growth of the cancer, at least temporarily, with drugs.

"This has been a tough period for me," I explained. "And I don't know if it has affected my ability to give 100 percent of what I normally give you guys. But I know there've been times when I've been more withdrawn than usual."

I began to tear up while I was talking, and the players seemed genuinely moved. Still, looking back, I'm not sure this was the right decision. Although telling the truth is never a mistake, there can be serious repercussions. And timing matters. I wondered if my confession would help unify the team or just make the players feel sorry for me. They'd never seen me before in such a vulnerable state. I was supposed to be the "Zen guy," the man they could always count on to be cool under pressure. Now what were they supposed to think?

In retrospect, I should have anticipated what would come next. But I'd never had one of my teams fall apart in such a strange and spooky way before. After all, the team was finally returning to championship form as we polished off the Hornets in the next two games. In fact, I was so impressed by the team's performance in game 6, I told reporters that I thought this squad had "the potential to be as good as any team I've coached with the Lakers."

Needless to say, I spoke too soon.

It wasn't that our next opponent, Dallas, was such a huge threat. The Mavericks were a talented veteran team that had finished the year with the same record as ours (57-25). But we'd always dominated the Mavs in the past and had beaten them handily in March to win our regular season three-game series, 2–1, and home-court advantage against them in the playoffs.

However, Dallas created some serious matchup problems for us. First, we didn't have anyone who could keep pace with the Mavs' quick diminutive point guard, José Juan Barea, who, like Chris Paul, was surprisingly good at breaking down our new defense. We'd hoped that Steve Blake, who is quicker and more nimble than Fish, could be our defensive stopper in the backcourt, but he wasn't back up to speed after his bout with chicken pox. Second, the Mavs were able to wear Kobe down with DeShawn Stevenson, a tough, muscular guard, and virtually neutralize Andrew Bynum with the bigman tag team of Tyson Chandler and Brendan Haywood. What's more, with Barnes and Blake not 100 percent, our bench had a tough time keeping up with Dallas's second unit, especially sixth man Jason Terry, who was devastating from the three-point line.

One of the biggest disappointments was the performance of Pau, who'd played well against the Mavs in the past. But the refs allowed Dallas forward Dirk Nowitski to push Pau and prevent him from establishing a solid post-up position, which hurt us badly on offense. I urged Pau repeatedly to fight back, but he was grappling with a serious family issue and was distracted. True to form, the media made up stories to explain Pau's less-than-stellar performance, including gossip that he'd broken up with his girlfriend and had had a falling out with Kobe, neither of which was true. Still, the rumors disturbed Pau and compromised his focus.

Game 1 was a mystery to me. We established dominance early and built up what looked like a solid 16-point lead in the third quarter. Then, for no obvious reason, we stopped playing on both ends of the floor and the energy shifted to the Mavs. By the end of the fourth quarter, we still had a chance to win, but we uncharacteristically flubbed several opportunities to put the game away. With five seconds left and the Mavs up by 1, Kobe stumbled trying to get around Jason Kidd and bobbled a pass from Pau. Next, after Kidd was fouled and hit one of his free throws, Kobe missed an open three at the buzzer to give the Mavs the win, 96–94.

The plot took a more ominous turn in game 2. We came out with fire in our eyes, but that feeling quickly dissipated. Not because the

Mavs' performance was so spectacular—it wasn't—but because they trumped us on aggressiveness and were able to capitalize on our slow-acting defensive game. The big surprise was Barea, who was virtually unstoppable, weaving his way effortlessly through defenders to pick up 12 points (which equaled the output of our entire bench) and 4 assists. Nowitski also had an easy time outmaneuvering Pau and scored 24 points to lead the Mavs to a 93–81 victory. In the closing seconds of the game, Artest was so frustrated he clothes-lined Barea, who was trying to put pressure in the backcourt, and was suspended for the next game. Not one of Ron's proudest moments.

Losing Artest hurt but it wasn't catastrophic. We replaced him in game 3 with Lamar and made a concerted effort to move the ball inside to take advantage of our bigger front line. That worked for most of the game and helped us to build a 7-point lead with five minutes remaining. But then Dallas, which was loaded with good three-point shooters, started exploiting our weakness in guarding the perimeter, particularly when we were using a big lineup. Led by Nowitski, who scored 32 points and 4 of 5 threes, the Mavs waltzed to victory, 98–92.

After that loss, my son Charley called to tell me that he and his siblings, Chelsea, Brooke, and Ben, were planning to fly to Dallas to see the next game. "Are you guys crazy?" I asked.

"No, we're not missing your final game," he replied.

"What do you mean my final game? We're going to win on Sunday."

Ever since I was a coach in the Continental Basketball Association, my kids had been in the stands for my big games. In those days we could drive to many of the games from our house in Woodstock, and June would turn the trips into family adventures. After I joined the Bulls, the kids, then in middle school and high school, would travel to away games during the finals, courtesy of the team. The ritual continued when I moved to L.A., by which time they were old enough to enjoy the parties connected to the series. By 2011, they'd been to so many finals—thirteen, to be exact—that they liked to say the NBA threw a big party for them every June.

My favorite moment was when they showed up in Orlando for the 2009 finals and presented me with a Lakers yellow basketball cap embroidered with the Roman numeral X to commemorate my tenth championship. Would there be an XII cap?

The vultures were already circling. When I saw my friend, NBA photographer Andy Bernstein, arrive in Dallas, I greeted him half-jokingly as "dead man walking." Still, even though it may seem like magical thinking now, I really believed that we were going to win game 4 and take the series back to L.A. To be honest, I hadn't given much thought to how I wanted my career to end or what I was going to do next. I was just trying to stay in the moment and get through the next game.

That was the message I delivered to the players: Win the game, get the series back to our house, then put the pressure on the Mavs to win. Maybe I was missing something, but I didn't have the sense that the players had given up or thought the series was already over. Nor did I think that they'd tired of playing together as a team.

Of course, when you're a coach, you don't have the same kind of apprehension you do as a player. When you're a player, you obsess about not screwing up and making a mistake that will blow the game. But when you're the coach, you think, how can I get these guys keyed up and on their game? What kind of insight can I offer them so that they can play more spontaneously? And what kind of coaching change can I make to give them an edge?

My concern in game 4 was trying to get Pau to push back against Nowitski and stake out a better position in the post. Our key to victory was a strong inside game, and that began with Pau. In game 3 I got so tired of watching him get shoved around that I thumped him on the chest as he walked off the floor just to get a rise out of him. The media had fun with that, but Pau understood what I was trying to do. Unfortunately, it wasn't enough.

I'm not sure any magic coaching fixes would have made much of a difference in game 4. The Mavericks had the touch from start to finish, shooting a remarkable 60.3 percent from the field and 62.5 percent from the three-point line, as they danced and laughed and partied their way to a 122–86 blowout. Much of the damage was done by the Mavs' backup players, particularly Terry, who hit a playoff-record-tying 9 three-pointers and scored 32 points; Predrag Stoyakovic, who went 6 for 6 on threes; and Barea, who scored 22 points while dashing around the court like Road Runner outwitting Wile E. Coyote.

The first half was so lopsided, it was almost laughable. By halftime, we were down 63–39, but I refused to surrender. I told the players that all they needed to do was to get a few defensive stops, make some shots, and turn the game around. And they started to make that happen. Then, midway through the third quarter, Fish stole the ball and tossed a long pass to Ron, who was speeding up court all alone. This could have been a game-changing drive. But as Ron rose toward the basket, he looked as if he couldn't decide what to do with the ball, and it slipped out of his hands and careened against the bottom of the rim. Soon after, Terry nailed a three-pointer and put an end to what turned out to be our final threat.

The next part was painful to watch. During the fourth quarter, Lamar took a cheap shot at Nowitski and was ejected from the game. Moments later Bynum struck Barea with a dangerous right elbow that sent him crashing to the floor. Andrew was immediately thrown out of the game and later suspended for five games. As he walked off the court, he tore off his jersey and bared his chest to the fans—an embarrassing, bush league move.

It was all over.

The late Lakers' broadcaster, Chick Hearn, often used to proclaim when he thought a contest had been decided: "This game's in the refrigerator, the door is closed, the lights are out, the eggs are cooling, the butter's getting hard, and the jello's jigglin!"

Those words rang true now. Not just for the game, but this championship run and my tenure as head coach of the Lakers.

Everything was in the refrigerator.

I've never been very good at dealing with loss. Like many competitors, one of the main driving forces in my life has been not just to win but to avoid losing. Yet for some reason this fiasco didn't affect me as much as some of the other losses I've endured in my basketball life. In part, that was because this wasn't the finals. It's much easier coping with an early-round loss than a game in which you're closing in on a ring. But even more than that, the way in which the Dallas finale unfolded was so over-the-top absurd, it was hard to take too seriously.

I wasn't pleased with how the players handled themselves at the end of the game. Still, as we gathered one last time in the locker room it didn't feel right to deliver a lecture on NBA etiquette. "I think we played out of character tonight," I told them. "I don't know why that happened at this particular time. The media will probably make a big deal out of this. But you shouldn't look at this game as a measuring stick of your ability or your competitiveness. You're better than this." Then I walked around the room and thanked each of the players individually for the great work we'd done together over the years.

As a rule, players usually have an easier time dealing with loss than coaches. They can go in and take a shower, then come out and say, "I'm tired and hungry. Let's go get something to eat." But coaches don't have the same kind of release that comes from playing a grueling physical game. Our nervous systems tend to keep firing long after the arena has cleared.

For me, the nerves usually kick into high gear in the middle of the night. I'll sleep for a few hours, then—bang!—my brain is up and spinning. "Should I have done this, should I have done that? God, what a terrible call in the fourth quarter. Maybe I should have called a different play?" And so on. Sometimes I have to sit and meditate for a long time before the noise settles down and I can go back to sleep.

Coaching takes you on an emotional roller coaster ride that's hard to stop, even when you've diligently practiced letting go of your desire for things to be different than they actually are. There always seems to be just a bit more to let go of. Zen teacher Jakusho Kwong suggests becoming "an active participant in loss." We're conditioned to seek only gain, to be happy, and to try to satisfy all our desires, he explains. But even though we may understand on some level that loss is a catalyst for growth, most people still believe it to be the opposite of gain and to be avoided at all costs. If I've learned anything in my years of practicing Zen and coaching basketball, it's that what we resist persists. Sometimes the letting go happens quickly; other times it may take several sleepless nights. Or weeks.

After talking with the players, I walked down the hall in the American Airlines Center to another room where my kids were waiting. They were distraught. A few had tears in their eyes; the rest were in a state of disbelief. "I can't believe this happened," Chelsea said. "That was the most difficult game we've ever had to sit through. Why did it have to be *this* game?"

That's a question I've asked myself a few times since. There's a tendency to search for someone to pin the blame on when an unexpected disaster occurs. The columnists had a field day accusing everyone from Kobe to Pau to Fish to Ron to Lamar, and, of course, me for the loss. Andrew told reporters that he thought the team had "trust issues," and there may be some truth to that. But I think there were a number of factors that stopped this Lakers' team from joining together into the integrated championship-winning force we'd been so many times before.

Fatigue was a big factor. It takes a lot of grit—physically, psychologically, and spiritually—to win *one* championship. By the time you're shooting for your third in a row, you've played so many games, it gets harder and harder to tap into the inner resources that make winning possible. What's more, many of the key individuals on the team—including me—were distracted by personal issues that made it difficult for us to compete with the same invincible spirit we'd known before. As Lamar said simply after the game, "There was just something missing for us."

Buddhist sages say that there's only "a tenth of an inch of difference" between heaven and earth. And I think the same can be said about basketball. Winning a championship is a delicate balancing act, and there's only so much you can accomplish by exerting your will. As a leader your job is to do everything in your power to create the perfect conditions for success by benching your ego and inspiring your team to play the game the right way. But at some point, you need to let go and turn yourself over to the basketball gods.

The soul of success is surrendering to what is.

LIFE IS A HIGHWAY

A man travels the world over in search of what he needs
and returns home to find it.

GEORGE MOORE

My first thought was to hit the road. Once I got my body back in shape, I figured I'd get a dog and head across the country in a van, à la John Steinbeck. It was the perfect time to explore all the hidden corners of America I'd never seen.

I've been a rambling man at heart ever since my high school days, when my teammates and I would drive for miles across the plains en route to our next game. I love the freedom of the open road. I love the fact that you can never be entirely sure what awaits you over the next rise. As Steinbeck put it, "A journey is like marriage. The certain way to be wrong is to think you control it."

For me, the highway is a form of meditation. Throughout my life, I've turned to the open road when my life was in turmoil. Driving long distance makes me feel more engaged in the moment and transports me into a calmer, more contemplative state of mind. When I was experimenting with meditation in my twenties, I was inspired by the musings of another famous road warrior, Robert Pirsig. "You look at where you're going and where you are and it never makes sense," he wrote in *Zen and the Art of Motorcycle Maintenance*, "but then you look back at where you've been and a pattern seems to emerge."

This time, however, my body wasn't cooperating. First, right after the 2011 playoffs, I had to undergo prostate surgery, which laid me up for most of the summer. Then I had to lose weight and get myself in condition for a difficult knee replacement operation. The surgery went well, but the recovery was brutal. To make matters worse, I injured my Achilles tendon during the following summer in Montana and was still limping around after months of sporadic workouts. Disheartened, I put my travel plans on hold and returned to L.A. in the fall determined to make healing my number one job.

In late September 2012, Mitch Kupchak, the Lakers' general manager, invited me to lunch to see how I was doing. He asked me if I was planning to get back to coaching any time soon, and I said I had no intention of doing that, especially if it meant moving to another city. At that point, I was more interested in exploring more sedentary front office positions, and I had a few possibilities in the works.

So I was surprised in early November when my fiancée, Jeanie, came home after meeting with her brother Jim, the Lakers' head of basketball operations, and asked me to "please just hear him out" about returning to coach the team. Over the summer Jim and Mitch had made deals with two major stars—point guard Steve Nash and center Dwight Howard—creating a "dream team" that prognosticators predicted had a good shot of winning the championship. But Mike Brown, who had taken over as coach the year before, had trouble getting the players to gel together at the start of the 2012–13 season and Jim decided they needed to replace him after the team went 0–8 in the preseason and dropped four of the first five regular games.

The meeting took place at my house on Saturday morning. Jim brought Mitch along and we talked mostly about whether I was up for doing the job. By then, I'd recovered from my Achilles tendon problem and I told them that I felt capable of handling the travel grind. To be honest, though, I was still ambivalent about returning to coaching. Now that I had begun to recover from my surgeries, I finally felt strong enough to start enjoying my retirement and I wasn't keen on becoming a slave to the NBA schedule again.

Still, the idea of going after one more ring with Kobe, Pau, and my other former players intrigued me. My biggest concern was whether this team could beat the reigning champs, the Miami Heat. In my mind, there's nothing worse than making it all the way to the Finals and losing. As they were leaving, I told Jim and Mitch that I needed time to think it over, but I'd be ready to give them an answer on Monday.

Most fans know what happened next. Mitch called me around midnight on Sunday and told me they had decided to hire another coach, Mike D'Antoni. I was a little stunned at first, but, on reflection, I realized why things fell apart so quickly. I was thinking of the job as a one-season gig, but Jim and Mitch were looking for a coach who could help them rebuild the team over the long haul. They were also eager to turn the Lakers back into the sort of fast-paced, high-scoring team they were in the Magic Johnson "Showtime" era—and D'Antoni was certainly a coach who might make that happen.

The overriding issue, however, was the state of owner Jerry Buss's health. He'd been in and out of the hospital during the previous several months battling prostate cancer and other ailments. But things had taken a turn for the worse recently, and his family hoped that a turn in the Lakers' fortunes might bring some joy into his life and, with luck, help speed his recovery.

That late-night phone call from Mitch was a big turning point for me. I realized that I had to distance myself from the Lakers, and I began to talk to several other teams about jobs, including the Brooklyn Nets, Toronto Raptors, and Phoenix Suns. I also did a brief stint with the Detroit Pistons advising the owner on his search for a new coach.

The prospect that most captured my imagination didn't involve any coaching. In December 2011 my son Charley introduced me to Chris Hansen, a successful hedge fund manager who had put together a group of investors who were trying to bring an NBA team back to Seattle. Hansen's plan was to buy a majority share of the struggling Sacramento Kings franchise, then persuade the NBA to let him move it to the former home of the Sonics.

What I liked about Chris was his innovative thinking about sports and community. He wanted me to help him create a new kind of culture, focusing on the team itself rather than individual superstars. His goal was to make the fans feel as if they, too, were part of the family. One of Chris's ideas, inspired by the Seattle Sounders soccer team, was to hold large pep rallies before each game to get the fans juiced up as they made their way to the arena. Another idea was to create a low-priced standing room section behind the baskets, complete with beat boards to rev up the noise level. Chris even wanted to remove the players' names from their jerseys to shift attention away from individual players. I told him the marketing department of the NBA might have a problem with that one.

My loosely defined job was to be keeper of the flame, overseeing the hiring of key staff and setting the tone for how everyone worked together. I wouldn't be the hands-on general manager—recruiting players, orchestrating trades, and negotiating deals. Instead, I'd focus on the big picture, making sure that all the pieces fit together and contributed to creating a positive, integrated culture. This was something I'd done on a small scale with the Lakers, but in Seattle we were talking about applying those principles not just to the players, but to the organization as a whole.

One reason this idea interested me was that it seemed like an anti-dote to the transformation that was occurring in the NBA due to the league's most recent collective bargaining agreement with the play-ers' union. That agreement, which was designed to create more parity in the league, put strict limits on how much teams could spend on talent—levying escalating fines on those that exceeded the designated salary cap and rewarding those that kept their payrolls below the line. The idea was to give the small-market teams, some of which are losing money, a greater chance to compete against well-heeled teams such as the Lakers.

In response, most teams have already begun to change the way they recruit talent. The Oklahoma City Thunder, for example, un-loaded star guard James Harden to Houston because, under the new agreement, the team wouldn't be able to afford him, given what it was already committed to paying their other stars, Kevin Durant and Russell Westbrook. Similarly, the Lakers have retooled their roster so that they will have only three players under contract at the end of 2013–2014, and will be able to make a serious bid for players in the upcoming free-agent market.

Sadly, what inevitably is getting lost in this shift is a sense of con-tinuity over time. Not only will the new agreement make it virtually impossible for teams—no matter how fat their wallets—to assemble lineups with more than two or three bona fide stars, it will also sig-nificantly reduce the number of players who can play the bulk of their careers on the same team. When I was with the Knicks, most of the key players on our championship teams—including Bill Bradley, Willis Reed, Walt Frazier, and Dave DeBusschere—were together for six years or more. That may never happen again. Instead we're going to see a lot of teams made up of one or two stars and a cast of inter-changeable specialty players on short-term contracts. As a result, it will be even more difficult to build the kind of group consciousness necessary to excel. The only remedy is to create a culture that empowers the players and gives them a strong foundation to build upon. Otherwise they'll be too insecure to focus their energy on bonding together as a team.

As fate would have it, Hansen and his partners weren't able to close the deal. Things looked promising in January 2013 when they arranged to buy a controlling interest in the Kings from the majority owners, the Maloof family. But Sacramento's mayor (and former NBA All-Star) Kevin Johnson secured an agreement from the league that gave investors committed to keeping the team in place an opportunity to make a competing bid. Johnson also persuaded the city council to approve a financing plan to raise $447 million for a new arena downtown (including a $258 million public subsidy). In May the NBA's board of governors voted to prevent Hansen and his partners from moving the franchise, and later that month the Maloofs accepted an offer from a local group led by software mogul Vivek Ranadive. That put an end to the dream.

Before the curtain came down on the Seattle deal, Jeanie and I had to grapple with a more serious personal loss. In late 2012, Dr. Buss gave Jeanie a list of people he wanted to see before he died, including Magic Johnson, Kareem Abdul Jabbar, Jerry West, and many others. In October, Jeanie had hoped that her dad would get well enough to come to a game at the Staples Center. By December, his ordeal had turned into a long vigil.

During that period, I decided to propose to Jeanie. Marriage was something we'd talked about before, but had always found reasons to postpone. The thought came to me during Thanksgiving at my daughter Brooke's house in Santa Barbara. All my children and their families were gathered together, except for my oldest daughter Elizabeth and her tribe, who live in Virginia. It felt good being there with Jeanie and seeing how comfortable she was with everyone, and I began thinking that the time had come to pop the question. In the back of my mind, I also thought that our engagement might give Dr. Buss some peace of mind in his final days.

When we returned home, I bought a ring and presented it to Jeanie on Christmas morning. She was delighted and took the ring to the hospital to show her father. But that day he wasn't feeling well enough to share in her excitement.

In February I went to the hospital to say good-bye. Even though Dr. Buss was barely conscious that day, I thought it was important to reassure him that he didn't have to worry about Jeanie. "It's okay," I said, putting my hand on his shoulder. "We're all going to be fine. You've made a good plan for your family's future. It's okay to let go. You've suffered enough."

A few days later he passed away.

It wasn't until Dr. Buss died that I realized that how many people were dependent upon him. The list included not just his six children, but also his former partners, his devoted personal staff, and the whole Lakers organization. Jerry was a warm-hearted, larger-than-life guy who'd had a hardscrabble childhood growing up in Wyoming. He never forgot how much the kindness of others had allowed him to climb his way out of poverty and achieve success.

One of the most impressive things about Dr. Buss was the caring relationship that he developed with his players. Magic, who referred to himself as Jerry's "adopted son," spoke movingly at the memorial ceremony about the extraordinary support Dr. Buss gave him when he was diagnosed with HIV in 1991—crying when he heard the news, finding him the best doctors, and making sure he took his meds every day. Jerry also formed a strong bond with Kobe. When Kobe was demanding to be traded in 2007, we had a meeting with him and his agent during which Dr. Buss said, "Kobe, if I had a diamond of great value, four or five karats, would I give up that diamond for four diamonds of one karat? No. There's no equal value that we can get for you. A trade would not match what you bring to this team." Eventually Jerry won Kobe over and he agreed to stay.

Dr. Buss left detailed instructions about how he wanted his children to run the Lakers after he was gone. He designated Jeanie to be in charge of business operations, Jim to oversee basketball personnel, and their older brother, John, to have a high-level advisory role. After the funeral, however, Jim and John were surprised to learn that Dr. Buss had named Jeanie as the Lakers' voting member on the NBA's board of governors. That decision essentially gave Jeanie final responsibility for the Lakers franchise.

The tension escalated later that year when an excerpt from an updated edition of Jeanie's book, *Laker Girl*, appeared in the *Los Angeles Times* revealing how blindsided she felt by the way the coaching search had been handled. That led to a number of emotional but constructive conversations between Jim and Jeanie in which they hammered out a more effective way of communicating with each other. If nothing else, those conversations gave them both more clarity about their respective roles.

Of course, it didn't help matters that the Lakers had struggled all season to make the playoffs. Not only was Steve Nash out for the first part of the season with a fractured left leg, but Dwight Howard, who was coming back from major back surgery, got off to a worrisome start. What's more, Pau Gasol was having trouble fitting into the new, faster offense. At the All-Star break, the Lakers were three and a half games behind the Rockets for the Western Conference's final playoff spot. After the break, driven by Kobe's leadership, they went on an 8-2 drive and finally scrambled over the .500 mark. Then, five days before the end of the regular season, Kobe tore his Achilles tendon in a game against Golden State, and the Lakers barely managed to eke out a place in the playoffs by beating Houston in overtime of the final game. Without Kobe, however, they weren't able to do much against the San Antonio Spurs in the first round and got swept in four straight.

In the midst of all this, friends asked if I had any feelings of schadenfreude and I said definitely no. The Lakers were family. More than anything, I wanted the team to succeed.

After the playoffs, Mitch Kupchak came over to my house to discuss the team's strategy for luring Dwight Howard, or D12, as he had come to be known, to stay with the Lakers. The competition was stiff. It included the Atlanta Hawks (his hometown team), Golden State Warriors (a young team loaded with talent), Dallas Mavericks (a former champion led by Dirk Nowitzki), and Houston Rockets (a strong championship contender). As Dwight's current employer, the Lakers had an advantage of being able to offer him a package totaling $30 million more than the other teams', plus an additional year on his contract, but that didn't guarantee anything.

During his post-season interview, Dwight asked for assurance that I would be coming back to coach the team, but Mitch quickly disabused him of that notion. He asked me to back him up on that and not send out a conflicting message. I agreed and told Mitch that I would reach out to Dwight and encourage him to sign with the Lakers. He never answered any of my messages.

Critics poked fun at the Lakers' D12 campaign, which included putting up billboards all over town with a giant photo of Dwight in Lakers purple and gold and a one-word headline: STAY. But some of the other teams were no less hokey. Dallas owner Mark Cuban created an animated feature starring D12 for his presentation, and the Rockets' GM put together a video of several local children, including his own daughter, pleading with Dwight to move to Houston.

The Lakers invited Kobe and Steve to the final pitch meeting to help persuade Dwight to come on board. It sounded like a good idea. Steve sent out an amusing tweet before the meeting: "Dwight Howard we're coming for you. You're going to love the statue we build for you outside Staples in 20yrs!" And Kobe made a moving speech during the pitch, promising to teach Dwight the secret of winning championships that he'd learned from the best in the game.

If the meeting had ended there, it might have worked. But after the presentation, Dwight asked Kobe what he was planning to do after he recovered from his Achilles injury. Was this going to be his last year? "No," replied Kobe. "I'm planning to be around for three or four more years."

At that point, according to others in the room, Dwight's eyes went blank and he drifted away. In his mind, the game was over.

A few days later Dwight announced that he was signing with the Rockets.

Jeanie wasn't happy when she heard the news. She was convinced that the result would have been different if her father had still been alive and healthy enough to be involved in the negotiations. In all his years with the Lakers, Dr. Buss had lost only one prime player to free agency: A. C. Green to Phoenix in 1993. If he were in charge, she said, he would have formed a supportive relationship with Dwight and been able to steer the talks in the right direction.

That may be true, but I'm not sure this turn of events was an unmitigated disaster. In fact, I thought it was not only a good wake-up call for Jim and Mitch, but it would also give them more flexibility budget-wise to create a young, speedier team more closely aligned to Mike D'Antoni's free-flowing approach to the game. And the recent signing of Kobe to a two-year extension shouldn't compromise that strategy.

Not long ago, I had lunch with the president of the Union Theological Seminary and we got into a wide-ranging conversation about how to create community for people who consider themselves spiritual but not necessarily religious. At one point, she suddenly looked at me and said, "You know, you really are a minister."

Her remark caught me by surprise. It reminded me of my parents' aspirations for me as a child. When I was young, I always thought that I might return someday to that calling after my basketball career was over. Once, when I was between jobs, I even explored the possibility of going to grad school in theology. But I got turned off when I visited a seminary in Missouri and saw how mercenary the profession had become. As I was touring the campus, the young man showing me around said, matter-of-factly, "You can really make big money in this field. Maybe even 150K a year."

In general, I've been a loner in my spiritual quest, in part because of my peripatetic traveling schedule, but mostly because of my deep-seated aversion to organized religion. But perhaps this woman saw something in me I needed to pay attention to.

Recently my Zen teacher asked me to consider taking the bodhisattva vow, which involves pursuing one's own spiritual development for the sake of all beings, not just oneself. As Chögyam Trungpa put it, "Taking the bodhisattva vow implies that instead of holding onto our own individual territory and defending it tooth and nail, we become open to the world we are living in. It means we are willing to take on greater responsibility."

This calling is not unlike the traditional Christian concept of living in grace. In October I went to a panel discussion on the ascetic life at Loyola Marymount College led by a friend, author Kathleen Norris. She told a story about a monk in the Middle Ages who traveled to a nearby city to visit a famous ascetic who turned out to be a merchant living in a busy market district. That night, while they were praying, the monk was rattled by the noise some drunks and prostitutes were making in the street and asked the merchant "How on earth can you stand this every night?" The merchant replied, "I just say to myself, 'They're all going to the kingdom.'"

Kathleen, who is a devout Christian, told this story because she often uses it in her own practice. Once when she was staying in a private club in Chicago, the man next door came back to his room with a call girl and they started making an unholy racket. "I had to make a choice between being disturbed or not disturbed," she said. "Then I remembered this story and just said to myself, 'We're all going to the kingdom.'"

There's a part of me that has always longed to lead a simpler, more ascetic life. But I've had to balance that with the demands of constantly being in the public eye. When I retired in 2011, Jeanie told me she thought I needed to stay "relevant," but to do that meant marching to a tune that no longer resonated with me the way it had before. Someday that may change and I may get drawn back into the game I love, but right now I'm more interested in dedicating my life to service.

On the domestic front, that means stepping back and helping Jeanie succeed in her new role, not just as an adviser on basketball issues, but as chief cook and bottle washer, as well. For years I've had people in the background taking care of me; now I'm the one buying the groceries, making dinner, and taking care of our home. (Okay, so I don't do windows. Still.)

As for my spiritual life, I've been quietly exploring letting my "inner minister" come out of hiding. I recently taught a meditation class in

L.A. and I'm considering traveling to New York to mentor students at the Union Theological Seminary. As long as they don't call me "Reverend," I should be okay.

I've always had trouble with so-called spiritual teachers who espouse a proscribed way of life. I'm not interested in becoming anyone's guru. I'm just feeling my way forward, trying to live my life mindfully and, to quote William Blake, catch "joy as it flies."

Someday, I hope, that might even include the road trip not taken.

ACKNOWLEDGMENTS

The work on this book began during the winter of 2011–12 in the living room of Phil's house in Playa del Rey, California, a sleepy beach town. The room, a long floor-through overlooking the Pacific, is filled with mementoes: an Edward Curtis photo of a Kutenai brave gathering rushes in a canoe on Flathead Lake, a totemlike painting of the Bulls' second three-peat team, a giant replica of the Lakers' 2010 championship ring. Outside the full-length windows, Olympic hopefuls could be seen practicing volleyball on the beach, while a parade of Angelenos in brightly colored exercise wear streamed by on inline skates, bicycles, razor scooters, and other earth friendly vehicles.

Every now and then, Phil would stop expounding on the wonders of the triangle offense for a moment and gaze dreamily at the ocean. "Look," he'd say, pointing to a fishing boat heading out to sea or a small pod of dolphins frolicking in the waves near shore. We'd sit in silence and watch for a while until Phil decided it was time to get back to unraveling the mysteries of the Blind Pig or some other arcane aspect of the Jacksonian game.

Tucked away in the rear of the room is a small meditation space enclosed by Japanese-style paper screens, where Phil sits *zazen* most mornings. On one wall hangs a beautiful calligraphic drawing of enso, the Zen symbol of oneness, with these lines from Tozan Ryokai, a ninth-century Buddhist monk:

> *Do not try to see the objective world.*
> *You which is given an object to see is quite different*
>   *from you yourself.*
> *I am going my own way and I meet myself which includes*
>   *everything I meet.*
> *I am not something I can see (as an object).*
> *When you understand self which includes everything,*
> *You have your true way.*

This is the essence of what we've been trying to convey in this book: that the path of transformation is to see yourself as something beyond the narrow confines of your small ego—something that "includes everything."

Basketball isn't a one-person game, even though the media lords sometimes portray it that way. Nor is it a five-person game, for that matter. It's an intricate dance that includes everything happening at any given moment—the tap of the ball against the rim, the murmur of the crowd, the glint of anger in your opponent's eyes, the chatter of your own monkey mind.

The same is true with writing. Creating a book of this kind goes far beyond the solitary work of two guys banging away at their laptops. Fortunately we've been blessed throughout this project with an extraordinary team of men and women who have contributed their insights, creative energy, and hard work to make this book come to life.

First, we would like to thank our agent, Jennifer Rudolph Walsh at William Morris Entertainment for helping give birth to this book and nurturing it along the way. Big thanks also to agent extraordinaire Todd Musburger for his perseverance, integrity, and gift for putting all the pieces together.

We owe a great debt to our publisher and editor, Scott Moyers, for holding the vision of *Eleven Rings* from the start and making that vision real. Kudos, as well, to Scott's assistants, Mally Anderson and Akif Saifi, and the rest of the editorial team at The Penguin Press for their Jordan-like grace under pressure.

We'd especially like to thank the players, coaches, journalists, and others who took the time to share with us their personal reflections about Phil and the events chronicled in these pages. In particular, we're grateful to Senator Bill Bradley and Mike Riordan for their insights re the Knicks; Michael Jordan, Scottie Pippen, John Paxson, Steve Kerr, and Johnny Bach re the Bulls; and Kobe Bryant, Derek Fisher, Rick Fox, Pau Gasol, Luke Walton, Frank Hamblen, Brian Shaw, and Kurt Rambis re the Lakers. Thanks also to Bill Fitch, Chip Schaefer, Wally Blase, George Mumford, Brooke Jackson, and Joe Jackson for their invaluable contributions.

We're especially indebted to writers Sam Smith and Mark Heisler for their guidance and in-depth knowledge of the NBA. *Chicago Sun-Times* columnist Rick Telander was also a great help, as were reporters Mike Bresnahan of the *Los Angeles Times* and Kevin Ding of *Bleacher Report*.

A tip of the hat to Lakers PR wizard John Black and his team for parting the waters as only he knows how. We're also much obliged to Tim Hallam and his crew at the Bulls.

Special thanks to Phil's collaborators on previous books, authors Charley Rosen (*Maverick* and *More Than a Game*) and Michael Arkush (*The Last Season*), and photographers George Kalinsky (*Take It All!*) and Andrew D. Bernstein (*Journey to the Ring*). We've also benefited from the perspectives of other authors in these works: Bill Bradley's *Life on the Run*, Phil Berger's *Miracle on 33rd Street*, Dennis D'Agostino's *Garden Glory*, Red Holzman and Harvey Frommer's *Red on Red*, Roland Lazenby's *Mindgames* and *The Show*, David Halberstam's *Playing for Keeps*, Sam Smith's *The Jordan Rules*, Rick Telander's *In the Year of the Bull*, Elizabeth Kaye's *Ain't No Tomorrow*, and Mark Heisler's *Madmen's Ball*.

In addition, we'd like to thank several journalists who've covered Phil and his teams throughout his career for their insights, especially Frank Deford, Jack McCallum, and Phil Taylor (*Sports Illustrated*); Tim Kawakami, Tim Brown, Bill Plaschke, T. J. Simers, Ben Bolch, and Broderick Turner (*Los Angeles Times*); Melissa Isaacson, Terry Armour, Skip Myslenski, Bernie Lincicome, and Bob Verdi (*Chicago Tribune*); Lacy J. Banks, John Jackson, and Jay Mariotti (*Chicago Sun-Times*); Tim Sullivan and Mark Ziegler (*San Diego Union-Tribune*); Howard Beck and Mike Wise (*New York Times*); Mike Lupica (*New York Newsday*); J. A. Adande, Ramona Shelburne, and Marc Stein (ESPN); and Michael Wilbon (*Washington Post*).

Researchers Sue O'Brian and Lyn Garrity did an exceptional job of making sure we got our facts straight. Deep bows to Kathleen Clark for creating the wonderful picture gallery, and to Brian Musburger and Liz Calamari for their tireless effort promoting the book. Thanks also to Chelsea Jackson, Clay McLachlan, John M. Delehanty, Jessica Catlow, Rebekah Berger, Amanda Romeo, Gary Mailman, Amy Carollo, Caitlin Moore, Kathleen Nishimoto, Gayle Waller, and Chrissie Zartman, for assistance beyond the call of duty.

Most of all, we are humbled by the love and support of the book's biggest champions, Barbara Graham and Jeanie Buss.

From the beginning Barbara has poured her heart and soul into this project and lifted the book with her masterful editing and creative vision.

And if it weren't for Jeanie, this book might never have been born. She is the reason Phil came back to the Lakers for his second run. We have Jeanie to thank, along with the late Dr. Jerry Buss, for giving Phil the chance to win his last two rings.

Phil Jackson and Hugh Delehanty

INDEX

CREDITS